The Pathway Paradox

BASED ON TRUE STORY

By OTILIA NICOLETA FLOREA

"A book is a dream that you hold in your hand."

-Neil Gaiman.

COPYRIGHT © 2024 by Otilia Nicoleta Florea
ALL RIGHTS RESERVED.
No part of this book may be reproduced or transmitted in any form by any means, electronic or mechanical, including photocopying and recording, or by any information storage and retrieval system, except as may be expressly permitted in writing from the author.

DEDICATION

To My Dearest Emma,

In the pages of my life, a story unfolds,
"The Pathway Paradox," with lessons untold.
From childhood dreams to present day,
I hope you'll learn, in your own special way.

Mistakes I've made, decisions I've faced,
In your eyes, I hope, no judgment is placed.
For every choice, both right and wrong,
Has shaped the mother you've known all along.

Emma, my love, my only child,
May your heart be kind, your spirit wild.
Elegant and clever, may you always be,
A reflection of the best parts of me.

Trust in yourself, with courage and grace,
In every challenge, find your place.
Know that my love is a guiding light,
By your side, both day and night.

For the rest of my life, and beyond,

My bond with you will remain strong.

No matter what, through joy and strife,

I'll be with you, my Emma, for all of life.

May your days be filled with laughter and cheer,

With dreams that soar, and skies so clear.

In every step, in every stride,

I'll be your anchor, your constant guide.

When the world feels heavy, and shadows fall,

Remember my love, standing tall.

In your heart, you'll find my embrace,

A timeless bond, no time can erase.

So, my dear Emma, as you grow and explore,

Know that my love is forevermore.

With every sunrise, with every night,

I'll be with you, my guiding light.

Be happy, my dear, in all your days,

Let joy and laughter light your ways.

No matter the storms that life may send,

I'll be by your side, until the very end.

And even beyond, in realms unseen,
My love for you will always gleam.
So, Emma, my child, hold your head high,
For you are my heart, my moon, my sky.

In moments of doubt, when shadows fall,
Remember my voice, my love, my call.
You have the strength to conquer all fears,
With courage and hope through all the years.

Dream big, my darling, reach for the stars,
Know that my love is never far.
In every success, in every trial,
I'll be there, cheering, mile after mile.

*"Love me or hate me, both are in my favour.
If you love me, I will always be in your heart,
and if you hate me, I will be in your mind."*

-William Shakespeare

TABLE OF CONTENTS

A Father's Legacy, A Brother's Promise 11

First Love: A Tapestry of Dreams and Heartache 22

Whispers in the Shadows 33

A Night of Unspoken Desires 37

Fragments of Love and Loss 44

A Journey Through Heartache, Healing, and Self-Discovery 49

A Christmas Encounter 53

New Year's Enchantment 61

Shadows of Desire 65

Whispers of Unspoken Desires 71

Whisky and Goodbyes 74

Autumn of Longing 76

Unspoken Ties 84

The Crossroads of Hearts 86

An Uncertain Farewell 93

Shadows of the Past 104

Echoes of the Past 107

Weight of Unspoken Words 110

Fragments of a Dream 119

Unconditional Love 122

A Baptism of Love and Resilience 126

Lessons in Humility and Hope 130

Threads of Hope	133
A Home Away from Home	139
The Missing Piece	142
A Family's Odyssey	146
Woven in Time	149
Between Two Flames	162
Shadows of the Past	167
Wagered Hearts	174
Journey of Contrasts	176
Wheels of Freedom	179
Festive Fragility	181
Snowbound Secrets	192
Dreams and Discoveries	205
Fragile Ties	210
Reunion	216
Torn Between Love and Deception	221
A Spy in My Own Life	227
The Price of Success	232
A Moment of Solitude, A Lifetime of Triumph	236
Whispers of the Open Road	238
In Her Footsteps	244
A Tribute to Grandmother	246
Shattered Bonds	249
The Quiet Victory	257

The Elegance of Timing 261
The Breaking Point 269
Beyond the Silence 279
Goodbye, Andrew 291
Fragments of Us 294
When Fate Calls 298
Rebirth of the Soul 309
My Guiding Star 1
Life Lessons and Reflections 6
Life's Gambit: Trust and Betrayal 14
Reflections on Identity, Society, and the Beauty of Romania 16

A Father's Legacy, A Brother's Promise

"Coincidences are the scars of fate."

-Carlos Ruiz Zafón.

"I do not believe in meaningless coincidences. I believe every coincidence is a message, a clue about a particular facet of our lives that requires our attention."

-Deepak Chopra.

"Coincidence is a messenger sent by truth."

–Jacqueline Winspear.

There was a princess who lived in a splendid castle, her days filled with love and grandeur under the watchful eyes of her father, the King, and her mother, the Queen. The air carried the perfume of romance, and her life seemed like a dream. But this is not my story.

The rich girl lived in a grand mansion, where the hum of luxurious cars filled the driveway, and every room was a testament to wealth. Yet, even amid all this opulence, my story took a different path, one that didn't follow the expected script.

The little girl, with dreams as vast as the sky, had a heart full of curiosity and a mind that wandered far beyond her modest surroundings. Her eyes sparkled with wonder, reflecting a world she longed to explore. She didn't dwell in castles or palatial homes, but her spirit soared high, reaching for more than the ordinary.

And this is where my story truly begins—a tale not of riches, but of dreams, resilience, and the journey to find something more meaningful than gold.

In the heart of mist-shrouded mountains, where the air tasted of pine and the essence of dreams, lay a small village—a sanctuary of simplicity. Modest homes lined the hillsides, their thatched roofs whispering stories of generations past. Here, life unfolded like pages from an ancient book, every soul woven into the village's tapestry of resilience and quiet beauty.

Amidst this world, I found my solace in the arms of my grandmother. She was my North Star, her laughter etched in the lines of her face, earned through countless seasons of joy and sorrow. When my mother's work pulled her away to distant places, it was my grandmother who anchored me and became my guiding light.

She taught me lessons that could never be spoken aloud. Her wisdom was in the kneading of bread, the scent of wildflowers pressed between the pages of her favourite books, and the quiet way she listened to the whispering wind. Together, we wandered the forest trails, our feet leaving imprints on mossy paths. She told me stories of spirits that danced among the trees, their laughter echoing through hidden glens. And as the sun dipped behind the mountains, she'd share tales of love, of strength, and the silent courage that bloomed within the hearts of everyday people.

My grandmother was my sanctuary—a blend of parent, teacher, and confidante. She knew the healing power of warm soup on a chilly evening and the magic of stargazing from our rooftop. When doubts clouded my young mind, she'd say, "Child, life is a winding river. Follow its bends, and you'll find your purpose."

And so, under her patient gaze, I learned to choose my path. Not the grand highways paved with gold but the winding trails that led to hidden meadows and forgotten shrines. My heart whispered its desires, and I followed, knowing that my grandmother's love would light the way.

In her kitchen, magic was created out of scarcity. The sunlight filtered through lace curtains, casting a warm glow on the worn wooden table where countless meals had been prepared. Pancakes, rare and precious, were our celebration of joy, emerging only on the brightest of days. She'd look at the meagre ingredients before her—an egg, a pat of butter, a handful of flour—and say, "Child, we'll make magic today." And we always did. With a whisk of love and a dash of hope, she'd transform those humble items into golden pancakes, each one a testament to her strength and grace.

When I was three years old, my parents went through a divorce. Although I was too young to fully comprehend the situation, the impact was significant. My brother, Charlie, and I were separated as a result. After the divorce, I lived with my mother in my grandmother's house, while my brother stayed with my father. My father eventually remarried, and our interactions were limited to summer, Christmas, or Easter holidays. Occasionally, my father would take me to spend time with his new family, but most of the time, my mother brought my brother to my grandmother's house so we could play together.

Having my brother by my side made me the happiest child in the world. However, it was hard for me to ignore the fact that my mother favoured him over me. On the other hand, my grandmother always held a special place in my heart, and I felt more attached to her than to my own mother.

My father loved us both fiercely, and I remember the days he would visit, his arms full of treats and toys, his love as boundless as the sea he once showed me. I still hold dear the memory of our seaside holiday, where he taught me to swim, where we built sandcastles together, and where, for those few magical days, I felt like the most cherished child in the world. Even when my salt-soaked hair tangled beyond repair, and he had to cut it, I knew he was trying his best to make me smile."

I also remember that, at the time, I had long, silky blond hair that became hopelessly tangled from the salty seawater. My father, unable to comb it, made the decision to cut it. Initially, I was upset, but eventually, he managed to calm me down by giving me lots of sweets, toys, and new dresses. Looking back, it remains the most beautiful vacation of my life—a cherished time spent with my father.

After our seaside adventure, my brother came to stay with me at my grandmother's house. Charlie was overjoyed because my grandmother had a small farm. She owned a cow, a few sheep, some chickens, a dog, and a cat. Additionally, her large garden allowed us to grow various vegetables and flowers, and we eagerly helped with farming and gardening. Our little farm provided endless activities to keep us busy, and Charlie even made friends with other children in the village. As the sun set, we played outside with our neighbours until nighttime.

After the summer holiday, my mother decided to enrol Charlie in school, hoping that my father would allow him to live with us so we could grow up together. At that time, my brother was eight years old, and I was seven. Going to school alongside Charlie made me feel safe and protected, and I couldn't help but feel incredibly proud of him. In the schoolyard, Charlie struck up a friendship with a classmate named George, and during every break between classes, we met and played together. It felt like I had two brothers, and those moments were precious.

However, our happiness was short-lived. About two weeks later, my father appeared in the schoolyard and took Charlie away. Tears welled up in my eyes as I watched them leave. I never understood why he did this—why he took my brother and left me behind. Why couldn't we stay together? As far as I know, when they divorced, the lawyer decided that I should stay with my mother, and my brother should stay with my father. Perhaps my father had to comply with the law at the time, which is why he took only my brother. Additionally, Charlie was supposed to attend school in the town where my father lived with his new family.

I was inconsolable, my tears flowing freely as my father carried Charlie away. George, who had witnessed the heart-wrenching scene, rushed to my side. His own eyes were red from crying, but he didn't hesitate. Wrapping his arms around me, he whispered, "Please stop crying! From now on, I'll be your brother, and I'll take care of you forever."

Those words etched themselves into my soul. George became my steadfast companion, a brother born not of blood but of shared pain and determination. We navigated the schoolyard together, our bond growing stronger with each passing day. During lunch breaks, I'd eagerly unwrap my sandwiches and offer half to George. He'd grin, accepting the simple meal with gratitude.

George's life mirrored mine in many ways. Like me, he had grown up under the watchful eye of his grandmother. His parents had left for a distant country in pursuit of work, leaving him in the care of his older brother. Two other siblings had moved to different cities, seeking employment opportunities. Our shared experiences forged an unbreakable connection—one that transcended mere friendship.

As the seasons changed, George and I faced life's challenges side by side. We laughed, cried, and dreamed together. And though my biological brother was miles away, George filled the void, becoming the brother, I never knew I needed. His promise echoed in my heart: "I'll take care of you forever." And in that promise, I found solace and strength.

As time flowed swiftly, a vivid memory remains etched in my mind—the day my father visited. His arms overflowed with candies, chocolates, toys, and an elegant red dress. Matching shoes completed the ensemble. As I twirled before the mirror, he watched, eyes filled with tenderness. At that moment, I felt like the most exquisite princess.

Yet, beneath the surface, something weighed on him. His tear-filled eyes revealed the truth: he planned to work in Italy. The allure of treats and the beauty of the dress momentarily distracted me, but I understood the gravity of his words. He would be abroad for a while, leaving me with both gifts and a bittersweet ache in my heart.

"Daddy, promise me you won't stay long in Italy and that you'll come back soon! I'm going to miss you," I pleaded.

"I'll miss you too, my little princess!" His voice held both tenderness and determination. "I'll earn more money, and in a few months, I'll return. We'll even start our own company. You'll be Dad's accountant. I'll always be proud of you. Promise me you'll be good and listen to your mother and grandmother."

"I promise, Daddy." My voice wavered. "I'll be a good girl, study hard, get good grades at school, and wait for you!"

As soon as he said goodbye, the weight of his absence settled over me. An ache formed in my heart, and I stood there, watching his car recede into the distance, tears streaming down my face.

Nearly two months after my father left for Italy, my mother returned home from work early. Her eyes were swollen with tears, and a sense of foreboding settled over me. I wondered if perhaps my paternal grandmother had passed away. My mother couldn't provide details; we simply hurriedly dressed and set off. Our footsteps quickened as we made our way to the train station. She gripped my hand tightly; her own emotions held in check.

The two-hour train journey felt interminable, each passing minute laden with anticipation. Finally, during that time, my mother mustered the courage to share what had transpired.

"Nobody wants to die," she began, her voice trembling, "even people who want to go to heaven. But God needed an angel, and He decided to take your father."

I shook my head, tears streaming down my face. "No! That's not true! God already knows that I need my Daddy here; he cannot help me from Heaven."

She tried to console me. "Your dad is an angel now, and he will take care of you from Heaven!"

Desperation filled my heart. "Please, mummy, please! Tell me that's not true! Please tell me that nothing happened to my father!"

Her gaze softened. "When someone we love dies, we never get to see them again, but we will always feel them because they live on in our hearts and our memories."

Even though I couldn't comprehend what my mother was saying, I clung to the hope that it wasn't true. The weight of this devastating news, received when I was nearly nine years old, was unbearable.

My life veered onto an unexpected path, forever altered by destiny. My father's life ended tragically in a car accident in Italy. One ordinary morning, as he set off for work, a car materialized out of nowhere and struck him. For three agonizing days, he teetered between life and death in the hospital, but ultimately, he lost the battle. His heart ceased to beat, leaving us shattered.

Our family rallied together, determined to bring his body back home. We spent two weeks raising funds and navigating grief and logistics. Just three days before the funeral, I learned of this heart-wrenching truth. My mother grieved silently, unable to utter the words that my brother and I no longer had a father. It was too soon for him to leave us—too abrupt, too unfair.

Life, it seemed, was both fragile and unpredictable. From that moment on, I carried a pang of silent guilt, wondering why fate had dealt such a cruel hand. Life is fleeting—each moment is precious. For the rest of my days, I'll harbour regret because I never told him a million times, "I love you, Daddy." When he visited and gifted me the red dress, I should have expressed my feelings, but I remained silent. It dawned on me how a single second can alter everything—bestow or take away. People depart, even after countless promises of return. Death is inevitable, but losing a parent always feels sudden and hard to accept.

Dear Dad,

I miss you more than words can express. The ache in my heart is a constant reminder of your absence, but I find solace in the love and memories we share. You will always be an angel in my life, watching over me from heaven. I hope you're proud of what I've accomplished and the person I've become, guided by your wisdom and love.

The emptiness you left in my heart is a void that no one else can fill. I cherish the unforgettable moments we shared, the laughter, the lessons, and the love. When I gaze at the night sky, I see the stars twinkling and remember that destiny took away my life's brightest star. Someday, I'll find my Prince, but Daddy, you will always be my King. No matter how old I grow or whose love brings me happiness, I will forever be your little princess.

In the quiet moments, I feel your presence, like a gentle whisper in the wind, comforting and reassuring. Your love surrounds me, and I carry it with me wherever I go. You taught me strength, resilience, and kindness, and your legacy lives on through the way I navigate life's challenges. Thank you for being my guiding light, my rock, and my hero.

Sometimes, I catch a glimpse of your smile in my reflection, and it warms my heart. Your love transcends time and space, and I hold it close like a precious treasure. I promise to live a life that honours your memory, filled with the values and love you instilled in me. Dad, you are forever in my heart, and I will never stop loving you.

Every day, I strive to make you proud and to live up to the example you set. Your strength and courage inspire me to face my fears and overcome obstacles. I remember the way you always knew how to make me laugh, even in the toughest times. Your sense of humour and your kindness are qualities I carry with me, hoping to spread the same joy and compassion you did.

When I achieve something, big or small, I imagine your proud smile, and it fills me with warmth. Your belief in me gives me the confidence to pursue my dreams. I know you're watching over me, guiding me with your love and wisdom. Your spirit lives on in every step I take and in every decision I make.

Dad, you are my hero, my guardian angel, and my eternal source of strength. Your love is a beacon that lights my way, even in the darkest moments. I miss you dearly, but I find comfort in knowing that you are always with me, in my heart and in my soul. Thank you for being the best dad anyone could ever ask for. I love you, now and forever. "Sometimes I wish I were an angel, and sometimes I wish I were you."- "An angel" by Kelly Family.

Life carried on, as it always does, but my father's memory stayed with me. Every step I take, every achievement I reach, I think of him. I wonder if he'd be proud of me if he'd smile and tell me that I'm doing well. I still feel his presence, a gentle whisper in the wind, a warm embrace in my dreams. He will always be my hero, my guardian angel, the one who taught me to be strong, even in the face of the deepest loss.

My grandmother, with her gentle wisdom and unwavering strength, stepped in as our caretaker. She became the anchor of our household, providing stability and comfort. Meanwhile, my mother toiled tirelessly to make ends meet. Her modest income often fell short of our needs, but we learned to find contentment in the little things—never asking for too much and always expressing gratitude for our health and the roof over our heads.

At school, both Charlie and I excelled academically, earning excellent grades that made our mother proud. After lessons, we would rush home to lend a hand to Grandma on our small farm. The heavy tasks, though exhausting, became a way for us to contribute and feel useful. Our circle of friends—both at school and in the neighbourhood—became our support system during those trying times.

Charlie and George shared a close bond. Together, they assisted neighbours in need, and their efforts were sometimes rewarded with small compensations. These acts of kindness not only helped others but also brought a sense of purpose and community to our lives.

First Love: A Tapestry of Dreams and Heartache

Time slipped away, and before I knew it, I had blossomed into a young woman. At fourteen, I entered high school—a milestone that marked the beginning of a transformative chapter in my life. My dream? To follow in my father's dreams and become an accountant, just as he had always hoped. Parents see boundless potential in their children, and every girl with big dreams eventually grows into a woman with a vision. When you nurture a dream, you have to hold onto it tightly and never let go. As Mariah Carey sings in *Hero*, *"Dreams are hard to follow, but don't let anyone tear them away."*

During the weekdays, I stayed on campus in the school's dormitory, but on weekends, I returned home. One particular day, while travelling home by train, I ran into Raul. We had attended the same secondary school, though we had never exchanged words. He was attending a different high school in a nearby town. Raul was cute, intelligent, and charming, but he didn't match the image of my ideal partner. I had always imagined my boyfriend would be a bold fighter like Jean-Claude Van Damme or Sylvester Stallone, with the rugged charm of a Spanish telenovela actor and the fiery love of Leonardo DiCaprio in Titanic. I dreamed of a prince straight from a fairy tale, ready to rescue me from the dangers of life. Yet, despite my preconceived notions, I decided to give Raul a chance—just as a friend, I told myself.

The next day, we met for what turned into a light-hearted conversation filled with laughter. As he shared stories about his family and school life, I began to appreciate his kindness and respect. After a few hours together, he surprised me with a hug and my first kiss—an unexpected, intimate moment. But unlike the magical experiences my friends had gushed about, this kiss left me feeling unsettled, as if something were missing. Sometimes, reality doesn't match our fantasies, and life takes unexpected turns that reshape our journey.

Despite my initial reservations, our relationship continued, and we met every weekend. My brother, Charlie, wasn't thrilled about it—constantly warning me to stay away from Raul. I suppose he still saw me as his little sister and wanted to protect me. George, on the other hand, exhibited strange behaviour whenever Raul was around. His jealousy was puzzling, and I couldn't quite understand why he acted that way, which only added a layer of intrigue to our interactions.

Raul soon asked me out on a proper date, suggesting a romantic evening at a restaurant. I wasn't ready for that, so I declined, opting instead to meet him at the local club. The nightclub in our village was more of a rustic pub where young people gathered to dance, party, and have fun. I had always dreamed of the day I would be old enough to join them, imagining the thrill of dancing beneath the flashing lights. When the time finally came, I asked my brother to take me, but he refused, saying he didn't want to babysit me. Thankfully, my grandma intervened, persuading my mother to let me go with my friends on the condition that I return by 10 PM.

The following day, I spent hours pleading with my brother to take me to the club. Unfortunately, he refused, citing his reluctance to babysit me there. Despite my best efforts, I couldn't sway him. Thankfully, my grandma intervened and persuaded my mother to allow me to go with my friends. The condition was that I had to return home within four hours—I knew I couldn't break that rule and arrive after 10 PM.

Excitedly, I dressed in a pair of jeans and a cute white lace top. My best friend Samantha and I headed to the club, bubbling with anticipation. When I saw Raul, I noticed one of my friends was vying for his attention, but his focus remained solely on me. I basked in the energy of the night, feeling special in a way I had never felt before.

Then, about thirty minutes later, George stormed into the club with his girlfriend, Adelle. His eyes flashed with anger when he saw me dancing with Raul. He wasted no time confronting me, pulling me aside for a heated exchange, even though the music drowned out most of our conversation. "What are you doing here?" he demanded. "Where's Charlie? Why aren't you with your brother?

"What are you doing here?" George demanded, his voice sharp. "Where's Charlie? Why aren't you with your brother?"

I met his anger with defiance. "Charlie didn't want to take me, and I'm here with my friends. I'm allowed to be here for a few hours. What's your problem?" His reaction seemed over the top, and I couldn't understand why he cared so much.

George's jaw clenched. "I don't care if she's watching. Be cautious about your actions. I'm keeping an eye on you, and don't you dare wander off. You're too young to be at the club."

I shot back, my frustration boiling over. "I'm old enough to take care of myself. Whatever's bothering you, it's your issue. Mind your own business."

His grip tightened on my arm. "Let's go home! I'll take you home!"

Despite this new awareness, I ignored George and returned to Raul, swaying to the music in his arms. But George didn't stay away for long. He approached me again, insisting we talk outside. When I resisted, he became more forceful, pulling me away from the dance floor. Outside, we argued. He claimed Raul wasn't right for me, that I deserved someone better. His words frustrated me, and I challenged him, asking why he cared so much. His response caught me off guard: "I promised to look out for you. You're like a sister to me, and I know what's best for you.

Only then did I realize just how captivating he really was. George possessed a boyish cuteness and undeniable handsomeness. In my mind, I repeated a mantra: "Don't be fooled by appearances." He was like a friend, almost a brother, and I didn't want to jeopardize our relationship. Besides, he had a girlfriend, and I certainly didn't want to be the cause of any trouble.

Despite other girls vying for George's attention, I chose to ignore him. I stood up from the sofa and made a beeline for Raul. He pulled me close, and we swayed to the music. George watched us, but I feigned indifference. After about an hour, he approached me, urgently asking if we could step outside for a chat. His grip on my hand left no room for protest. Outside, our argument began. I held my ground, refusing to be intimidated.

"I'm not leaving now!" I shot back. "What about your girlfriend and Raul? What will they think about that?"

"I don't care! Anyway, Raul's not the right boyfriend for you. You need somebody better than him and trustworthy."

My frustration bubbled up. "How do you know if he's right for me or not? Why do you care? This is not your problem! Who are you to decide what is good or bad for me?"

He stepped closer, his voice low and intense. "It's my problem. I've known you since you were a little girl. I promised that I would be like a brother to you, and I know what is best for you. Also, I'm older than you, and I know how bad people can be."

I couldn't help but laugh, even in this tense moment. "You're nearly three years older than me. How can you know how bad people are? Go and take care of Adelle."

His eyes narrowed. "Are you jealous? Why do you keep telling me about my girlfriend? Stop arguing with me and listen to me. I'll take you home!"

I tilted my head, feigning innocence. "I am not jealous, and I'm not going home. I still have one more hour to dance and stay with my boyfriend! He will take me home later. What's going on with you?" I flashed a smile, surprised that I had just used the word 'boyfriend.'

His grip tightened. "I don't want to see you with Raul anymore!"

I raised an eyebrow. "Should I tell you that I do not want to see you with Adelle anymore?"

He scowled. "Wherever, but you're smaller than me, and you have to listen to me."

I remained utterly perplexed. How could George presume to know what was best for me? Why did he assume this protective role without explanation? Despite my inquiries, he remained tight-lipped. So, I continued to observe him, attempting to decipher the hidden meaning behind his intense gaze. It was as if George harboured his own secret, and I was merely a piece in his intricate puzzle.

His words hung between us, heavy with an unspoken truth. I was left utterly perplexed. I had always seen George as a friend, almost like a brother. But now, I wasn't so sure. His protectiveness seemed to hint at something deeper. I couldn't argue anymore. He took my hand, and without saying goodbye to Raul, I left with him, curiosity swirling in my mind. As we walked home, the silence between us was heavy. I wanted to ask him why he was acting this way, but I couldn't find the words. When we finally stopped, I turned to him and asked, "Why can't you just tell me what you feel?" His answer whispered softly, took my breath away: "I want you to be mine."

His eyes bore into mine, unwavering. "I just want you to be mine," he whispered, "and you'll be mine forever."

His response sent my heart racing. He pulled me into an embrace, locking eyes with me. His gaze felt like twin arrows piercing my soul, and I could practically feel the blood coursing through my veins. I had lost all sense of reason. At that moment, if he had asked for my name, I wouldn't have been able to recall it.

His confession left me reeling, but before I could fully process it, he pulled me into an embrace and kissed me. Time seemed to stop. In his arms, I felt something I hadn't felt before—a magnetic pull, an intensity that left me breathless. His kiss was everything I had imagined my first kiss should be and more. After what felt like an eternity, we pulled away, both aware of the weight of the moment. We stood there in front of the church, making promises we were too young to fully understand. "Promise me you'll always love me," he whispered. I found myself whispering back, "I promise."

We were like two kids wielding big, powerful words. After he kissed and embraced me, I hurriedly left to ensure I'd be home on time. George returned to the club, where Adelle awaited him.

Jealousy tugged at my heart, yet my happiness and newfound love eclipsed any other concerns.

The days that followed were a blur. George and I agreed to keep our secret, but the memory of our kiss lingered in my mind, replaying over and over. I couldn't share it with anyone—not even my brother. The risk of ruining George and Charlie's friendship was too great. George confided in me that he wanted to break up with Adelle, but her threats of self-harm made him hesitant. I believed him, though I suspected a setup involving Raul and Adelle, who had both used similar tactics in the past. Raul, too, had once threatened self-harm when I tried to break up with him, but I had seen through his manipulations.

A few days later, George confided in me that he wanted to break up with Adelle. However, she had threatened to harm herself if he left her. I believed him because Raul had said something similar when I discussed ending our relationship. Initially, I suspected a setup orchestrated by Raul and Adelle, but it turned out to be genuine. I told Raul that our relationship wouldn't work and that it was best to break up, but he pleaded with me not to give up on him. Despite lacking feelings for Raul, he remained unconvinced. He even mentioned the possibility of self-harm due to our breakup, although I knew it was a desperate ploy. Still, I chose to continue our relationship, hoping he'd eventually realize its emptiness.

Shortly after this conversation with George, I faced another twist of fate. My mother decided to marry Adelle's father. Destiny made me stepsisters with George's girlfriend. Although their relationship didn't last long, I maintained a friendly connection with Adelle. She was nice, but the glitch in our friendship was her association with George. I kept my distance from him, guarding our secret. George and I agreed to forget the small gestures between us and focus on Adelle and Raul.

After a while, just when I thought my relationship with Raul was finally on track, I discovered he was cheating on me with my friend Hellen—a long-standing crush of his. Nervous, I ended things with Raul, hoping to put him behind me for good. Strangely, I didn't feel upset; instead, anger simmered within me. I realized I'd wasted precious time on someone who had played games and used emotional manipulation, threatening self-harm if I dared break up with him, only to betray me later.

As time passed and the dust settled, I assumed George had moved on, forgetting our shared history. But fate had other plans. One day, my phone buzzed, revealing a message from him: "Next weekend is my birthday party, and you're my special guest. Don't keep me waiting too long! I'll see you soon." His message hung in the air, a tantalizing promise that set my heart racing. I resisted the urge to reply immediately, feigning indifference. But deep down, I couldn't wait to see him.

As the day wore on, I sat in class, pretending to be busy while my mind raced with anticipation. The evening arrived, and he called me.

"When you come home on Friday," he began, his voice carrying a hint of hesitation, "would you want to come over to my house?"

I raised an eyebrow, curious. "Why should I come?"

His tone softened, almost pleading. "I need you. I have to make the shopping list. Saturday is my birthday party, and I must buy a lot of stuff. I don't know exactly how much to buy and what I should buy."

I tilted my head, considering his request. "Why don't you ask Adelle to help you?" I suggested, trying to sound casual.

His response was swift and tinged with a touch of bitterness. "Because we broke up."

"Oh... I'm sorry to hear that!" I said, attempting to sound sympathetic, though my voice wavered slightly.

He chuckled a dry, humourless sound. "Oh... I know you're not sorry. Why are you lying?"

On Friday, after class, I packed my bag with meticulous care, ensuring I had everything I needed for the weekend. I dressed in my favourite outfit, a soft blue sweater and jeans, and left the student house with a mix of nervousness and excitement. Boarding the train, I embarked on a two-hour journey, my excitement palpable with each passing mile. The countryside whizzed by in a blur of green fields and quaint villages, but my mind was focused on the destination.

And there he stood—George—waiting for me at the train station, his face lighting up as he saw me. He looked effortlessly handsome in a casual jacket and jeans. He invited me for a drink, and together, we headed to his house, chatting animatedly about our week. As I stepped through the door of his cosy home, the warmth and inviting scent of freshly baked cookies greeted me. I asked for more details about the party, curious about the evening ahead.

Pulling a piece of paper and a pen from my school bag, I prepared to jot down the shopping list. His smile played on his lips, a mischievous glint in his eyes, and I wondered what surprises awaited me.

"There won't be any birthday party!" George confessed, his voice soft but clear.

"What? Why?" I was taken aback, my mind racing with confusion.

"I mean, you're my only guest," he explained, his eyes locking onto mine with sincerity. "I want to celebrate my birthday with you."

"But it's your birthday," I protested, feeling a mix of surprise and warmth. "You told me you're going to have a party."

He chuckled, a sound that made my heart flutter. "I don't need any party. I just wanted to see you, and I needed a good reason to make sure you'd accept my invitation and be here with me."

I looked at him, surprised and ready to yell at him for lying to me. But then he hugged me, and he kissed me. With every touch and every kiss, everything intensified.

"Do you want to be mine," he whispered, "or do you want us to stop here?"

"I'm a little worried," I admitted. "You know this is the first time, and you told me that for your birthday, you want me to give you as a gift, just a little sweet kiss."

He leaned in, his eyes intense. "Can you change it and give me this precious gift? Do you think I deserve it? I want you!"

I hesitated. "I admit, I've been thinking about it a lot, and I want this moment to be special."

"Trust me!" he promised. "We'll never forget those moments."

That night with George was unforgettable. As I lay in his arms, I felt safe and cherished. We had created a secret world, a place where nothing else mattered. First, love is like that—intense, consuming, and unforgettable. It leaves a mark on you that time can't erase. The memories, the emotions, the first taste of love—they shape who you become. And no matter where life takes you, your first love stays with you, a reminder of the innocence and intensity of youth. As Kelly Clarkson sings in *Because of You*, *"I never stray too far from the sidewalk."* First, love teaches you, shapes you, and stays with you forever.

First love—we carry it with us; an indelible mark etched into the fabric of our existence. The memories of that initial date, the tentative first kiss, and the whispered "I love you" linger, woven into the tapestry of our lives. Why is it that we remember our first love so vividly? Perhaps because it's the one that leaves its mark—the one that breaks our hearts and shapes our understanding of love.

No matter where life takes us, regardless of the paths we traverse or the companions we choose, that first love remains a beacon. It might have been a tempest, a whirlwind of emotions that left us breathless. Or perhaps it was a gentle breeze, fleeting yet profound. Regardless, its purity and innocence endure—a cherished memory that time cannot erase. The laughter, the tears, the dreams shared under starlit skies—they all form a part of who we are, a testament to the power of love in its most untainted form. The lessons learned, the joy, and the pain all contribute to the person we become, forever influenced by that first, unforgettable love.

Whispers in the Shadows

Falling in love with George was like stepping into a secret world, one where only we existed. It was intoxicating and thrilling but always teetering on the edge of disaster. For months, we hid behind the veil of friendship, carefully navigating around my brother's watchful eye. The fear of his disapproval loomed over us, casting a shadow on every shared glance, every stolen moment. But hiding wasn't just about fear—it became the very essence of our love, a love too fragile to withstand the harsh light of reality. We clung to it, even though we knew deep down that living in the shadows could never last.

But that peace didn't last. Just when everything felt perfect, a storm began to brew. George's ex, Adelle, reemerged, flooding him with desperate messages—calls and texts begging for another chance. Seeing her name flash on his phone cut deeper than I expected, stirring up a fit of jealousy I could barely contain. Our love, once fragile but pure, faced its first real fracture.

Why is she still texting you?" I spat, trying to hide the hurt that laced my words. "Why haven't you told her you don't want to be with her?"

"I did," George sighed, running a hand through his hair, frustration cracking through his calm. "She doesn't believe me."

"You should have been more convincing!" I snapped, the words tasting bitter in my mouth.

His eyes darkened, his jaw clenched. "I've tried. I've ignored her completely."

"Well, you didn't convince me either," I shot back, my voice colder than I intended.

His gaze softened, pleading. "Why are you so jealous? You know I only want you. I love you.

"But she still wants you," I argued. "I don't have time to play games and end up fooled. Go talk to her, solve your problems, and if you really love me, no one will text you."

"Please calm down and let me explain!" George pleaded.

"There's nothing more to explain," I declared, my resolve unwavering. "I understand everything. Please leave!"

His words fell on deaf ears. My stubbornness, my fear, my jealousy—they built a wall he couldn't break through. I pushed him away, convinced he needed something different—something that wasn't hidden, wasn't secret. Maybe he needed a love he could show the world, not one confined to whispers and stolen moments. Despite his attempts to bridge the growing chasm between us, I refused. I believed I was protecting both of us.

For weeks, I cut George off completely. I ignored his calls, and his texts, convinced myself he deserved more. He deserved a love he could share, one that wasn't shrouded in secrecy. In time, he drifted back to Adelle, and I forced myself to accept that reality. But the hollow ache it left in me was unbearable.

Then, Raul reappeared in my life. Every Friday after school, he waited for me at the train station, his apologies pouring out like a broken faucet. In my heartbreak over George, I let Raul back in, hoping maybe this time things would be different. I gave our love another shot, though my heart remained numb.

George occupied so many roles in my life: sometimes a brother, sometimes my best friend, sometimes my secret lover. But we always existed in the shadows, in the unspoken spaces between us. I wondered why we couldn't just declare our love openly and wear it proudly for the world to see. Were we fools, clutching a dream of a private world where only our hearts spoke while reality constantly threatened to tear us apart?

Even as we played the parts of best friends in public, our jealousy simmered just beneath the surface. Raul and Adelle became the unwitting pawns in our game. We ventured into public spaces—restaurants, clubs, parties—always together but never truly with each other. I could see the discomfort in George's eyes when he watched me with Raul, the same way my stomach churned when I saw him with Adelle. But neither of us spoke, both too afraid to disrupt the fragile balance we had built.

Friendships are a currency, valuable but fragile, easy to forge yet infinitely harder to maintain. As Octavia Butler once wrote, being a friend requires timing—knowing when to hold on, when to let go, and when to pick up the pieces after everything has fallen apart.

Time passed, and George began confiding in me more. He told me about his family, his parents' bitter divorce, and how his mother had remarried and moved to another city. One day, he told me he was going to visit her and invited me to come along.

"Why me?" I asked, suspicion and annoyance lacing my voice. "Why not Adelle?"

"I did ask her," George said a tired smile on his lips. "But she doesn't want to come."

"Then why should I?" I snapped. The tension between us was palpable.

"Because I love you the most," he whispered, his voice barely audible.

"Don't say that" I begged, my resolve weakening. "I don't want to hear those words anymore."

"They're not just words," he said, his voice firm, but my heart was already closing off.

"Shhh…"

Despite my resistance, George convinced me to go. But on the day of our departure, Adelle changed her mind. She wanted to come after all. The moment I found out, I refused to join them. I couldn't understand why George was so desperate for me to be there. He was supposed to go with his girlfriend, not me.

George's mother was a kind, respectable woman, and when we arrived, she welcomed me warmly into her home. He introduced me as his best friend, but I saw the questions in her eyes. She knew there was more to our story. George was skilled at sidestepping her inquiries, but the truth lingered just beneath the surface. His eyes said more than his words ever could, and I knew she saw it, too.

During the visit, we shared meals and stories, the moments sweet but tinged with an unspoken sadness. As we left, I promised to keep in touch with his mother. But I never did. Our lives, tangled as they were, felt like they could unravel at any moment. And I wondered, as I so often did, how much longer we could keep this love hidden before it consumed us both.

A Night of Unspoken Desires

Adelle became my roommate when she transferred to my high school, and since we were from the same village, it was convenient to travel back home together every Friday to spend weekends with our families. My grandmother eagerly awaited my arrival each week, counting on me to help with farm chores. As she grew older, managing everything on her own was becoming harder.

On a Sunday afternoon, I packed my bags, preparing to return to school. Near the train station, George and Adelle were waiting. Their plan involved spending a few hours at the club, followed by a hotel stay until morning. George implored me to stay, worried that Adelle would be alone if I left. Raul was away in Bucharest for work, so this night was theirs.

Initially, I wanted to leave. Watching their closeness felt unbearable, but George held my hand, asking me to stay. I agreed though I had a hidden motive: to teach George a lesson, to let him feel the jealousy I felt seeing him with Adelle. I couldn't fully explain why, but I was determined. This time, I'd show him what it was like.

My intention was to leave and let them be, as I didn't want to witness their togetherness. However, George held my hand, pleading with me not to go. In the end, I agreed to stay, but secretly, I had a plan. I wanted to teach George a lesson—to see how jealous he could get and to show him what it felt like when I saw them together. I couldn't quite pinpoint why I felt compelled to do this, but I was resolute. Next time, he wouldn't ask me to stay. So, I analysed every moment, ready to seize any opportunity to execute my plan.

At the club, a boy noticed me sitting alone and, mustering his courage, approached. I returned his smile politely, accepted his compliments, and even took the drink he offered. As the evening progressed, I invited him to join our table—a playful move designed to catch George's attention. Ever watchful, George observed my interactions closely.

In the dimly lit club, I found myself engaged in conversation with a boy. We delved into mundane topics—the end of the world, the Second World War, climate change, and global warming. Despite my forgetfulness regarding his name, we shared laughter over my dull jokes. Later, as George remained silent, I extended an invitation to the boy to join us at the hotel. That's when George's jealousy erupted, and our voices escalated into heated shouting.

"I will never talk to you again; I don't trust you anymore," he declared. "I'll never trust a woman like you! Why do you play such foolish games?"

"Why?" I retorted. "Because I'm tired of your games! I told you to let me go. Why did you want me to stay? You should have convinced your girlfriend to stay with you without me."

"You wanted to leave because someone special was waiting for you?" he pressed. "Why did you want to go?"

"No one was waiting for me," I replied, my resolve unwavering. "And you already know why I want to leave."

"You're lying!" George's anger flared. "I don't believe anything you say to me anymore. I don't want to see you!"

"Then I'll call a cab and leave," I shot back. "Next time you want to spend time with your girlfriend, forget about me!"

"Don't make me angrier than you already have," he warned. "You're not going anywhere!"

"You just said you don't want to see me!" I countered.

"I'll keep my eyes closed," he muttered.

"I just want to go as far away from you as I can," I confessed.

"But you just can't," he replied, a smile playing on his lips.

"One day I will!" I vowed.

As we left the club, it was too late to ga to the student's house. The student house curfew loomed—arriving after ten o'clock would trigger a call to my mom, and this could cause numerous troubles. George held my hand tightly, ensuring I wouldn't slip away. Haddaway's lyrics echoed in my mind: "What is love? Baby, don't hurt me, don't hurt me, no more.

The hotel, nestled amidst picturesque surroundings, exuded charm. Beyond its walls, near a serene lake, stood a row of quaint cottages. George had arranged for us to stay in one of these cosy abodes—a single-bedroom cottage with a spacious living room. As I stepped inside, I casually draped my coat over the couch. George, ever the gentleman, promptly took my coat and hung it up.

"Why do you wear my coat?" I asked him. "Can't you see it's too small and doesn't fit you?"

"It doesn't matter," he replied. "I'm heading to the bar to buy some drinks, and I want to make sure you're not leaving. I'll be back in five minutes."

"If I want to leave," I asserted, "I'll do so without my coat."

"Then I'll take you with me," he declared.

He led me to the bar, gesturing for me to sit at a table. Moments later, he ordered two glasses of wine.

"Why only two glasses?" I questioned. "You're supposed to buy drinks for everybody and go back. Adelle is waiting for you!"

"Let her wait," George said firmly. "Now we need to talk."

"What do you want to talk about?" I asked.

"Let's talk about us," he said, his gaze intense.

"What about us?" I wondered aloud.

In my mind, I started singing the lyrics: *"Hold on tight, hold onto me, 'cause tonight, it's all about us"* from T. A.T.u's song "All About Us." The melody echoed through my thoughts, intertwining with the emotions of the night.

"Why are we sad and feel empty," he asked, his eyes revealing a hidden sorrow, "when we can have everything and be together?"

"Can we really have everything?" I pondered. "It feels like a dream, hard to achieve. Perhaps we're merely playing, pretending we're in love."

"I just love you," he insisted, "and I don't pretend. But you keep pushing me away. Why?"

"Because life is full of coincidences," I replied, my voice soft yet resolute.

We continued our conversation, ignoring the others waiting for us. The bar was our refuge, but as it closed, we ended up sitting by the lake. The wine had flowed freely, and that night marked my first intoxication. Together, we gazed at the moon and stars, their brilliance casting shadows on our hearts.

"Tell me," he whispered, "what do you see when you look at the stars?"

"I see that destiny took away my life's brightest star," I confessed, "and that star was my father."

"Do you miss him?" he inquired.

"Yes," I replied, my voice catching. "I miss him terribly. I feel so alone."

"And what do you see?" I asked, turning the question back to him.

"I see that you're mine forever," he said, his gaze unwavering. "I love you beyond the moon and the stars."

"I love you too," I whispered, "but... I don't believe in fairy tales anymore."

"Shhh..." he hushed me, pulling me close. His kiss ignited a passion that swept us away—a moment when control slipped through our fingers, and desire bloomed under the moon and stars.

As dawn approached, we reluctantly returned to the cottage, our hearts entangled in a story that defied logic and embraced the magic of that unforgettable night.

The boy from the club, whom I had invited to join us, had already left. Adelle sat on the sofa, her eyes fixed on us, waiting for an explanation. Her gaze bore into us, the hurt palpable. All night, she had imagined scenarios of our whereabouts, but explanations seemed futile. The truth was etched across our flushed faces and tangled limbs.

"Where were you?" Adelle's voice trembled, her fingers gripping the edge of the sofa. "Why did you leave me alone?"

George sat up, torn between guilt and defiance. "Adelle," he began, his voice hoarse, "sometimes life takes unexpected turns. We can't always predict where our hearts will lead us."

"And what about me?" Adelle's voice cracked. "What about the promises we made?"

I watched, torn between sympathy and my own selfish desires. George had been my weakness, my forbidden fruit. But Adelle—she was the one who had stood by him. Did she know that 'forever' could be fragile, shattered by a single night of passion?

"Adelle," I finally spoke, my voice barely audible, "we didn't plan this. It just happened."

"Happened?" Her laughter was bitter. "Is that what you call it? A moment of weakness? A betrayal?"

She didn't know about my hidden relationship with George. Adelle deserved honesty, but my passion blurred the lines. Guilt weighed on me.

"It's not that simple," George interjected. "We've all made mistakes. But love isn't always neat and convenient. Sometimes, it's messy, painful, and—yes—unpredictable."

Adelle's eyes flickered between us, anger warring with heartache. "And what now? What do we do with this mess?"

"We'll figure it out," he whispered as if trying to convince himself. "We'll find a way to navigate this mess."

"Why?" she asked, her voice raw. "Why did you both choose this path?"

"One day," I whispered, "we'll find our answers."

As the sun rose, we hurried to catch the train, heading back to the student house by 6 a.m., burdened by the weight of a night that had changed everything.

Fragments of Love and Loss

After my pivotal moment with George, everything changed. Serendipity favoured us, and George embarked on a fresh journey, working with his brothers in Bucharest. His relationship with Adelle unravelled once again, but he found contentment working at his brothers' construction company.

At the same time, I ended things with Raul, and George and I quietly embraced our own love story. However, our secrecy couldn't last—my brother discovered our relationship, leading to a painful, catastrophic argument that shattered his long-standing friendship with George. I was left reeling, caught between my love for George and my brother's refusal to accept our bond.

Amid these upheavals, extraordinary news arrived: our family's legal battle over my father's accident finally bore fruit. Seven years later, we were victorious, receiving compensation from the responsible party. With those funds, I was able to secure my own apartment near my high school while my brother moved to a new place in another town.

My life entered a new chapter. With success and newfound financial stability, my childhood friends drifted away, perhaps driven by jealousy or resentment. But I chose self-improvement over competition. In the mirror, I saw my true adversary: myself. Surrounded by a world teeming with deceit, I embraced solitude over the company of false friends.

Life shifts—love slips away, friends fade, and fragments of yourself scatter. But unexpectedly, those pieces return. A fresh chapter unfolds, bringing better companions and a wiser reflection in the mirror.

Life took a turn, and suddenly, I found myself a homeowner, juggling responsibilities and living solo. Once I'd furnished my apartment and gathered everything I needed, I decided to rent out a room. It seemed like a practical way to earn extra income and split the bills. Initially, I considered offering the room to Adelle, but I hesitated. Our past friendship had been lukewarm, and it was time to forge new connections.

Enter Anna—a fellow high school alum, though we'd been in different classes. When she learned about my available room, her interest was piqued. Having experienced student housing, she appreciated my reasonable price. Within days, Anna became my roommate, and I felt fortunate to have her as a friend.

Anna brought warmth and positivity to our shared space. Her laughter echoed through the apartment, transforming mundane moments into cherished memories. She was considerate, tidying up after herself and respecting boundaries. Late nights were spent sharing stories and dreams, creating a bond that felt like family. Anna turned my house into a warm embrace—a true friend in this exciting new chapter of life.

My clandestine relationship with George continued. Weekends became our sanctuary, where we revelled in stolen moments before he returned to work. In his arms, I felt like a radiant princess, and our time together transcended ordinary boundaries.

But then came the day George shared life-altering news. He had an opportunity in London—one that promised stability and financial independence. He hoped to buy his own place while I was about to graduate from high school. Our future together felt uncertain.

"What are you saying? When will you come back? What about us?" I pleaded.

"There won't be an 'us' anymore," George replied, his voice heavy with regret. "Our relationship ends here. I don't know when I'll return, and I don't trust you enough. You're young—you won't wait for me. Perhaps someone better awaits you."

"Why don't you trust me?" I implored. "You've known me for so long. I'll wait for you.

"It's better for both of us to stop here," he insisted. "Let's not make promises."

But I clung to our shared promises. "I promised to be yours forever! I won't give up on us!"

"Maybe you'll be happier without me," George murmured, his sadness palpable.

"You'll search for me in another person, but you'll never find me. I promise! You're not brave enough to love me; you're just a coward. All this time, you pretended to love me. You can't just leave if you truly love someone."

Tears streamed down my face as I faced the painful truth. Love wasn't convenient; it demanded courage and unwavering commitment. At that moment, I vowed to hold onto our promise, even if George chose a different path.

His words pierced my heart like arrows, leaving behind scars—remnants of my first colossal mistake. Perhaps I shouldn't have accepted his departure, but love, it seemed, was both my salvation and my undoing.

That night, our tears mingled with passion as we made love. I traced his skin as if it were the last time, the bittersweet ache of impending separation hanging heavy in the air. My grandmother's wisdom echoed: "If you love someone, you have to let them go. If they return, they're yours; if not, they never were."

As our paths diverged, I whispered, "I'm going to miss you." His voice, tinged with sadness, replied, "Maybe one day, we'll meet again."

I fought back tears as he left, knowing that his departure signalled our paths diverge. The unexpected ending fractured my heart, yet they say what shatters you won't necessarily heal you. True love, they insist, won't abandon you.

The following day, George boarded a London-bound flight. I clung to hope—maybe we'd keep in touch, exchange phone calls. Perhaps he'd miss me, reappear at my doorstep. But it remained a fragile fantasy. Countless thoughts swirled: Did we not fit? Was it simply wrong timing? Six months slipped by, and his call never came. *"E io aspetto ad un telefono, litigando che sia libero, con il cuore nello stomaco"*—Laura Pausini's words etched into my soul.

During that time, I changed. Craving attention, I wore a mask of false happiness. My heart grew cold, and I played with love, only to vanish when others grew close. Lucas, a kind childhood friend, confessed his feelings, but my heart was too broken to respond. I left him just as George had left me.

In that dark period, I hurt someone undeserving. One day, I accompanied my cousin Mary to a club, and there, I encountered Lucas. We'd known each other since childhood—playing hide-and-seek in my grandmother's garden. Lucas, with newfound courage, confessed his feelings. He liked me, he said, and I was the first girl he'd ever fallen in love with. His confession touched me, but I explained that my heart had closed its doors. Still, he persisted, urging me to unlock them once more.

For two weeks, we exchanged calls and texts. He invited me out repeatedly, but I declined. Yet, there he stood—patient, romantic, and kind—waiting near my house. Sometimes with a bouquet of flowers, sometimes ready to accompany me home after classes. Lucas hoped that one day I'd love him, but I shattered his heart. My selfishness blinded me to his efforts. I vanished from his life, leaving no trace, believing my absence might somehow complete the missing piece of his puzzle.

Despite his hopeful encouragement, I couldn't touch him. Love remained elusive; a distant star I dared not reach for. Instead, I played with words, weaving a trap that ensnared him. It was as if I lifted him to the clouds, only to release my grip and watch him plummet. Perhaps honesty should have been my compass from the start—sharing my story, revealing why love was an uncharted territory for me. Had I bared my soul, he might have glimpsed the game I played.

In those days, I wore cruelty like armour, my heart encased in ice. A stranger even to myself, I sought no peace. Yet, a whisper echoed within: "One day, love will pierce harder than any pain you've caused." Lucas, unaware of my true reasons, remained a mystery—a thread lost in the folds of time, unanswered questions trailing behind.

Years passed, and through my cousin Mary, I learned of Lucas's inquiries. He sought me out, desperate to bridge the gap. But fate conspired against us. Lucas never married; his heart remained steadfast, unable to trust another. And then, a digital echo: a Facebook friend request. I blocked his profile, sealing our unfinished tale.

A Journey Through Heartache, Healing, and Self-Discovery

After some time, weary of my circumstances, I decided on a brief visit to my mother and grandmother. In my grandmother's embrace, I sought comfort and the peace that had long eluded me. My mother couldn't stay with me, her duty lay with my ageing grandmother and their small farm. As we both grew older, my mother assumed the role of caretaker, tending to the farm. A few hours helping her yielded unexpected rewards—a bag full of home-grown goodies.

On my way to the train station, fate intervened. Raul crossed my path once more. We exchanged brief words, and impulsively, I invited him to my place. I couldn't explain why. Raul could never replace George; I had no illusions about that. He wasn't my type, and there was no attraction. But perhaps it was time to move forward, to loosen the grip of the past. I spent time with Raul, knowing he couldn't mend my heart but hoping he might help me turn a new page.

Everyone did what was best for them; now it's my turn," I whispered to myself. Change beckoned—a chance for new beginnings. And as Cher's lyrics echoed in my mind, I found myself wondering: *"Do you believe in life after love? I can feel something inside me say, I really don't think you're strong enough.*

I thought I could trust Raul and decided it was worth giving him another chance. After visiting my grandmother, I invited him to my apartment, and we spent some time together. We shared moments of joy, and both tried to make the relationship work. But happiness lasted only two weeks.

Raul's jealousy became suffocating. Even a simple trip to the store for bread triggered scenes of possessiveness. I attempted to reassure him, but his lack of trust persisted. Our time together turned into arguments, and I finally suggested breaking up. His desperate threat of self-harm weighed heavily on me.

Sometimes, we rush into love to avoid loneliness, making compromises we think we can endure. Yet, we wake up in stories where we no longer recognize ourselves, unsure how to escape. I felt responsible for Raul's emotions, hoping love would eventually prevail.

But not everything is meant to be. Despite our efforts, some relationships don't work out. It's essential not to fear losing what wasn't meant for us and to accept that certain things remain beyond our understanding. Everything happens for a reason. Live, love, and learn from it.

I grappled with guilt over Raul's shifting moods and emotions, convincing myself that I was responsible for every twist in his life. My intention was never to harm him; I genuinely wished him happiness. Yet, he lacked self-trust, making it impossible for him to fully trust me. Still, I persisted in the relationship, hoping time would strengthen our connection. But life doesn't always unfold as we expect, and sometimes, despite our best efforts, things unravel. It's essential to accept that some mysteries will remain out of reach. Embrace life, love it, and learn from it.

There are moments when life quietly demands that we pause and listen to the whispers of our hearts. To reflect on the choices we've made, and wonder if they have led us to the happiness we crave. To gather the courage to follow the dreams that truly belong to us. To ask our hearts if they are full—or if a single, missing piece awaits someone who can make them whole.

Negative thoughts and hidden emotions are our strongest adversaries. If we don't break free from these destructive patterns, we become prisoners of our own minds, and our hearts suffer in silence. Life needn't be as intricate as our minds often paint it.

Take a moment to pause and look deep within yourself, to uncover who you truly are. Contemplate the dreams that stir your soul before they drift beyond your reach. Ask yourself whether the path you walk honours your heart's deepest desires. As Dr. Alban so powerfully sings, 'It's my life, take it or leave it, set me free.' Let those words be a reminder to claim the life—and love—you were meant to embrace.

I wear my scars with pride; they testify to my resilience against life's trials. Looking back, I see pain, missteps, and heartache. Yet, in my reflection, I find strength, wisdom from hard-earned lessons, and pride in my journey. When I peer into my own eyes, I ask, "Am I truly content?" The answer is elusive, but I seek a new direction, a way to navigate life's complexities.

The crucial realization? Even when the world questions me, I choose to trust in myself. Self-belief is a quiet, potent magic, capable of reshaping the very soul. I have changed—the person I once was no longer fits this life I am meant to live. Transformation is inevitable, and every twist of fate carries purpose. Though the path may feel chaotic now, one day clarity will arrive, and everything will fall beautifully into place.

The mirror becomes my confidante, reminding me of my essence. It whispers encouragement: 'Trust yourself, persist.' My grandmother's wisdom echoes: 'Feel pain but wear your smile as armour.' Our world harbours both disguised monsters and scar-adorned angels. Kindness matters, yet we learn to shield ourselves from harm as we grow. Life, like a cryptic puzzle, has revealed both its shadows and its hidden gems. Amidst chaos and uncertainty, I've learned to seek pockets of happiness wherever I stand. Life's curriculum taught me to fiercely defend my dreams and prioritize my well-being. Even when the world seemed like a tempest, I anchored myself in self-awareness and unwavering desires.

A Christmas Encounter

One week before Christmas in 2007, a new chapter unfolded in my life. Raul proposed we spend the holiday with his family at their parents' home, mentioning that his sister Evelin and her husband, Andrew, would also be there. After much contemplation, I decided to join them for a festive gathering. With bags packed, I hailed a taxi and embarked on the journey to Raul's childhood home. Along the way, I wrestled with self-doubt and reservations but clung to the hope of a memorable Christmas.

Upon arrival, Raul's parents welcomed us with open arms, treating me as one of their own, which helped ease my nerves. Later that day, Evelin and Andrew arrived. Though I had seen Evelin during my school days, we had never spoken. Destiny, or perhaps life's complex weave, brought us together once more. When I greeted Evelin, she seemed genuinely pleased to see me beside her brother and introduced me to her husband, Andrew. The moment he took my hand, time seemed to halt. His eyes held a peculiar familiarity, an unspoken connection, and in that instant, I felt as though I had met him in a dream. His endearing smile captivated me, and in that moment, my world shifted irrevocably. Strength and vulnerability, beauty and imperfection—all seemed to converge within me.

I extended my hand to introduce myself, trying to appear composed while my mind raced. A whirlwind of impossible thoughts stirred; I felt like a girl lost in a fairy-tale. Andrew's smile, both charming and mysterious, held me spellbound, and his gaze, powerful and magnetic, pierced through my defences. Those deep brown eyes, framed by long lashes, left me breathless, and I couldn't break away as though ensnared by fate.

Andrew remained polite, yet his voice resonated deeply, setting my heart aflame. I teetered between strength and vulnerability in a beautiful paradox that would be forever etched in memory. As the day unfolded, everyone chatted and made plans for Christmas. Raul's family were welcoming, but I never felt they were truly mine. My heart wasn't with Raul; we clung to our relationship out of reluctance to part during the holiday season. Raul understood—the unspoken awareness lingered between us like mistletoe.

I eventually slipped outside, seeking quiet in the winter air, and lit a cigarette, lost in a storm of thoughts. Why had Andrew stirred me so deeply? It was as if I'd fallen under a powerful spell. Remembering my grandmother's words—''Hate has logic, but love doesn't''—I realised life orchestrates encounters for a reason. Some people are fleeting, while others become woven into our existence. As I reflected, I saw Andrew tending the grill despite the biting cold, flames reflecting my inner turmoil. *"This girl is on fire,"* Alicia Keys sings—a fitting anthem to my feelings.

I tried not to stare, but Andrew's yellow sports jumper with white stripes on the sleeves and black athletic trousers lent him a striking look. His gaze seemed to read my thoughts, and when he invited me closer, my cheeks flushed.

"Why stand there in the cold?" he asked. "Come warm up by the fire."

"Thank you," I replied, "it truly is chilly outside."

"Vodka warms the soul," he offered. "Stand near the fire and get hot", he invited me.

''Your vodka is welcome," I said, my mind racing. "But do you think I can get hotter than this?"

His eyes glittered. "You're already too hot. I'll tread carefully not to get burned."

"Play with fire, get burned," I quipped, emboldened.

He stoked the flames. "Let's keep the fire alive. I must grill some meat."

"I can assist," I volunteered, drawn into our shared warmth.

Our smiles lingered, our glances full of unspoken words. After a few minutes, with the help of another vodka shot, our conversation flowed easily. We tended to the grill, the sizzle of the meat punctuating our talk. Time stretched as we savoured each other's presence, feeling as though we had known each other forever. Evelin interrupted us, checking on the nearly charred meat. As we moved inside for dinner, laughter filled the room.

Around the table, everyone shared funny stories. Despite his marriage to Evelin, Andrew seemed like an outsider, a reminder of the formality between Raul and me. A silent tension simmered between Evelin's parents and Andrew, but I dismissed it as a holiday strain. Love often hides silent sorrows.

I remained by Raul's side until nearly midnight, eager to engage in their discussions and share amusing stories. Amidst their banter, I discovered that Andrew was roughly eight years my senior. At that moment, I reassured myself: "Age is irrelevant; Andrew's life experiences make him dependable." But what truly mattered was the way Andrew occasionally met my gaze and offered a warm smile—a silent affirmation of something more between us.

Even the most brilliant minds struggle to convey love to those who haven't experienced it. Sometimes, words become superfluous for those who already hold the answer within. When Andrew's eyes met mine, butterflies danced in my stomach. I fell in love with him from the very first second, I laid eyes on him. His enchanting gaze set my heart racing. My emotions felt like déjà vu—I sensed that I'd glimpsed his eyes in another time, another existence. Despite the familiarity, I dismissed the uncanny feeling. As Adriana Mezzardri sings in 'Marcas de Ayer' (with English subtitles), *"I feel like I've known you for so long, from another millennium and another sky."*

The next day, I awoke to an empty room and noticed it was nearly 10 AM. I dressed, tidied up, and noticed Evelin's wedding dress hanging in the closet. This was my first close look at such a gown. Without thinking, I slipped it on, intending to show Raul. Instead, I encountered Andrew in the hallway, his gaze sparking with amusement.

"Good morning, princess," he said.

"Good morning, my prince!" I replied, my heart fluttering.

Andrew smiled. "I believe you're lost. Allow me to guide you back to your castle."

I straightened my imaginary crown. "I need to reclaim my empire. We've been invaded, and an evil prince now rules our kingdom. It's time to gather my strength and prepare for battle."

As I entered the kitchen, Raul's mother stood there. Our eyes met, and we exchanged smiles before I hurriedly passed by her. However, the moment she caught sight of me in the wedding dress, she erupted in anger.

"You're going to steal Evelin's destiny!" she snapped. "Wearing a used wedding dress brings bad luck."

"I'm just trying it on," I explained. "I want to see how I look in a wedding dress."

"Go and change it now!" she demanded.

Back in the room, I pondered her words. Could wearing a second-hand wedding dress truly affect my fate? Did the previous bride's destiny somehow transfer to the gown? I'd seen movies where people sold or auctioned their wedding dresses. Why, in this case, looks different? In the end, I decided to let it go because there was no answer. When I returned to the kitchen, Raul's mom acted as if nothing had happened. But the mystery lingered—was there more to that dress than fabric and lace?

The remainder of the day slipped by swiftly. Everyone bustled about, preparing for Christmas Eve—cooking, cleaning, and setting the stage for festivities. Andrew's presence cast a comforting spell, his handsome smile momentarily erased thoughts of Raul and my troubles. Unfortunately, I never found an opportunity to converse with Andrew or steal a few precious minutes in his company.

Christmas Eve and Christmas Day unfolded harmoniously, enveloping us in the spirit of the season. Laughter and joy permeated the air, and everyone behaved as expected. As evening approached, we all agreed to head to the club for more merriment. The pulsing beat of the music echoed the lyrics: *"Your love feels so good, and that's what takes me high"* (from Sonique's "It Feels So Good"). My heart fluttered as I anticipated returning to the same club where I'd first noticed George's striking features and felt his gaze upon me. I allowed myself to imagine—perhaps he would be there too, and our paths would cross once more. In my daydream, he'd stride over, seize my hand, and passionately declare that Raul wasn't the right match for me, affirming that I belonged to him.

At the club, surrounded by friends, I danced freely, laughter bubbling forth. Two glasses of whiskey and ice lent a pleasant warmth, though I wasn't overly concerned. Raul, on the other hand, had indulged a bit too much. Yet, with Andrew nearby, I felt secure.

Evelin's whereabouts remained a mystery, but when Andrew extended his hand, inviting me to dance, I knew I couldn't refuse. The night held promise, and destiny swirled around us like the music on the dance floor.

He took my hand, gently hugged me, and then squeezed my waist tightly while looking into my eyes. For a second, I felt like George was holding me, and Andrew's eyes looked exactly like George's. The whiskey and Andrew's perfume drove me crazy. His arms were strong, and he guided me to the rhythm of the music. I don't know what song was playing, but we danced like tango experts as if there was no one else around us and the dance floor belonged solely to us. It was like a dream. *"With my body and my soul, I want you more than you'll ever know"* (from "The Time of My Life" by Bill Medley and Jennifer Warnes).

At some point, we stopped dancing. He held me tight, and then we almost kissed. 'Let's make history even if everyone's against us,' I told myself in my mind. One of life's biggest mistakes is never having the courage to risk and lose the chance. I felt his lips, but somehow, I slipped. It was as if an evil force pushed me away, and we fell.

In a way, it was fortunate that we fell. If we had kissed, Raul or Evelin might have seen us, leading to a massive argument and other unfavourable outcomes. However, part of me wished I could have kissed him at that moment. Everything happens for a reason. He quickly got up and then helped me to my feet, both of us laughing. These events were simultaneously funny and serious. I remember wearing an elegant white shirt, white jeans, a red coat, and red boots. When we fell, I got completely dirty—my white jeans and shirt were no longer white. He apologized for what happened and went to retrieve my coat. I put it on, and together, we went in search of Evelin and Raul.

Outside, in front of the club, Evelin was arguing with the security guy. Andrew went to see what was going on, and Evelin claimed that her purse had been stolen. Everyone gathered around and watched that unpleasant scene. Luckily, her purse was found immediately, but Evelin overreacted and exaggerated, taking advantage of being in the centre of attention. Maybe it was because of the whisky, or perhaps that was just her personality. When Raul came over to me, I asked him to go back home, and then we took a taxi and left. When I got home, I went straight to bed so I wouldn't see or hear anyone else. In my mind, there were only those moments when I was dancing with Andrew. *"Follow me to a place where we can be absolutely free"* (from Sky by Sonique).

The next morning, I resolved to talk to Raul. I needed to leave to create distance from Raul, Evelin, and Andrew. Just as I was about to start, Evelin joined us, her expression hiding a surprise. She revealed Andrew hadn't come home. He'd argued with her about the purse incident and stayed out. When Andrew finally returned, visibly drunk, he confessed in private that his absence wasn't because of me—he couldn't handle being close to me and distant at the same time.

Just as I was about to broach the topic with Raul, Evelin joined us, her smile masking unexpected news: Andrew hadn't come home the previous night. She returned alone from the club after a heated argument with him about the stolen purse incident. The whole situation felt surreal, reinforcing my desire to leave. So, I told them I wanted to go. Raul looked upset, and Evelin asked me to stay longer. She suggested we spend New Year's Eve together—shopping, cooking, and having fun. She wanted me to stay with

Raul, not leaving him alone even on New Year's Eve. Despite my reluctance, her proposal to celebrate at my place appealed to me. Perhaps it was because I felt safer and stronger there. With no other choice, we waited for Andrew to come home.

The next day, Andrew stumbled home, almost drunk. During our brief moments alone, he confessed that his absence wasn't because of me. He explained that he couldn't simultaneously be so close and so distant from me. His alcohol-induced state made it hard for me to believe what he was saying. Despite our physical proximity, true connection eluded us. Strangely, it felt as if we'd known each other for years, not just a few days.

Evelin asked Andrew where he had been, and he replied—while looking directly at me—that he had been at his brother Michael's house. Evelin seemed to accept his answer without question and didn't press him further. I found myself studying their relationship, trying to make sense of it. Whatever Andrew did, it didn't appear to bother Evelin—or perhaps she simply chose not to care. Strangely, I realized I felt more jealous than she did. A part of me longed to ask Andrew where he had really been and why he hadn't come home. Why hadn't he taken Evelin with him to visit his brother? Later, I learned that one of Andrew's brothers lived in the same village, barely ten minutes from Evelin's parents' house, while another lived in a nearby village.

New Year's Enchantment

The next morning, we got ready to return to my apartment. During the drive, I learned something that surprised me: Andrew's father and grandparents actually lived in the same town as I did. Since he had been raised by his grandparents, he knew the city well—its streets, its schools, and its familiar corners from childhood. Before heading to my place, we stopped at the supermarket to pick up a few things for the New Year's Eve party. As we shopped together, I couldn't help but feel a warm thrill knowing Andrew was coming to my home. I wanted everything to be perfect, to make him feel as comfortable as possible. To me, he wasn't just another guest—he was the special one. As the song says, *"When you have your private party, I hope that I'm invited"* (Enrique Iglesias, Push It).

We both felt it—that something extraordinary was unfolding between us. Out of the millions of people in this world, he was the only one I wanted, even though deep down I knew I could never truly have him. Everything between us carried the weight of being forbidden, even the smallest, most innocent glance. Maybe that's the strange allure of the forbidden—it tempts the heart all the more. Each time my eyes met his, it was as if I were committing a quiet sin, one that both thrilled and tormented me. As the lyrics say, *"There is no sweeter innocence than our gentle sin"* (Hozier, Take Me to Church).

New Year's Eve unfolded in the kitchen with Evelin, where we busied ourselves preparing the meal and setting the table for the night's celebration. When everything was ready, I slipped away to steal a few moments for myself. I wanted to look perfect. Following tradition, I chose something red—symbolizing luck in love—and slipped a coin into my pocket for prosperity. I settled on an elegant cream blouse with red-dotted sleeves and curled my hair in soft waves. As I caught my reflection in the mirror, a flutter of innocence and anticipation washed over me, as if I were a schoolgirl again, nervously waiting for something magical to happen. In that instant, Britney Spears' words echoed in my mind: *"Oh, baby, baby, the reason I breathe is you. Boy, you've got me blinded."*

All through the evening, Andrew's gaze carried a quiet intensity, his smile both endearing and disarming. The passage from one year into the next felt almost enchanted with him by my side. As midnight drew near, he handed me a crystal flute of champagne, his voice warm and steady as he reminded me to make a wish. I returned his smile, my heart fluttering with unspoken feelings. In that brief, shimmering moment, Nicholas Sparks' words echoed in my mind: *"In the blink of an eye, something happens by chance—when you least expect it—that sets you on a course you never planned, into a future you never imagined.*

Minutes later Andrew leaned in, his voice a soft murmur. "Did you enjoy the champagne?"

"It's delightful," I said, savouring the sweetness. "A little bit magical, too."

He chuckled. "I don't like it."

"Why not?" I asked, pretending innocence. "Don't you like sweet things?"

His lips brushed my ear as he whispered, "I do — and you're the sweetest thing here."

His words made me blush; my mind scrambled for an answer. Sensing my reaction, he folded me into a warm embrace, and I felt bolder. "Happy New Year," I managed, breathless. "I made my wish. Did you make one, too?"

He grinned, mischievous. "Oh yes. A crazy wish."

"Did you know," I teased, "that telling your wish makes it more likely to come true?"

He leaned closer, eyes dancing. "Hmmm… you're a witch, aren't you?"

I laughed. "Yes — a witch, and I'll put a spell on you."

His eyebrows shot up. "Well, that was my wish."

I lowered my voice. "But I didn't say whether I'm a good witch or a bad one. Do you still want me to enchant you?"

His fingers brushed mine; I smiled. "You've already enchanted me," he said.

His words held me captive, my heartbeat quickening as he gazed at me. "You're merely enchanted," I thought to myself, "but you stole my heart from the very beginning." I felt as if I was floating, only to come crashing back to the reality that kept us apart.

His words intensified my desire for him, yet I knew he couldn't be mine. Our mutual attraction was undeniable; my intuition had not led me astray. But the harsh truth remained: reality diverged from our shared longing.

As Annie Lennox's haunting lyrics echoed in my mind—"I put a spell on you because you're mine"—I grappled with the enchantment that bound us.

The New Year's party slowly came to an end as guests began to leave—everyone except Raul. He lingered, clearly wanting a chance to speak with me. As we tidied up together, our conversation remained light and amicable. To my surprise, he admitted that he agreed with my decision to end things between us, and we promised to stay in touch.

Before leaving, Raul mentioned that he would be spending a few more days with his parents before returning to his job in Bucharest. Then, almost casually, he added something that caught me off guard: he was one of Andrew's employees. As if that revelation weren't enough, he went on to say that Andrew co-owned a construction company with his brother, James. His words lingered with me long after he left, adding yet another layer of mystery to Andrew—and leaving me with far more questions than answers.

Shadows of Desire

As the new year settled in, life gradually returned to its familiar rhythm. Anna came back to my flat after the school Christmas holidays, and together we threw ourselves into studying, with exams drawing closer each day. Time seemed to blur, the hours swallowed up by endless reading and revision as I focused intently on my goals.

Meanwhile, Raul remained a steady presence in my life. He bridged the distance with regular phone calls and visited every few weeks, his company a welcome break from the monotony of study. Yet, even in his presence, my mind often wandered elsewhere. Unfinished stories lingered in my heart, and George's memory haunted me like an unanswered question. Where had he gone? Why had he left so suddenly? His silence weighed heavily on me, leaving an ache I couldn't quite put into words—a shadow I carried quietly with me.

Even though that chapter had closed, George remained in my thoughts. I couldn't stop wondering—where was he now, what was he doing, and why had he chosen such heartless silence after leaving? The ache of missing him gnawed at me, his absence like an unanswered question that echoed endlessly through time.

Days turned into weeks, and weeks into months, yet the same worn-out phrase lingered on our lips: 'I'm okay.' Six months slipped by in the blink of an eye, and suddenly the school summer holiday had arrived. Anna flew to Italy to spend time with her mother, while I stayed behind with no plans of my own—no travels, no companions, only long, sun-drenched days that stretched out before me in solitude.

But life, ever the trickster, had its own plans. Just when I had stopped expecting anything new, Raul's call shifted everything. He invited me to spend a week at his sister's apartment in Bucharest. While he would be busy with work, I was to explore the city with Evelin and Andrew—an adventure I hadn't dared to imagine.

Raul arrived to pick me up the following morning, his cheerful energy a sharp contrast to my quiet anticipation. The drive to Bucharest stretched on for four hours, the passing landscapes giving me time to wonder about Andrew. Would he be the same as I remembered? Would he even notice me among the bustling city?

When we finally arrived, Andrew was waiting calm, composed, and impossibly magnetic. Raul handed me over with a teasing grin, instructing him to look after me, even joking that he should hold my hand to make sure I didn't wander off. Andrew's hand found mine with effortless familiarity, and a warmth spread through me at the simple touch. It was as though our connection required no words— just the quiet understanding of hands brushing together, and I knew then that I'd follow him anywhere.

The city stretched out before me, calling to be explored, yet the long drive had left me drained, my hunger and fatigue pulling against my desire to keep going. Andrew didn't let go of my hand. He stayed beside me, calm and steady, as if reading my thoughts without a word. When I finally asked how much longer it would be, he met my gaze and whispered gently, "Just thirty minutes." It felt as though he understood not only my question but the quiet longing beneath it.

People vary; some remain oblivious even after hours of conversation, while others grasp your soul with a single look. Andrew fell into the latter category—a silent understanding that transcended words.

Finally, we arrived home, where Evelin was waiting. Her greeting felt a little forced, her smile carefully masking something she wasn't ready to share. I sensed the tension in the air, a quiet unease that lingered even as we settled in. Yet by the evening, when Raul returned from work, the atmosphere softened. His presence brought a natural warmth, easing the edges of strain and allowing moments of genuine connection to peek through.

The next morning, the scent of coffee filled the air. I smiled, thinking, "Love is in the air, and it smells like coffee." Andrew stood in the kitchen, brewing my coffee for the first time. "Life begins after coffee," I thought, "and today, I need it more than ever.

"Good morning!" I greeted him, inhaling deeply. "It smells amazing."

"Your coffee is ready," Andrew replied. "How much sugar would you like?"

"Two teaspoons, please," I said, grateful. "And where's Evelin?"

"She's at work," he explained. "Probably forgot to mention it last night. But don't worry—I'll be your tour guide today. I know Bucharest like the back of my hand. Lived here since I was sixteen."

I grinned. "Perfect! You can be my personal guide. Just promise it won't break the bank."

Andrew chuckled. "Consider it a discount."

"Thank you," I said, feeling lucky. "Today must be my day."

As I sipped my coffee, I marvelled at the unexpected turn of events. Sometimes, the universe conspires to grant our wishes—even the seemingly impossible ones. And today, with Andrew by my side, I was ready to explore Bucharest, guided by fate and a touch of magic.

After coffee, we both changed into white outfits by chance—a coincidence that felt like a silent pact. Hand in hand, we set off to explore the city, blending in with the tourists, lost in each other's company. From the towering Palace of Parliament to the bustling streets, we wandered, laughing and sharing secrets as we went.

At lunchtime, we found ourselves on a terrace overlooking a lake in Youth Park. Flowers bloomed around us, sunlight sparkled on the water, and across the table, Andrew's gaze held a promise I dared not speak aloud. We shared a cold lemon beer, and as the conversation deepened, we both felt the pull of something unspoken—a shared desire too precious to voice. Yet the weight of reality lingered, a reminder of the people we'd hurt if we crossed that line.

As we sipped cold lemon beer, courage flowed. Our conversation delved deeper, unravelling secrets. We both sensed the gravity of our attraction, yet reason whispered caution. Forbidden territory lay ahead—we couldn't risk hurting Raul and Evelin. So, we maintained distance, our eyes aflame with desire, hearts yearning for more.

Our footsteps danced through the park, his hand in mine—a silent promise to follow him anywhere. As long as he held on, I'd journey to the ends of the earth.

"Movie?" he asked, interrupting our reverie. Before I could respond, he halted, eyes locking with mine. His approach was gentle and deliberate. And then, his lips met mine—a kiss that unravelled time. In that stolen breath, I glimpsed decades ahead: 80 years mapped out in the press of our mouths.

We clung to each other, barely breathing, lost in the moment. Reality blurred; we wished those stolen seconds could stretch into eternity. Robbie Williams' lyrics echoed: *"I just want to feel real love, 'cause I've got too much life running through my veins."*

When our lips finally parted, we returned to the world—aching, guilty, and forever changed. Our silence spoke volumes. Our gazes are a mix of guilt and passion. Hand in hand, we headed to the cinema, opting for the X-Files movie. As the film played, our lips were too busy to notice the plot. In the dim theatre, the eerie X-Files soundtrack enveloped us. The twist? We became the movie's antiheroes, our connection a tantalizing enigma. The only difference between the X-Files movie and reality was that we became the negative characters from the movies—we were the criminals. Our actions felt sinful, yet we revelled in those beautiful, forbidden moments—until Raul's call shattered our guilty reverie.

Raul had just finished work and called me to meet him near his sister's house. He suggested we go to a restaurant for dinner. Raul shared the exact location with Andrew and me, and we hurried to catch the bus, eager to get there. After about fifteen minutes, we arrived at the spot. Raul stood in front of the restaurant, scanning the buses, looking for us. Unfortunately, luck was not on our side—Raul saw me kiss Andrew through the bus window. In that moment, I had kissed Andrew for the last time to express gratitude for a wonderful day and the great moments we'd shared, without realizing Raul could see us.

After stepping off the bus, we encountered Raul. Without warning, he slapped me across the face and confronted us about witnessing our kiss during the bus ride. I stood there, stunned, unsure of how to respond. Andrew, on the other hand, denied everything vehemently. He dismissed Raul's account, claiming it was a product of an overactive imagination. Andrew couldn't bring himself to tell the truth, and I understood that revealing it would be equally problematic. Strangely, in that moment, I hoped Andrew would confess. I wished he'd acknowledge our shared humanity, recognizing that everyone makes mistakes. But perhaps it was too early for such honesty. After all, courage is a rare trait—few are willing to admit their faults.

After numerous debates and fabricated explanations, Raul somehow chose to believe us. Perhaps indifference or jealousy clouded his judgment, leading him to dismiss his own suspicions. He even apologized for the slap, acting as if nothing had transpired. Later, after dinner, we returned home together. My emotions were a tumultuous mix of devastation, misery, guilt, and confusion.

Later that night, as I lay alone, I longed for solitude, desperate to escape the weight of my thoughts. I wanted a love that would stand by me, but I realised, perhaps too late, that I'd chosen the wrong hero. Bonnie Tyler's lyrics echoed in my head: *"I need a hero."* But heroes don't dwell in shadows, and I couldn't live as the "other."

Raul was mine, but the passion was gone, no spark, no fire—just the hollow comfort of possession. Andrew was the spark, but a love built on secrecy couldn't last. And so, with a heart full of questions, I waited for morning, hoping for a new beginning.

Yet, how naive was I to consider Andrew my hero? Our connection couldn't transcend an affair, and I despised the role of the mistress. It wasn't me. I didn't want exclusive ownership of him; I didn't want to share him either.

Whispers of Unspoken Desires

Over the weekend, I stayed at home with Raul, Evelin, and Andrew. We cooked together, played music, and watched films, slipping into a comfortable rhythm that made the past feel like a distant memory. Yet beneath the surface, none of us were truly content. Each of us performed our part with the precision of seasoned actors, but genuine happiness remained elusive. Life often assigns us roles, and we play them dutifully, knowing that within those roles, true victory or fulfilment is out of reach. Sometimes, our strength lies not in continuing the act but in stepping away from the stage and moving forward.

Each morning offered a fresh start, a chance to rewrite the story in small, quiet ways. That particular Monday, I woke to the rich aroma of coffee, a sign that Andrew was already in the kitchen. The weight of our shared secret lingered in the air—the unspoken truth that tied us together in ways no one else could understand. As I stepped inside, a tangle of emotions gripped me. Should I remain distant and composed, protecting myself? Or let my heart speak freely, ignoring the boundaries we had carefully drawn?

"Good morning," I said, my voice steady but my heart racing. "Thank you for the coffee."

Andrew met my eyes, and I saw our reality mirrored in them. Guilt, regret, disappointment—they swirled between us. He tried to apologise, but his words failed. We both knew there was no easy escape, no path that wouldn't hurt someone. "There's no way to tell the truth, "He finally whispered. "We're not ready for the consequences."

I nodded, my throat tight. "It's better this way," I agreed. "For everyone."

His sad smile tore at my insides. "Then forget everything," he said, his voice barely audible. "If you can."

And so we continued, coffee in hand, carrying our hidden truths like a quiet weight between us—a fresh start shadowed by the burden we could neither share nor escape. Andrew's gaze held a subtle melancholy, his attempted smile failing to hide the emotion beneath. Some things, I realized, were better left unsaid. The tension hung in the air, delicate yet persistent, threatening to upset the fragile balance we maintained.

"Do you want to explore the city together again?" he asked, trying to shift our focus away from the weight of our situation. "Let me be your guide once more."

I hesitated, then whispered, "Only if you hold my hand."

At that moment, I felt invincible. With Andrew's warmth beside me, the outside world ceased to matter. We sipped our coffee, cocooned in our shared secret, and I decided to take a daring step. After a quick shower, I emerged in white shorts and a simple T-shirt. Without overthinking, I handed him the sun cream.

"Could you please apply this to my legs?" I challenged, surprising even myself. It was a daring move, a silent invitation. I didn't know where this would lead, but I wanted to find out.

Andrew's eyes met mine, and in that silent glance, he understood. The television murmured in the background, a programme detailing a high-stakes experiment called the Black Hole unfolding in Germany. Yet in that moment, we were participants in our own experiment—a fragile dance of desire and consequence. He reached for the sun cream, choosing us over the distant chaos on the screen.

He settled beside me on the sofa, and as he took the cream, I rested my legs across his lap. His touch was deliberate, careful, each movement imbued with intention, his gaze holding mine longer than necessary. On the screen, the presenter began a tense countdown from ten, marking the start of the experiment. The stakes were cosmic—the fate of the universe itself seemed to hang in the balance. My pulse raced, a mix of fear and exhilaration, and I instinctively clung to him. Then, with a sudden release, the presenter declared the experiment a success. Relief washed over me, and in that suspended moment, I pressed my lips to Andrew's. The kiss sparked between us like an unseen fuse, ignited by the universe's narrow escape and the electricity we had been holding at bay.

He kissed me with a deliberate slowness, his touch igniting a fire within me. Our bodies pressed together; our breaths stolen by desire. In that moment, reality eclipsed any dream. Some of the best moments in our lives are the ones we can't tell anyone about. I'm built from every mistake I've ever made, and when I get older, I will remember that I held in my arms a truly beautiful soul. *"Can you feel my love, can you hear my thoughts, can you feel everything?"* (Blaxy Girls, If You Feel My Love).

Whisky and Goodbyes

After surrendering to our gravest mistake, guilt clung to us like a shadow. The city's beauty—its museums and palaces—faded into irrelevance. All that mattered was Andrew's presence, his warmth beside me. Seeking solace, we retreated to a dimly lit pub, where whisky poured freely, and time seemed to taunt us with its relentless pace. Tomorrow, I would leave, and reality loomed over us like a spectre. In defiance, we made a pact: to explore every pub nearby and drown our sorrows together. It was reckless, exhilarating, and a small rebellion against the inevitable. As we stumbled home, giddy and intoxicated, our laughter echoed through the night. Only the wise live each day as if it were their last.

On my final day in Bucharest, every moment with Andrew felt priceless. Wrapped in his arms, we shared coffee and stories, savouring lunch at a nearby café. We both knew our time had an expiration date, an unspoken truth that hung heavily between us. Thoughts of Andrew consumed me—my dreams, my hopes, my heart. Even as I prepared to leave, a part of me clung to the faint hope that I wouldn't lose him entirely. I'd known from the start that he was never truly mine, yet the ache cut deeply all the same.

Later that afternoon, Andrew was my guide to Raul's workplace. Raul awaited me there, ready to drive me home. When we arrived, Andrew's eyes held mine in silent protest. Neither of us wanted this parting. Goodbyes weighed heavily on my soul. We embraced tightly before facing Raul.

In Raul's presence, I maintained a careful distance from Andrew, avoiding his gaze. I climbed into the car, glancing back only to see Andrew fade into the distance. It felt like breathing without oxygen, an emptiness swelling within me. Tears threatened, but I held them back—Raul was watching. The lyrics of *No Air* echoed in my mind, capturing my sense of loss: *"Losing you is like living in a world with no air."* Jordin Sparks feat. Chris Brown

As I journeyed home, Andrew's memory clung to me like a persistent melody. The path to seeing him again remained elusive and forgetting him proved impossible—I missed him deeply. Yet, an inexplicable void echoed within, as if my heart harboured an incomplete puzzle. It whispered, urging me to keep searching for the missing piece that would fill the emptiness.

Arriving home, I returned to a different reality. Raul and I had agreed it was time to end things, but he held tightly to denial. Threats of self-harm and emotional manipulation coloured his words, but my heart was already detached and distant. My mind wandered elsewhere as I maintained sporadic contact, hoping he might find healing and eventually release his distressing grip.

Fortunately, Raul's work in Bucharest kept him away most days, sparing me from the weight of daily interactions. Our phone conversations were few and restrained, a delicate balance between understanding and distance—dance around the fragments of what we once shared.

Autumn of Longing

As summer slipped into memory, early autumn wrapped the world in a sombre embrace, and I stepped into my senior year of high school, feeling adrift. Time-pressed forward, yet happiness seemed to slip further away, leaving a lingering ache. I clung to the quiet hope that someday, someone would hold me close, mending the fractures etched into my soul. Memories, like fragile petals, clung to my heart, unyielding even as life marked me with its inevitable scars.

In the quiet corners of our souls, we harbour emotions too fragile to share. George, the enigma who had slipped away, never called. His absence echoed through the corridors of my heart. And Andrew, the one who had ignited sparks within me, remained silent. My heart, once a fortress, now crumbled like a forgotten castle. *"Where are you now? Was it all a figment of my imagination? Where are you now? Were you merely an illusion?"* The lyrics of Alan Walker's "Faded" echoed in my mind, a haunting melody for my fractured heart.

After nearly two months of silence, the phone rang at midnight. The unfamiliar number flashed on the screen, and for a fleeting second, hope flared. Could it be George? But as I answered, the voice that reached me was not his. It was Andrew—the one who had left me breathless, the one who had shattered my castle walls.

My heart raced, caught between longing and uncertainty. The past collided with the present, and I wondered if this unexpected call would mend or break me further. My heart was beating out of my chest.

"Hello," he said, his voice trembling slightly. "How are you?"

"I think I was asleep," I replied, my voice drowsy. "Am I dreaming now?"

"No," he assured me softly. "You're not dreaming."

"How are you? You remembered about me so…late." My words came out with a mix of surprise and regret.

"I've never forgotten you," he confessed, his voice filled with sincerity.

"Stop stealing my heart away," I responded, half teasing, half serious.

"If I steal your heart," he whispered tenderly, "I promise to keep it safe always."

"Where are you now?" I asked, hearing the faint sound of music in the background.

"I'm in a club," Andrew admitted. "There are many ladies around me, but none of them can replace you."

"Maybe none of them can replace me because you're married," I shot back, the bitterness slipping into my voice.

"Believe me," he said earnestly, his voice filled with longing. "I miss you! I want you only! Don't you miss me?"

"I miss you too," I confessed quietly. "You'll never find another me there in the club! If you miss me, come here and see me!"

"I will!" he promised enthusiastically. "Let me see how I can disappear for a few days. I'll call you again. Have a good night."

"I'll have a good night if you go back home and sleep," I said softly, my heart aching.

"I'll go, don't worry," he promised gently.

"Good night!" I couldn't resist adding, "I'll send you a kiss."

"How long before the kiss arrives here?" he asked playfully.

"Wait for it," I replied with a smile. "It will arrive in twenty minutes."

"Great! In twenty minutes, I'll be home. Good night!"

"Good night," I whispered, hanging up, my heart tangled in hope and uncertainty.

In the dim hours that followed, sleep eluded me. I imagined him at that crowded club, wondering if he, too, felt the same pull I did. Perhaps he sought a distraction, or perhaps—just maybe—he longed for more than superficial connections. In a world of fleeting encounters, I wanted to be something deeper, a place where he could find solace.

Beyond those club walls existed a sea of women, each a universe of allure. By societal standards, many might surpass me in physical enchantment—graceful curves, captivating eyes, and beguiling smiles. Yet, I yearned to offer more than mere appearances. Beauty, I believed, transcended skin-deep allure. It resided in the size of the heart, the strength of character—the ability to weather life's storms.

Imperfections wove our shared tapestry, threads of vulnerability and courage. In the quiet of the night, I wondered if Andrew sensed this too if he carried our unfinished story within him as he navigated the crowded club. Perhaps, just perhaps, he longed for more than fleeting connections—a heart that beat with purpose, a soul that dared to love beyond the surface.

And so, as the clock ticked toward morning, I held onto hope. Hope that our paths would intersect again, that fate would weave us together once more. For in the tangled threads of longing and uncertainty, there lay the promise of something extraordinary—a love that defied the ordinary and embraced the imperfect beauty of our shared existence.

The next day, he called to say he'd visit in three days. My heart fluttered with a mix of joy and trepidation. Waiting for someone I might never truly have wasn't fair, but I couldn't deny the excitement building within me.

Excitement bubbled up—I longed to hug him, look into his eyes, feel his lips, and hear his voice. As each second passed, he drew closer, inexorably approaching my house. Amidst whispers, I realized my own beauty only when he spoke. His gaze, like a compass, pointed toward self-acceptance. Love transformed me through his eyes. The Kelly Family's lyrics echoed: "I fell in love with an alien, fell in love with her eyes..." Our connection defied norms, defying gravity and logic. His eyes held galaxies, and I revelled in their pull.

As I eagerly awaited my special guest, I busied myself with preparations. I scrubbed the entire house until it gleamed, and the air filled with the aroma of a special recipe simmering on the stove. I dressed in my finest clothes, the fabric soft against my skin, like whispered promises. My favourite perfume clung to me; a fragrant veil woven from anticipation.

And then, my imagination took flight. I pictured the exact moment when he would arrive—the gentle knock on the door, time suspended. My heart fluttered like a tempest, a whirlwind of emotions. When the door finally yielded to his touch, I leapt forward, propelled by sheer joy. His arms enveloped me, and suddenly, I was that kid on Christmas morning, unwrapping the most coveted gift from Santa Claus himself. His gaze held love, a universe within those eyes, and when our lips met, it felt like the cosmos aligned.

In his embrace, nothing else mattered. Love flowed through my veins, intoxicating and heady. With each touch, I ascended—closer to the clouds, closer to life itself. The mundane dissolved, leaving only the raw essence of existence. Bon Jovi's anthem echoed: "I just want to live while I'm alive. It's my life." And in that stolen moment, I understood: This was living. This was love.

We spent the entire week together. During the day, the walls of my apartment cocooned us, but as evening unfurled its velvet wings, we ventured out. Dinner at the restaurant became our nightly ritual, or sometimes we strolled hand in hand through the park. Our footsteps traced a map across the town—we walked every street, every corner. It was as if we inhabited an alternate reality, a world woven from our shared breaths and whispered secrets. Our world felt intimate and infinite.

Each moment etched itself with depth. One morning, sunlight filtered through the kitchen window as we prepared breakfast. The radio hummed softly, a companion to our mundane tasks. And then, like a serendipitous note, his favourite song began to play. He swept me into his arms, and we swayed—a dance choreographed by fate. The lyrics enveloped us: *"She's taken my heart, but she doesn't know what she's done."* Patrick Swayze's voice echoed our own unspoken truths.

Andrew was an enigma, a mix of silence and intensity. His passion for fishing was like his personality—quiet yet purposeful. He knew the patience it required, the communion it created with nature. I became entangled in his quiet charm, drawn in like a fish on a line.

But as the days slipped by, our time drew to a close. Andrew belonged to another life, another woman—Evelin, who waited for him at home. She thought he was on a business trip, and I was left to grapple with my role in his life. I wanted him to stay, to choose me, yet I knew the impossibility of my wish.

As he prepared to leave, he placed the key to his house on the table. I rushed to the window to see him one last time, calling out as he exited the building. Holding up the keys, I called down, "I have the key…to your heart."

"Whatever I do, I'll come back to you!" he called back, a promise or a wish—I couldn't be sure. And with that, he was gone, the echoes of his presence lingering in the air.

Also, like a skilled fisherman, he had his repertoire of funny jokes, although not everyone grasped their nuances. His humour was infectious, and he knew precisely how to coax laughter from my lips. But Andrew was more than punchlines; he was an enigma wrapped in surprises. He oscillated from one extreme to another, a chameleon of emotions. Sometimes, he'd sweep me off my feet with romance; other times, he'd ignite flames of desire—a tantalizing blend of passion and playfulness.

As beautiful moments waned, the inevitable hour arrived—the moment when Andrew had to leave. Our secret, wild affair ended again. Andrew carried obligations beyond our stolen week; he belonged to Evelin, his reality, his life, his wife. She believed he was away on business, attending a week-long meeting in another city. She waited for him at home while I grappled with my role—the keeper of secrets, the silent accomplice, the mistress.

She waited, and I was supposed to let him go. From the beginning, I knew he was married, yet this situation gnawed at me. Perhaps I shouldn't have become entangled, but once ensnared, escape proved elusive. I yearned for him to be mine eternally, to awaken in the dead of night and draw him nearby. Love arrives unbidden and leaves when needed most. *"Mai I ricordi non passano mai, stanno con noi"* (The memories of the heart never fade; they remain with us), as Amedeo Minghi's song echoed within me.

When Andrew left, he placed the key to his house on the table. Seeing it there, I hurried to the window, waiting for him to emerge from the building. As he stepped outside, I called out and displayed the keys. He asked me to toss them down, but hesitation gripped me—I longed for him to return, retrieve his keys, and share one more embrace. "I have the key… to your heart!" I whispered.

His response echoed: "Whatever I do, I'll come back to you!" And I, in turn, confessed, "I'm going to miss you." His voice, mixed with unhappiness, replied, "Maybe one day, we'll meet again."

A curious coincidence, I thought. This had happened before when George left, and now history repeated itself. Same words, same feelings, I pondered the paradox: what breaks us might not heal us, yet what loves us clings steadfastly. With this realization, I granted freedom to the man I loved. If he truly cherished me, he'd return and never leave again. I held firm to the belief that when two souls were meant to be, no distance was insurmountable, no time too long, and nothing could tear them apart.

Despite feeling alone, Andrew's calls and texts bridged the gap. He shared details of his days—where he went, what he did, what he ate—all except our relationship. His voice reassured me, and I treasured those moments. Life taught me patience; I understood that good things unfolded in their own time.

Also, sometimes, when Raul called me, he would inquire about my well-being. He knew I didn't love him, yet he clung to the hope that perhaps one day I would become his wife. He always used to gloat about it, revelled in the idea that one day we would walk down the aisle together and our lives forever entwined in matrimony. Maybe time would change our minds, make us more mature and responsible, and bring us together.

With each passing day, Raul sensed my growing indifference. He called me his "cold rain," his distant love, and sometimes I pitied him. He had a good heart, and perhaps he truly loved me. But I'd found my heart elsewhere, even if that meant waiting for someone who might never truly be mine. As Coco Chanel once said, *"Don't spend time beating on a wall, hoping to transform it into a door."*

In the end, love defies logic, a force that binds and breaks us, that challenges and transforms us. And as I waited, I clung to a belief that, if we were truly meant to be, no distance, no time, could keep us apart. For now, I cherished the memories, a promise etched in my heart, hopeful yet accepting, waiting for whatever the future would bring."

Unspoken Ties

Two months later, after returning home from class, my friend Anna dropped a bombshell: she was getting married and moving into her future husband's home. She'd planned to stay at mine for a few more days, which I didn't mind. Still, I felt compelled to sit her down, explaining that she was too young to marry. I urged her to finish high school first and then think about settling down. But love had blinded her; my words went unheard. Not long after, I discovered that she'd left school altogether. Despite my advice, her heart had led her down an unexpected path.

Around the same time, Andrew confided in me. He'd had a row with his brother James and was considering leaving the company they'd built together. Meanwhile, Raul remained loyal to James. Andrew wanted a fresh start—a venture of his own, free from family complications. His frustration spilt over, and I did my best to comfort him. Little did I know, he had another wild idea brewing, one I'd later learn from Raul. Life, it seemed, was brimming with surprises.

After Anna moved out, Raul called me. He asked if I'd be willing to rent out the spare room in my house to his sister Evelin and Andrew, who needed accommodation for a couple of months. At first, I thought he was joking, but it soon became clear he was serious. Unsure how to respond, I made up an excuse about a possible tenant and promised to call him back within the hour.

A week later, they moved in. My heart wrestled with my mind, yet I grew accustomed to the idea and welcomed them. I wondered if Andrew was a divine gift, or a punishment sent by fate. Though it felt more like the latter, my heart clung to the hope that there was purpose in this arrangement. "It doesn't make sense now, but one day it will," I reassured myself.

Once in the game, I committed to playing until the end. I vowed to stay calm, let life flow, and maintain a positive outlook. Sometimes, silence becomes our refuge; words can't fully express the inner turmoil. A successful person prevails because they're prepared to face failure.

Two days after I agreed to their proposal, Andrew and Evelin moved into my apartment. During their stay, I kept conversations with Andrew brief as if nothing had happened between us, like we just met—similar to a relationship between a landlord and tenant. He had set up a small company and was engrossed in a new project nearby. Evelin, on the other hand, worked as a chef in a hotel not far from my location. Her schedule alternated: three days at home and three days at work. When Evelin had time off, Andrew often returned home late or didn't come back at all. His excuses ranged from visiting his grandparents' house to being at his father's place. When Evelin was working, Andrew would occasionally come home, but our interactions remained minimal. Many times, I arrived home from class to find him waiting silently, our unspoken desires hanging in the air. In our peculiar situation, the conversation felt futile—we couldn't alter our circumstances.

The Crossroads of Hearts

After successfully passing my exams, I completed my four-year high school programme. Facing adulthood, I confronted the pivotal question: *what next?* I yearned to continue my studies at university, but the obstacle was daunting—no funds for tuition. My choices were stark: find work in the city or consider an opportunity my uncle proposed.

My uncle offered to take me to Italy, where I could work in my aunt's restaurant, earning money towards my education. He promised that in two months, we could set off together. In the meantime, I decided to find a local job, paving the way for both my ambitions—to work and study.

The most challenging aspect? Revealing my intentions to Andrew. How could I convey that I planned to go so far away? Andrew could have lived anywhere else, but I knew and felt that he wanted to be close to me, even though we didn't have a relationship and didn't communicate. We pretended as if nothing had happened between us. I needed to ask him to leave, and I couldn't understand why this decision hurt me. He was a married man, and it would have been better for both of us to stop interacting altogether. However, Raul and Evelin's opinions mattered little; the true struggle was my own reluctance to be separated from Andrew. Yet, deep within my heart, I sensed something missing—a puzzle piece left unfound. My emotions tangled, but I ignored their whispers, refraining from questioning my true desires.

Sometimes, leaving everything behind to start anew feels liberating. But how does one depart, leaving a part of themselves behind? Wrestling with these thoughts, I chose patience over haste.

I kept my plan hidden, waiting for the opportune moment, all while seeking employment.

Then, one day, Evelin asked if I could step in at her job for three days as a temporary replacement. One of her co-workers was pregnant and unwell. Though I had no work experience, I saw it as an opportunity to learn about hotel and restaurant work. The hotel where Evelin worked as a chef was nestled in a beautiful tourist area close to the mountains—a place I loved. I readily accepted, intrigued to learn more.

As I assisted Evelin, I noticed something intriguing from day one. She shared a remarkable bond with one of her colleagues—a waiter. He seemed to orbit around her in the kitchen while she cooked. Although she tried to conceal their relationship from me, it was unmistakably evident, especially when she wore a special smile every time he was near.

After our first day of work, in the evening, we returned to our room to rest. Unexpectedly, the waiter knocked on our door, extending an invitation to a club. Evelin hesitated, unsure how to react, but eventually, she accepted his offer. She had no choice but to invite me along. Assuring me that more colleagues would be there, she promised a night of fun. As we dressed for the club, she leaned in and whispered, "That's our secret," underestimating my perception.

I made no promises. It was impossible to comply with her request because my heart belonged to Andrew, though she remained unaware of my feelings. Throughout the night at the club, she nestled in her colleague's arms, treating me like her closest confidante. I played along, and indeed, we had fun. When we returned to the hotel from the club, it was already midnight. No one was going to sleep, so we decided to go to the hotel pool. Evelin and her colleague swam together in the pool, sharing drinks and laughter. Their connection was unmistakably that of lovers. As dawn approached, we retired to our room for a few hours of sleep, preparing for yet another day of work.

After those three days, I returned home, ready to tell Andrew the truth. Evelin didn't love him; their marriage was a sham, a tangle of lies neither dared to unravel. The events at the club had steeled me, yet I hesitated. Instead, I informed them of my decision to travel to Italy with my uncle and gently suggested they find another place to rent.

Andrew's reaction moved from surprise to sarcasm as he shared his own plans—to move to London, where his uncle and brother could help him find work. He would go alone initially but intended for Evelin to join him once he was settled. At first, I thought this meant the end of any connection between us, but disappointment quickly overtook me. I realised that in his life, I had been a fleeting adventure, a diversion from his real world. His decision to go to London seemed carefully designed to end his marriage peacefully—no mess, no scandal, just geographical distance.

Yet, as I fully grasped the implications, a mix of confusion and disappointment washed over me. For a fleeting moment, I didn't want to see Andrew anymore. The lyrics of Whitney Houston's "I Have Nothing" echoed in my mind: *"Don't make me close one more door, I don't wanna hurt anymore. Stay in my arms if you dare, or must I imagine you there?"*. It was a poignant reminder that emotions rarely follow logical courses.

My hopes clung to a fragile thread—I yearned for him to somehow intervene, to halt my departure to Italy, perhaps persuade me to stay. But it remained a wistful fantasy, fuelled by my innocent expectations. Solitude beckoned; I craved a few moments alone, perhaps with a drink to blur the edges of reality. Why did those I cared about always seem to gravitate toward London? George had long since departed; now, Andrew was preparing to leave while I was bound for Italy. Richard Marx's lyrics echoed in my mind: *"I took for granted all the time that I thought would last somehow."* by Richard Marx's "Right Here Waiting".

Gasping for air, I hastily dressed and stepped outside. Near my house, a river flowed, and I walked along its edge, attempting to corral my chaotic thoughts. "He's the most beautiful thing I can't have," I whispered to myself. The weight of unrequited longing bore down on me. No one else truly comprehended the tempest within; I stood alone. Yet, perhaps there existed someone who could decipher the language of our souls—their dreams, disappointments, beauty, and darkness. In life, we encounter countless conversationalists, but only a select few possess the ability to truly grasp our essence. These are the ones who listen differently, who glimpse truth merely by meeting our gaze.

A few hours later, when I arrived home, Evelin stood there alone. The air was thick with tension—the aftermath of their fight—and Andrew had already left. I craved solitude, an escape from the emotional turmoil. So, I retreated to my room, seeking solace in its quiet corners.

Three days later, Andrew reappeared while Evelin was at work. We found ourselves alone in the house—an opportunity to finally talk. But we didn't delve into our complicated relationship. Instead, we discussed mundane matters, the trivialities that masked the deeper currents between us. As the evening wore on, we shared drinks, and the lines blurred. We surrendered to the moment, our bodies seeking solace in each other's warmth.

I could have altered the course of everything, but I hesitated. Perhaps Andrew wasn't ready for a fresh start, for a new chapter. His failed marriage with Evelin had left scars, and now he craved freedom. They had wed with hope, but love had eluded them, leaving an empty space.

That night with Andrew left me feeling adrift as if my dreams had evaporated. Guilt no longer clung to me; I existed in a numb state, neither happy nor sad.

When Evelin returned home from work, I couldn't bear to witness their interactions. I hoped for an excuse to escape, but I proposed a journey to the bank to cash some money. Andrew agreed, without hesitation, to accompany me, and we stepped out together. Our destination shifted from financial transactions to our favourite pub. Two shots of tequila later, we ceased caring about consequences, about the tangled web we wove. At that moment, the universe held sway, and I realized that living life on my terms meant embracing the chaos, even if it defied convention.

It was complete chaos around me. At that time, in my mind, the only beautiful moments were when I was with Andrew; otherwise, it was a disaster. Despite despising the role of "the other woman," I continued playing it without guilt or concern for consequences. I wondered why I consumed so much alcohol, knowing it wouldn't solve anything. Most likely, I was in a depression, yet I resisted changing my situation—I wasn't doing anything right. The excessive drinking with Andrew should have been a wake-up call, but I merely resigned myself to the miserable circumstances I was in.

After an hour of indulging in alcohol, we stumbled back home, our senses slightly dulled. As we entered the building, ascending the stairs to my apartment, we paused on each step, sharing kisses that tasted of recklessness and longing.

At the door, reluctance tugged at me—I didn't want to step inside. Against the wall, a ladder leaned, its iron rungs beckoning us upward. Without hesitation, I seized it, ascending to the attic. The ladder groaned under our weight, echoing through the entire building. Our laughter stifled yet infectious, accompanied each step.

In the dim attic, Andrew's lips found mine, passion igniting between us. But reality intruded—the space was draped in spiderwebs, dust clinging to our skin. The arachnids disrupted our wild moment, and we descended hastily, laughter bubbling up once more. We were two lunatics, minds unshackled, living in the present, consequences be damned.

As we stepped into the building, Evelin's acute senses detected our presence. Then she heard all the noise we made and heard us laughing in the attic. The puzzle pieces clicked into place, revealing a clandestine relationship that had thrived in the shadows. Despite lacking irrefutable evidence, she intuited my role as Andrew's long-standing mistress and my peculiar connection to her brother—a web of secrets that had woven itself into an ugly, precarious situation.

The door to my apartment stood open, beckoning us further. Evelin awaited us, her demeanour eerily composed. She turned to Andrew, her voice steady, questioning whether he had ever spent nights away at his grandparents' or father's house since they moved from Bucharest. His silence spoke volumes. I glanced at Andrew, on the verge of asking where he spent those nights when he wasn't with me, but I held my tongue. Then, her gaze shifted to me, and she kindly requested my phone to make a call—her own phone lacking credit. I handed it over, observing as she dialled her colleague's number. She handed back my phone and then swiftly began packing her belongings.

Half an hour later, her lover arrived, and she left with him. The abruptness of it all left Andrew and me stunned. Relief warred with guilt as we stood there, locked in each other's gaze. We feared we had shattered her heart, but fate had other plans.

After Evelin's departure, Raul called me the next day. Unaware of the recent events, I confessed that I was now with Andrew—his ex-brother-il-law. As Andrew's 'girlfriend', I requested that Raul refrain from contacting me further. Although Evelin hadn't yet informed him, I felt compelled to share the truth.

Raul's initial reaction was laughter, but as the reality sank in, he understood that our relationship had reached its end. Maybe I had caused him pain, breaking his heart, yet our peculiar connection was destined to dissolve. Sometimes, bidding farewell is the only path forward. If we muster the courage, life rewards us with fresh beginnings—a new chapter waiting to unfold.

Evelin quickly filed for divorce, and years later, I learned through Facebook that she'd found happiness with her lover. Their photos showed a life full of laughter and two children. It was evident that she had emerged from the turmoil, stronger and more resilient than ever before.

As I scrolled through Facebook, Raul's profile caught my eye. His smile radiated genuine contentment, and beside him stood his wife—a partner who shared both his joys and sorrows. Yet, the most heartwarming sight was their little girl, eyes wide with wonder, a testament to the life they had woven together. Raul had found his happiness, and it was a beautiful sight to behold. As Einstein said, *"Life is like riding a bicycle. To maintain balance, you must keep moving."* In the end, life had given us fresh starts.

An Uncertain Farewell

After everything that had happened, I stood by Andrew's side for nearly two weeks. Though we shared a silent connection, we never spoke of labels. Caught in a state of uncertainty, we found happiness, tempered by the relentless march of time, slipping through our fingers like sand in an hourglass. Our plan had been decided months prior: one of us bound for Italy, the other for England. Dwindling funds pressed our decision forward. My uncle had secured a job for me in Rome, while Andrew's uncle and brother had arranged a place for him in London. The moment for goodbyes had arrived.

What we shared—the highs and lows—would remain in our hearts as cherished memories. Laughter mingled with tears, weaving together a tapestry of emotions. In his embrace, I glimpsed the essence of love—a desire both exquisite and rare. Yet he remained an incomplete part of my life, a beautiful fragment I could not fully possess. Whatever the outcome, I vowed not to regret following my heart's lead. Some people enter our lives and leave indelible marks, altering us forever. Time is now divided into two epochs: before and after.

Andrew's invitation to the restaurant hung in the air—a bittersweet promise of our final dinner together. I chose my elegant cream shirt, adorned with small red dots on the sleeves—the same shirt that had graced New Year's Eve. My hair, carefully curled, framed my face like a schoolgirl's, a deliberate reminder of the night I playfully vowed to cast a spell on him.

The restaurant he chose matched the gravity of our farewell. Throughout the evening, his hand held mine, and his gaze lingered—a silent conversation that stirred my heart, both exhilarating and painful. We spoke of everything and nothing, the weight of unspoken words hanging between us.

His admission came gently: "I hope you don't mind, but I'll leave my movies collection at your place. Perhaps, in the future, we'll cross paths again, and I'll retrieve it."

I smiled, masking the ache. "Your CDs will be a good reason for our paths to intersect once more."

"Maybe," he mused, "we'll find other reasons too."

"Perhaps," I replied, "unless you decide to marry again."

And so, in that dimly lit restaurant, we wove our final chapter—a tapestry of memories, regrets, and the fragile hope that life might surprise us yet.

Amidst the soft glow of the restaurant, we shared a bottle of wine—a libation that blurred the edges of reality. Andrew, ever the artist, deftly folded a napkin into a white rose, a fragile token of our fleeting moments.

"Why don't you come with me to London?" His question hung in the air, a bridge between possibility and impossibility.

"Because you're not taking me," I replied, my heart caught between longing and reason.

His eyes bore into mine. "I'll take you with me. Will you come?"

Tipsy and unguarded, I confessed, "We may be drunk, but I'll follow you anywhere as long as you hold my hand."

"We must find a way," he insisted. "I can't bear to lose you."

"But decisions made in this haze..." I hesitated. "Perhaps tomorrow, you'll forget this discussion."

"How can I forget," he murmured, "when all I want is not to lose you?"

And so, we set our dreams aside until morning, the weight of London, the scarcity of funds, and the fragility of our hearts all hanging in the balance. Back home, we lay side by side in the quiet darkness, staring at the ceiling. Was this our chance? Life, like a fleeting melody, offers no encore. As Eminem once asked, "If you had one shot, one opportunity to seize everything you ever wanted, would you capture it or let it slip?" The following morning, over coffee, I waited for Andrew to mention our conversation. His silence was laden with unspoken possibilities. After breakfast, we sat down to watch a movie, but as I began packing, he stopped me with a determined look.

"Don't pack," he said. "I have a plan—one that just might work. It involves us going to London together."

His words sent ripples through my heart. Andrew outlined his idea, and I found myself at a crossroads. Without hesitation, I picked up the phone, dialling my uncle's number. When he answered, I delivered the news: "I've changed my mind. Italy is no longer my destination." My uncle's fury erupted. He asked so many questions. He was worried. He demanded details about Andrew, probing for answers. Without hesitation, I asserted, "Andrew is mine. He's my boyfriend."

Also, my brother received a similar call, his surprise mingling with concern. "Why this sudden decision?" he wondered aloud. ''What's going on?'' ''Who's Andrew?''

Consultations ensued—my brother and our uncle huddled in discussion. Soon, they decided to convene at my apartment, their worry etched on their faces. My family feared for me, but sometimes, life demands swift choices. This was our chance—a fork in the road where love and destiny converged.

The following day, my family gathered at my place. Andrew, however, was absent when they arrived because he went to meet a friend to borrow some money. Just as we were growing impatient, Andrew finally arrived ten minutes later.

"Who is Andrew, and where is he?" Charlie asked his tone a mix of curiosity and frustration. "He knew we were coming; he was supposed to be here."

"He'll be here soon," I reassured them.

My uncle looked at me sternly. "You should have consulted us about this decision. Instead, Andrew's not even here to meet us. When he should be taking responsibility, he's absent?

"We were planning to meet and talk," I explained. "I didn't anticipate you'd arrive so quickly."

When Andrew finally arrived, there was a moment of tense silence. He introduced himself and placed a bottle of whiskey on the table. He poured whiskey into three glasses, took my hand, and we all sat down to talk. The conversation swung between humour and seriousness."

My uncle leaned forward. "I want to see your ID card," he said firmly. "I need to know who you are and who your parents are. Just in case something happens to her in London, I'll know who to look for."

Andrew nodded. "I promise I'll take care of her."

By the time our conversation ended, both my uncle and my brother had begun to place their trust in Andrew. Their initial doubts softened into acceptance, and they agreed with my decision to follow him to London. They believed I would be safe at his side, and together we could carve out a future. Even my mother, who later tried to dissuade me, couldn't sway my resolve. My heart had already chosen—what I wanted, more than anything, was Andrew.

After they left, Andrew confided in me. Though his friend had loaned him money, it wasn't enough, so he planned to borrow from his mother. He spoke with her over the phone, and she invited us to her home in another city until our departure. Yet, something in his story raised my suspicions. When I pressed him, he admitted he'd met an old friend involved in the drug trade, who had given him some marijuana to sell for a quick profit. He'd kept all the proceeds—enough for our tickets to London.

"You're crazy, Andrew!" I exclaimed. "Are we like gangsters now? Don't tell me you have a gun! Are we going to rob a bank and head to London as Bonnie and Clyde?"

Andrew chuckled. "Don't exaggerate. I had to do something to get the money quickly. Besides, it's not a big problem. Please don't worry!"

I wasn't worried, but I realised how little I truly knew about Andrew's past. I reassured myself that we'd have time to learn more about each other. At that moment, I was simply glad to be with him and for our dream to be within reach.

The following day, we packed our bags. But before heading to his mother's house, we made a stop to visit Andrew's grandparents and his father. Our mission was to inform them that Andrew and Evelin had broken up, and we were now a couple. Additionally, we wanted to share the news that we were bound for London.

As we stepped into Andrew's childhood home, his grandmother welcomed us warmly. She hadn't approved of his marriage to Evelin and hadn't attended their wedding, making it clear she felt relieved he was no longer with her. As we left, his grandparents wished us luck, playfully urging us to return from London with a brood of grandchildren. Andrew beamed with pride, clearly delighted that his grandparents liked me.

However, the atmosphere shifted when we reached his father's house. His father was firmly against our relationship, to the point that he almost barred me from entering. He angrily demanded to know why I had supposedly ruined Andrew's marriage. Andrew tried to explain, but his father refused to listen. In that tense moment, I clasped Andrew's hand and boldly declared, "Whatever you say, Andrew is mine!" His father stared at me, momentarily taken aback, before vowing to settle the matter later. Andrew looked at me with pride, and together, we bid his father farewell. As we walked home, Andrew cradled me in his arms, showering me with kisses.

Within me, possessiveness surges like a tempest—I am unyielding in my claim. You, my beloved, are mine, and I shall brook no rival. Your heart, those lips, the warmth of your arms—they belong solely to me. No other soul shall trespass upon this sacred territory.

'What if your mother doesn't approve of me either?' I asked Andrew, my nerves fluttering like startled birds.

He chuckled, his eyes crinkling at the corners. 'Simple,' he said. 'You just have to tell her, "Andrew's mine!"'

Despite my lingering worry, Andrew reassured me. His mother, he explained, was a woman of wisdom and kindness, her life's journey etched in the lines on her face. She would understand, he promised, and perhaps even welcome me into her heart.

The next morning, we gathered our belongings and set out for Andrew's mother's house. As we reached the familiar doorstep, a shiver ran through me—a strange recognition I couldn't ignore. I had been here before. Still, I prayed with all my strength that I was wrong. When the door creaked open, my heart sank. Standing before me was not a stranger, but a face from the past I had desperately hoped not to see George's mother.

In that instant, the world tilted. My chest tightened, my pulse thundered, and I clung to the impossible hope that there was some explanation—that perhaps Andrew's mother had purchased the house from George's family. But the truth came crashing down like a lightning strike: Andrew and my former love, George, were brothers.

My breath caught as my life unravelled in a dizzying flash of memories. Every stolen glance, every unanswered question, every lingering ache of George's absence suddenly made sense. The ground seemed to give way beneath me, yet I forced myself to stand tall, to mask the storm raging inside.

Andrew's mother greeted me with a warmth that cut like a blade. "Come in, my dear! Hang your coat, slip off your shoes—there's no need to be shy. We've met before."

I stumbled forward, my legs weak, my voice caught somewhere between confession and silence. Andrew's eyes widened as he turned toward me, confusion written across his face.

"You... know each other?" he asked, his voice trembling between disbelief and demand.

His mother's smile carried a weight I couldn't yet name. "Of course," she said lightly. "She's been here before—with your brother George, and his girlfriend."

Her words struck like a dagger. I froze, my tongue heavy, my lips unable to form a single sound. My mind reeled, scrambling for an explanation, while my body betrayed me—legs trembling, a weak smile forced onto my face. Across the room, Andrew's eyes locked on mine, wide with shock, demanding answers I wasn't ready to give. The silence thickened between us, until his mother, perhaps sensing the storm, excused herself with a gentle smile and slipped into the kitchen to fetch food.

Inside, I was unraveling. How had I not realized? Why hadn't the pieces fallen into place sooner—that Andrew and George were bound not just by circumstance, but by blood? How could I explain this tangle of past and present to Andrew without destroying everything we had built?

The truth of his family unfolded in fragments I barely managed to piece together. His mother had lived two lives, two marriages, each leaving behind sons divided by circumstance. From her first marriage came Lucas and Michael, who were raised far away by their paternal grandparents. From her second marriage came Andrew, James, and George. Even among them, the bonds of family were fractured: Andrew had grown up under the watch of his paternal grandparents, while James and George were raised by their maternal side. They knew they were brothers, but they had not shared the same childhood, the same roof, the same memories. They had grown up apart—connected by blood, but strangers in many ways.

And now, that complicated past had collided with my present, leaving me standing on the edge of revelation and ruin.

It wasn't until Andrew turned sixteen that he discovered Lucas was his brother. Though he'd always known he had an elder sibling—older even than Michael—the two had never crossed paths.

That revelation altered Andrew's world, just as mine was now shifting under the weight of our tangled destinies.

At seventeen, Andrew moved to Bucharest, where he secured steady work and began carving out a life of independence. Not long after, his younger brother James joined him, and together they shared a modest flat. With determination and ambition, they launched a construction company, pouring years of effort into building it from the ground up. In time, George joined them as well. For a while, they stood united. But cracks soon appeared—George, frustrated by what he saw as an unfair share of the profits, chose to break away and seek his fortune in London.

The company, strained by disagreements over money, eventually dissolved. Andrew, unwilling to let failure define him, seized the chance to return to his hometown and start anew. Fate, ever unpredictable, placed him in my very own apartment block, alongside his wife. It was there that our paths collided.

What a cruel, extraordinary coincidence. George—my first love, my unanswered question—was now waiting for Andrew in London, and I was to walk into his world by Andrew's side. My feelings for George had long faded, dulled by time and silence, but memories cannot be erased. They live in the shadows, waiting to be stirred. And as I looked into Andrew's eyes for the very first time, I had felt it—a haunting déjà vu. Now I understood why: Andrew and George shared more than blood. They carried the same magnetic charm, the same way of looking at me as though they could see straight through my soul.

That evening we stayed until midnight, Andrew's mother filling the hours with laughter, stories, and jokes. On the surface, everything was perfectly ordinary. Yet when night fell and the house grew still, my thoughts churned in restless silence. How would

Andrew react once I told him the truth? Would he believe me when I swore that George was part of my past, that my heart now belonged only to him? Or would he see me as a traitor, unable to trust?

We had endured so much to reach this point—but what lay ahead if he doubted me? How could I prove that my love for him was stronger than coincidence, stronger than history itself?

The next day Andrew went shopping with his mother for paint and tools—she wanted to transform the balcony into a little garden, full of flowers. The plan was simple: fresh paint first, then plants. Andrew stayed to help, and I couldn't shake the feeling that his mother might mention George. When they came back, he seemed quieter than usual. That evening he asked me to meet him for pizza—just the two of us.

"Mum told me you were George's girlfriend once," he began, voice low. "You two have a history, don't you?"

"We were together a long time ago," I answered, keeping my words measured.

"Is it really over between you and my brother? This is all so strange... I don't know how to feel." His eyes searched mine, trying to find proof.

"It's over," I said. "There's nothing left between us. We haven't spoken since he left. I never imagined George could be your brother." I tried to be as honest as I could.

"Are you sure?" he pressed. "I don't want to be deceived. Don't lie to me."

"I'm not lying," I whispered. "He's part of my past—just that." Even as the words left my mouth, a small doubt tugged at me. I hadn't lied, but uncertainty lingered. Questions turned in my head: How would I stand beside Andrew when we met George? What would it feel like when our eyes met across a room? Should I still go to London with him?

"Love takes many shapes," Andrew said, raw and earnest. "Whether it's steady love or something fierce and sudden—I care for you. If anyone ever hurts you, I won't stand for it. I want us to be honest, respectful, real."

"I promise I won't let you down," I breathed.

In that moment I believed it—believed in us, and in myself. It felt like the first true commitment between us: official, fragile, hopeful. We held hands as we left the restaurant, an outward sign of a decision made. Yet beneath the warmth of that touch, an inexplicable ache remained—a quiet warning that not everything had been resolved, and that the road ahead might still ask for more courage than either of us expected.

But we vowed never to give up, no matter the challenges. Life throws obstacles our way because it knows we're strong enough to overcome them. In this poker game of life, we might bend the rules, but we'll never surrender. *"Would you swear that you'll always be mine? Would you lie? Would you run and hide?"* (from "Hero" by Enrique Iglesias).

Shadows of the Past

Two weeks later, we arrived in London. George had refused to pick us up from the airport because of me sending his roommate to his place. Although he introduced her as his "roommate," it was clear she was more—likely his girlfriend. She seemed fully aware of our history, as she spent the entire way from the airport talking solely to Andrew. Each time I attempted to join the conversation, she pointedly ignored me.

Eventually, my hunger became unbearable, and I suggested stopping for a quick bite. She overheard and insisted we wait until we reached their house, dismissing the idea of a food stop. A few minutes later, she pulled two small packets of biscuits from her bag. She kept one for herself and handed the other to Andrew, who kindly shared it with me. At that moment, I realised I would need all my strength to face what lay ahead. She viewed me as an enemy, and it was evident we'd never find common ground. But sometimes, the very obstacles meant to tear us down end up forging a resilience we never anticipated.

When we arrived at George's house, he swung open the door and greeted us with a forced smile, but then he promptly ignored me. Not a glance, not a hello—just a cold dismissal. The moment hung awkwardly in the air, affecting all of us.

Seeing George again stirred complex emotions within me. It had been nearly two years since I last saw him, and he was no longer the George I remembered. His new demeanour exuded arrogance, selfishness, rudeness, and a surprising hardness. Strangely, I found his transformation beneficial for my relationship with Andrew. To borrow from Adele, it was as though the song played in my head: *"Hello, it's me. I was wondering if, after all these years, you'd like to meet."*

For nearly two weeks, the silence was relentless. Except for Andrew, no one acknowledged me. To them, I was a foolish girl, incapable of understanding, unworthy of respect. Andrew tried to defend me, making it clear that disrespect toward me was disrespect toward him. Yet their attitudes never shifted. Every glance, every word unspoken, painted me as the outsider—the unwanted guest. And in the quiet of those days, one truth settled heavy on my heart: I had become the enemy in a story I never meant to enter.

Andrew and George shared a deep bond. They worked side by side, leaving home in the morning and returning in the evening. One day, as Andrew prepared for work, I hugged him tightly, and we made a pact.

"Regardless of what happens," I said, "no matter how upset you are, promise me this: Every time you leave the house, you'll give me a kiss."

Andrew grinned. "Deal," he replied.

"But wait," I continued. "When you come home, don't forget the kiss."

"Got it," he said playfully.

"And even when you take out the trash," I added.

"I promise," Andrew assured me.

We nurtured grand dreams. Our goal was to save enough money to buy a house with a large garden—a place to build a fishpond, our very own peaceful retreat. Despite the fact that we didn't yet have work permits in the UK, we pressed forward. Andrew and I understood that no dream was too small or too ambitious. We clung to our vision, trusting that dreams are the creative compass guiding us toward the future.

Echoes of the Past

George and I had come a long way. The past was forgotten, and we had become close friends—almost like family. On weekdays, we toiled away in our jobs, while weekends were reserved for clubbing and revelry. Andrew and I had recently decided to move into a new home, seeking a bit more privacy. Our little haven was still close to George's place. Andrew, ever the diligent builder, had secured a steady job while I grappled with the challenge of finding work without the necessary UK documents. Each time I applied for the paperwork to work legally, my application faced rejection.

George, who worked night shifts, surprised me one morning. He knew I'd be home alone and needed help filling out a form. It was for his driving licence, and he asked me to assist. As I took up the pen to help, I couldn't help but wonder why George hadn't waited for Andrew to be home. However, Andrew already knew about George's request. After all, we were like family now.

When George arrived, he wore exhaustion like a heavy coat. He requested a cup of coffee, and I promptly brewed it before helping him with the form. After sipping his coffee, he sighed. "I'm utterly drained," he confessed. "Could I catch a few hours of sleep?"

I hesitated. "George," I said, "why not go home? Andrew might find it odd if he discovers you napping here."

George smirked. "What Andrew thinks depends on what you're thinking," he retorted. "Wake me up later, please!"

I frowned. "This isn't right," I declared. "You've lost your mind."

He chuckled. "It's not the first time," he admitted.

Allowing George to nap, I retreated to the kitchen to prepare a meal. Afterwards, I sat in the garden, unable to shake a growing feeling of unease. Something about his behaviour felt off. A couple of hours later, George woke up and, in passing, mentioned that his clothes now carried a faint scent of my perfume—bringing back memories of a time when we had been more than friends and more than just brother and sister-in-law. Back then, his cologne would linger on my clothes, too. He intentionally wanted me to remember.

"Thanks for letting me rest," he said, flashing a charming smile. He lit a cigarette and hurriedly left, leaving me speechless.

When Andrew returned home, he seemed both bewildered and a bit concerned. I managed to ease his worries, but I could tell that he, too, found George's behaviour a little suspicious.

I recounted the entire incident to Andrew while George was still at our house, hoping to restore normalcy. Yet, it didn't last long. Two days later, George visited again. Andrew knew about it, and I grappled with confusion—how long would these inappropriate visits persist?

This time, when George arrived, he seemed more worn out than ever. He mumbled something about an argument with his girlfriend, skirting around the details. Nonetheless, we spent the entire day together, chatting like old friends. George spoke at length about his life since moving to London, sharing tales of the challenges he had faced.

In the evening, Andrew returned home, and the three of us sat down for dinner.

"Do you want to watch a movie after we eat?" Andrew asked.

"Why not?" George replied. "I'd rather stay here than go home. Got any new films?"

Andrew nodded. "I've got one," he said. "It's a good movie—the lead actor usually stars in action films."

As the movie played, Andrew, the discerning critic, gauged its quality within minutes. But truth be told, the film didn't meet our expectations. Instead, we drifted into conversation, sharing stories.

Then, without warning, George turned to me. "Remember when we first watched Titanic?" he asked. "How much did you cry?"

I sighed, both confused and annoyed. "I remember," I replied.

The memories were vivid, but now wasn't the time for them. I feigned indifference as George delved into the past. Times when he'd held me, kissed me and teased me for crying over the film. I remembered everything: after the movie, when he'd playfully reminded me of his promise—a lifetime of love. We'd had a pillow fight, trying to chase away the lingering sadness from the screen.

Andrew observed us, puzzled but stayed silent. Why had George decided to bring up these memories now? I wanted so badly to move forward, yet somehow, these old memories clung to me. Perhaps George couldn't let go of them either. *"We'll stay forever this way. You are safe in my heart, and my heart will go on."* Celine Dion, "My Heart Will Go On."

Weight of Unspoken Words

The more time I spent with George, the more he resembled a haunting echo of our shared history. It felt like a relentless game—one I couldn't halt. "If I don't make peace with my past," I mused, "it will keep resurfacing in my present, casting shadows." But how could I break this cycle?

Andrew grew increasingly upset, and our arguments multiplied. I resolved to talk to George, waiting for the opportune moment to have a serious conversation. I needed him to understand that our past was hurting Andrew and that every small gesture he made affected our relationship. Perhaps it was partly my fault—I should have confronted him sooner, but uncertainty paralyzed me.

Just as I prepared to address the issue, George texted me. He'd be at my house in ten minutes, seeking coffee and help with a work document. His excuses always seemed credible, yet I knew they were wrong. That morning, I silenced my phone and chose not to answer the door, leaving George to wonder if I was home.

My plan had failed. George knew I was home, and he persisted. Knocking on my window, he burst into laughter. His breath reeked of alcohol. When I opened the window, I demanded he leave—I felt guilty about his visits while Andrew was away. But George pushed the window wide open, clambering into my room. His odd behaviour continued as he perched on my bed, casually requesting coffee.

"You're drunk," I said. "Why are you here?"

He shrugged. "You and Andrew are the only people I know here. No one else to visit."

"You have a girlfriend," I retorted, "and other friends."

"I'm bored of her," he confessed. "We fight all the time. My other friends live far away."

"Unbelievable!" I snapped. "I don't care. You need to leave!"

As I stepped into the kitchen to prepare coffee, I knew I needed to remain calm during our conversation. Yelling would only hinder honest answers. Handing him the coffee, I mustered courage, unsure how to broach the subject without misunderstanding. His gaze held both confidence and sadness.

"Why can't you just tell me what you feel?" I asked. "Your actions confuse me."

"You were supposed to be mine!" he declared.

"You were the one who left me," I countered. "I waited for you, but you never called. You forgot about me."

"I haven't forgotten," he said. "I made a huge mistake."

"That's how it was meant to be," I replied. "Leave the past where it belongs. Don't look back when you know you shouldn't. The past is just a story, and once you realize this, it has no power over you."

"But I can't," he replied. "You're telling me to leave the past behind and live in the moment?"

"You know what I mean," I said. "It's too late for regrets."

"Why did you choose Andrew? Why him?" he asked.

"I didn't choose him," I explained. "Fate and destiny brought him into my life, and I love him."

"Are you sure?" he challenged. "What's love? I was the one who showed you."

At that moment, as he asked, confusion overwhelmed me. It felt like I was unravelling. Before I could respond, he pulled me into his arms, attempting to kiss me. His perfume enveloped me, momentarily clouding my judgment. But as our lips met, clarity surged—I stood on the precipice of the biggest mistake of my life, and I halted.

"Please leave," I pleaded.

"I know," he replied. "I have to go. I'm sorry. The wheel is turning, and now you're pushing me away, but I need to tell you something."

"Don't say anything," I insisted. "Just leave."

I stood there, waiting for him to exit. He donned his jacket, then leaned close, whispering in my ear.

"I love you so much that I'm willing to betray my brother for you," he confessed. "Even though I know it's wrong, and I might regret it."

"You're about to make a colossal mistake," I countered. "I won't stand by and let you. It's too late to prove your love now. I don't trust you, and I refuse to carry guilt for the rest of my life. You forgot about me once, and now you have to do it again."

"The same applies to you," he shot back. "You forgot about me once, and now you have to do it again. I wish you all the best."

"You leave me no choice but to forget about you!" I implored. "Please... just go."

After George left, tears streamed down my face. Why did life have to be so complicated? Destiny played its cruel games, and I was caught in the middle. If only they weren't brothers—if only I hadn't met George again.

But Andrew… he meant everything to me. Leaving him seemed impossible, even though guilt gnawed at me. I decided not to tell Andrew about George's persistent visits. It was for the best, I thought.

However, fate had other plans. As Andrew approached the house, our neighbour intercepted him.

"I don't know what's going on," the neighbour said, "but there's a man who comes to your wife when you're not home. Maybe he's your friend—I've seen the three of you together."

Andrew sighed. "Yes, I know. He's my brother."

"Okay," the neighbour replied. "As you say. But it's strange—I saw him today, entering through the window!"

Andrew hesitated. "Maybe the door was broken," he explained, "or perhaps she lost her key."

That chat concerned Andrew. He didn't know what to believe anymore. That day, we had a very serious discussion—a heated argument where he sought the truth. Repeatedly, he asked me, 'Why did George enter through the window?' Everything was confusing, and I tried to explain to him that nothing had happened between me and George. He inquired whether the door was blocked or if I had lost the key. I simply replied that I hadn't heard him knocking at the door. Andrew sensed that something wasn't right, and eventually, he understood, though he remained sceptical.

I felt guilty; there was a desperation in my heart that prevented me from explaining the situation. I couldn't say anything to jeopardize their brotherly relationship. I wished for Andrew to trust me, but the circumstances were too complex for all of us to comprehend. As the song goes, *"I cannot always show it but don't doubt my love."* (quoting Calling You by Outlandish).

For almost a week, Andrew and I hardly spoke. He was upset, worried, and withdrawn, but gradually, we managed to overcome the situation. We reconciled, worked through our problems, and conquered our fears. George rarely visited us, and he stopped coming over when Andrew wasn't home. Additionally, I found a new job, and life returned to normal. I was content with Andrew, and then something happened that brought even greater joy.

One morning, I woke up feeling unwell—a strange sensation lingering. After returning from work, I decided to take a pregnancy test. Impatience gnawed at me as I awaited the result, emotions colliding within. I silently prayed for the test to be both positive and negative simultaneously. But when those few minutes passed, the test showed a clear positive result!

Staring at it, I felt torn—should I cry or laugh? How would I break the news to Andrew? Would he be thrilled? Was I ready to become a mother? Was he prepared to be a father?

By the time Andrew arrived home, my mind raced with a thousand thoughts. I didn't even know how to share this life-altering revelation. During dinner, he noticed my quiet demeanour and concern.

"What's the matter?" he asked. "Why are you upset?"

"I'm not upset," I replied. "I don't know if I'm happy or upset. I have some news for you."

"Is it something good or bad?" he inquired.

Taking a deep breath, I said, "I'm pregnant."

His gaze lingered on me for a few heartbeats, and then he pulled me into a tight embrace. Even he didn't know how to react. Emotions swirled within him—a blend of surprise, happiness, confusion, and worry, all compressed into a single moment. When news like this hits you, your mind races with a million thoughts, and finding the right way to respond feels like an impossible puzzle.

"Are you ready to be a mother?" he asked, his voice both gentle and concerned. "A child isn't like a puppy. You can't just abandon them in a shelter or sell them if you change your mind. Also, getting a dog is a lifelong commitment, but if you ever find yourself unable to care for it, consider finding a loving home through adoption. With a child is a different situation. Parenthood is a significant responsibility, and you're so young. In six months, you'll only be twenty years old."

I took a deep breath. "I'm ready," I replied. "If I'm pregnant, I want to have this baby. Do you want to be a daddy?"

His eyes softened. "Of course," he said. "I'm nearly twenty-eight years old—I think this is the perfect time for me to become a father."

I didn't overthink it. I was ready to become a mother. Andrew and I were over the moon, our hearts full of excitement as we eagerly anticipated parenthood. I immersed myself in parenting magazines, agonised over the perfect name for our baby, and bought all sorts of adorable clothes and toys. My life suddenly felt full of purpose—my dreams and my vision for the future all shifted as I embraced this new chapter. Yet, despite everything, I was the happiest I had ever been, knowing that soon, I would be a mother.

Deciding to have a child is a monumental choice—it's the decision to have your heart walk around outside your body forever. The most incredible thing about parenthood is that once you become a parent, you will never be your own priority again. You love your children more than you ever loved yourself or anyone else.

When the time came to share the news with our family, the reactions were filled with joy and congratulations—everyone, that is, except George. His response was strange, detached. He wouldn't meet my gaze, his words were few, and the congratulations he offered felt more like a formality than genuine warmth. With a forced smile, he quickly changed the subject, his indifference weighing on me.

The next day, George turned up at my house unexpectedly. I was about to head out for a walk in the park to clear my head when he arrived, looking unusually quiet and troubled. Sensing something was off, I invited him to join me. As we settled onto a park bench, he turned to me, his expression grave.

"Are you sure you want to be a mother? I've known you since you were a little girl, and we need to talk about this. Raising a child is a huge responsibility," he began.

"I'm absolutely sure. I'm thrilled about having a baby. We're committed to being responsible parents," I responded confidently.

"I understand, but you're very young, and you should think it over. You're not even married to Andrew yet."

"That's not an issue. We're planning to get married soon. Did Andrew ask you to talk to me about this?" I asked, curious.

"No, this is just me wanting to make sure you're making the best decision. Maybe you should take more time to consider it. If you ever feel uncertain, I'm here to support you. We can visit a private clinic together and consult a good doctor."

"I don't know why, but I have a bad feeling about this conversation, and I don't know what to believe. Is this some kind of test or game?" I asked, feeling uneasy.

I stood up from the bench and went home, feeling very annoyed. I hadn't considered the possibility that George had that conversation with me because he loved me and didn't want to lose me. If I become a mother, we'll never have a chance to be together again. He was hoping that maybe one day I'd realize I was not happy with Andrew and come back to him. I didn't even think for a second about what he was really trying to say; I thought it was a game and Andrew was testing me.

When Andrew came home, I initiated a serious argument.

"If you're not ready to be a father, you can just tell me. Talk to me! Why do you play games? Why did you ask your brother to talk to me about it?" I demanded.

"I don't know what you're talking about!" he replied, confused.

"Do you want to test me to see if I'm ready to become a mother?" I asked, my voice edged with frustration. "Today, George asked me if I'm sure about this decision. He even offered to help, just in case I change my mind."

Andrew's face darkened. "Are you sure this baby is mine? Maybe that's why he asked you," he said, his voice laced with suspicion.

His words hit me like a punch to the gut. At that moment, everything snapped into place, and I realised why George had brought up that conversation. Andrew hadn't been testing me—he genuinely believed that I was pregnant with George's child. Confusion and disbelief surged through me, and I found myself struggling to explain the truth. There was no intimacy between George and me, but how could I make Andrew see that?

Andrew knew about George's visits when I was home alone, and now his mind had spiralled into an unimaginable place. He was convinced that it was during one of those visits that I had become pregnant that I'd cheated on him with his brother. The more I tried to explain, the worse it seemed to get. The coincidences stacked up, the circumstances entwined in a messy, tangled web. It felt as though everything, even the universe itself, was conspiring against me. I wanted nothing more than to wake up from this twisted nightmare, but I knew that wasn't possible.

But in the end, Andrew chose to believe me. Despite his lingering questions and doubts, he understood that nothing had happened between George and me. At least, that's what he told me—he believed me. He knew that George still had hidden feelings for me, yet he remained silent. However, he became colder towards me. It was the first time my relationship with Andrew began to collapse. This became the initial step towards our falling apart and the first barrier between us. Additionally, Andrew decided to maintain distance, opting for more phone conversations with George rather than in-person visits. George, too, acquiesced, visiting us less frequently.

Fragments of a Dream

My relationship with Andrew seemed to be flourishing, and we thought we were happy. Yet, sometimes, I felt that something was missing—like my heart wasn't quite whole, as if the final piece of my puzzle remained elusive. I began to wonder if I had been mistaken in believing that Andrew was my missing puzzle piece. I felt lonely; I had no friends. Andrew was always away at work, and our evenings together were brief, with him often tired. Our touches grew infrequent, and I increasingly longed for love, tenderness, and understanding. I hoped it was just a difficult phase and that it would pass.

After many searches, even though I was pregnant, I finally found a job. I didn't have the necessary documents to work, but I secured a position as a housekeeper at a hotel. It was a very demanding job, but I was glad to leave home and not spend the entire day alone. Additionally, I was happy to have the opportunity to save money for the period when I wouldn't be able to work and would have to stay home with the baby I was expecting. The dreams I had when I arrived in London had shattered. There was no longer any chance to save money and return to Romania to continue my studies. My destiny had taken a different course, and I needed to build new dreams.

The following Christmas holiday, Andrew and I celebrated together—just the two of us. We did the shopping, cooked meals, and decorated the Christmas tree, eagerly awaiting Santa Claus as per tradition. It was our chance to spend quality time together and enjoy the present. Although we didn't have much money for gifts, we were content with what we had. During the two weeks of the holiday, we mostly stayed indoors, watching movies, shopping together, and cooking side by side.

One evening, Andrew and I sat down to watch a movie together. The film was called True Romance, and I found myself captivated by it. Christian Slater and Patricia Arquette, the stars of the movie, portrayed the perfect couple on screen.

The following week, while I was home alone, George's words kept echoing in my mind. He had pointed out that I wasn't officially married to Andrew, yet we were expecting a baby. The thought nagged at me. With Andrew's birthday approaching, I wanted to give him a heartfelt gift—something simple and original. So, I decided to create a marriage certificate as my present. Unfortunately, finances were tight, and I couldn't afford anything extravagant. Instead, armed with a crayon and a piece of paper, I meticulously crafted our fictional marriage certificate. As witnesses to our imaginary union, I inscribed the names of Christian Slater and Patricia Arquette.

When Andrew returned from work that day, I handed him the unique gift—a whimsical testament to our bond.

"If I sign this official document, does that mean you're officially my wife? Don't forget, this paper holds more value than a real marriage certificate," he said with a smile.

"I know, and I accept being your wife! I promise that for the rest of my life, I'll be there for you," I replied.

Laughing, we signed that paper. Then he hugged me tightly and led me to our room to spend our wedding night. As Jennifer Lopez sings in "Papi*,*" *"He let me wear the crown; I'll do my best to make him proud."*

I always dreamed of being a bride. Since I was little, I imagined myself in a white wedding dress, with a groom arriving on a white horse to propose, asking for my hand in marriage from my grandmother. I didn't dream of a grand wedding, but I wanted to follow tradition and the laws of marriage. However, we didn't have enough money for a wedding, and every time I told Andrew about my wish, he would say he didn't believe in marriage or wedding ceremonies—they were just unnecessary expenses.

He had been a groom when he married Evelin, and having gone through the wedding experience, he wasn't eager to repeat it. We weren't even engaged, and I didn't wear a ring. So, whenever I dreamed of becoming a bride, it remained a private wish for me.

Unconditional Love

Our lives changed radically when our little girl was born. We felt like the luckiest parents in the entire universe. Holding her in our arms for the first time, it felt as if nothing else in the world mattered. We named her Emma because her name signifies wholeness, completeness, and everything we cherish. She gave our lives meaning and purpose—a precious gift from God, a blessing that fills our days.

Emma is my treasure and Andrew's little princess.

Bringing a child into the world is like giving birth to a piece of your heart and nurturing it. Without that piece, you can never be whole again. To raise a child, you need boundless love, immense patience to overcome worries, hard work, and countless sacrifices. From the moment Emma was born, I vowed never to blame her for anything I did or will do for her; I do it all out of love. I promised her that I would never control her life or her decisions; instead, I'll conquer my fears and grant her the freedom to explore the world. I pledged to be by her side throughout her life, ready to help whenever she needed me. Since her birth, my purpose has revolved around her. I will celebrate her achievements and dreams, share in her joy, feel her sadness, and bask in the light of her smile.

Andrew, too, made similar promises. He committed to being a present and supportive father despite his demanding job. He wanted to ensure that Emma always felt loved and valued. His transformation into a devoted father was a journey of growth and self-discovery, one that deepened our bond as a family.

I hope that when she grows up, she won't see me as absurd or possessive but will understand my fears. I hope she realizes that since she came into my life, my greatest fear has been losing her and seeing her unhappy, hurt, or discouraged. I hope that a mother's love won't frighten her, bore her, disturb her, suffocate her, or drive her away. I want her to be honest with me, to see me as a good friend, and to share all her secrets and worries with me. I hope she understands that a mother's love is irreplaceable.

I will strive to be both a mother and a friend, a worthy example for her to follow and someone she can learn from. All I want is for her to be happy and to understand that she's truly perfect. I'll teach her to trust herself, to love herself, and to respect herself. I'll guide her to be independent, to succeed on her own, and not to rely on a man for her success. I'll tell her that a real woman values a man's love, time, loyalty, and commitment over his money or the car he drives.

I want her to know that she can always come to me, no matter what. Whether she's facing a challenge, celebrating a victory, or just needs someone to talk to, I'll be there. I'll encourage her to pursue her dreams and passions, to never settle for less than she deserves, and to always believe in herself. I'll remind her that she is strong, capable, and worthy of all the good things life has to offer.

I'll teach her the importance of kindness and empathy, to treat others with respect and compassion. I'll show her that it's okay to make mistakes as long as she learns from them and grows. I'll support her in every decision she makes, even if it's different from what I would choose. I want her to feel free to be herself, to explore the world, and to find her own path.

Most importantly, I want her to know that my love for her is unconditional. No matter where life takes her, she will always have a home in my heart. I'll be her biggest cheerleader, her confidant, and her safe haven. My greatest joy will be watching her grow into the amazing person I know she will become.

Life doesn't come with explicit instructions, but it gradually imparts its lessons. It isn't a scripted movie, yet it features an ensemble cast of remarkable actors. I'll guide her to keep her plans and desires close to her heart, letting her achievements speak for themselves. Envy can disrupt even the best-laid plans, so I'll encourage her to smile at those who hide envy and gossip behind her back, allowing them to believe she remains blissfully unaware.

I'll empower her to take care of herself and navigate any situation with confidence. She shouldn't expect anything from anyone, and if someone chooses to leave, so be it—only the right people will remain. I'll share everything I've learned and everything my grandmother taught me, equipping her to protect herself from hurt.

I'll teach her to be resilient and self-reliant, to trust in her own strength and abilities. I'll remind her that life's challenges are opportunities for growth and that she has the power to overcome any obstacle. I'll encourage her to be kind and compassionate, to treat others with respect, and to always stay true to herself.

I'll also instil in her the importance of self-love and self-respect. She should never feel the need to change who she is to fit someone else's expectations. I'll teach her to value her own worth and to never settle for less than she deserves. I'll show her that true happiness comes from within and that she has the power to create her own joy.

I'll encourage her to pursue her passions and dreams, no matter how big or small. I'll support her in every endeavour, reminding her that failure is just a stepping stone to success. I'll teach her to be brave and to take risks, knowing that I'll always be there to catch her if she falls.

Most importantly, I'll show her that she is loved unconditionally. I'll be there to support her, to celebrate her successes, and to comfort her in times of need. I want her to know that no matter what happens, she will always have a home in my heart. I'll be her biggest cheerleader, her confidant, and her safe haven. My greatest joy will be watching her grow into the amazing person I know she will become.

A Baptism of Love and Resilience

When Emma was about two months old, we felt compelled to follow our religious and cultural traditions by baptizing her. Selecting suitable godparents for our daughter became a significant decision, especially since we had few friends in London at the time and couldn't travel to Romania for her baptism. Just as we were searching for the right person, George approached us. He expressed his willingness to be our daughter's godfather, and we gladly accepted. Soon after, we scheduled the christening ceremony.

During that period, financial constraints weighed heavily on us. Andrew, in an effort to make ends meet, took on an additional job for a brief two-week stint. His days were filled with labour as a carpenter, followed by evenings at a more lucrative but risky part-time gig. His unusual task involved plastering inappropriate advertisements on phone booths across Central London. A co-worker had tipped him off about this opportunity, and given our urgent need for funds, Andrew decided to take the gamble. The first week went smoothly, but in the second week, fate intervened—the police apprehended him.

Before the christening ceremony, as per our tradition, we all had to attend church for confession. In the evening, I placed Emma in her pushchair and headed to the church. I was supposed to meet both Andrew and George there, but only George was waiting for me. Andrew had been apprehended by the police and taken to the station. Despite my repeated attempts to call him, his phone remained unresponsive. Anxiety gnawed at me, but George tried to soothe my nerves, assuring me that everything would be alright, and that Andrew would soon communicate with us. As we waited in the church for the priest to arrive for confession, George played with Emma.

"I may not have been destined to be the father of your children, but now I proudly embrace the role of Emma's uncle and soon, her godfather," he said.

"Indeed, it seems this was meant to be. My hope is to set a positive example, uphold your godfatherly promises, and nurture her growth with Christian values," I replied.

Considering that he's not a particularly faithful person and doesn't pray often, my response elicited laughter from him. He then harked back to a memory from our past.

"I always keep my promises. I vowed in front of the church that I would never lie to you, and I assured you that you would be mine forever," he said charily.

"That's true. We'll be together forever, but I can't be yours," I said.

"We'll never truly know! We can flee from anything; we can traverse the world, but we can't escape what resides in our hearts. We cannot release those we love; they accompany us everywhere because they dwell in our hearts eternally."

"Since we're in the church now, promise me once more that you'll love me like a sister-in-law and as a friend! Promise me you'll leave the past behind!" I said.

"I promise, I'll love you like…"

Just as he was about to complete his promise, the priest arrived, and George had to go to another room for confession.

"Don't forget to confess all your sins!" I reminded him as he followed the priest.

"I'll confess all my sins except one because God already knows that each of us lives trying to forget somebody," he replied.

After our confessions, George joined us at home, and we anxiously awaited any sign from Andrew. I kept calling him, but his phone remained switched off. Finally, at midnight, Andrew called.

"I'm at the police station; they arrested me while I was putting up posters. I have to go through some procedures, but please don't worry! I'll be home in the morning."

"I'm concerned, but I hope everything will be okay. I'll be waiting for you. Take care!"

"I will!" he assured me.

After my phone conversation with Andrew, a wave of calm washed over me, his reassuring words eased my anxiety, and I felt a sense of peace. George, sensing my need for company, stayed with me for another ten minutes, offering his support and comfort. Once he left, I nestled next to Emma, her gentle breathing lulling me into a much-needed sleep.

The next morning, Andrew walked through the door, safe and sound. Relief flooded over me as I embraced him, grateful for his return. He shared his decision to leave that risky job behind, prioritizing our family's safety and well-being. With the little money we had saved, we began planning a modest baptism ceremony for Emma. It wasn't extravagant, but it was filled with love and hope for our future.

We invited our few friends, creating a warm and intimate gathering. The ceremony was simple yet beautiful, a testament to our resilience and the strength of our bond. Despite the challenges we faced, we found joy in the small moments and cherished the support of those around us. This experience taught us the value of togetherness and the importance of making decisions that prioritize our family's happiness and security.

"Happiness doesn't always require a lot of money; as long as we're together, we have everything we need," I thought to myself. It's essential to appreciate what we already have and not constantly seek more to enjoy life. Quitting that job was a good decision, and we managed to celebrate a small christening ceremony with the funds we had.

Lessons in Humility and Hope

For three years, I stayed at home with Emma while Andrew worked tirelessly. Unfortunately, we lacked the necessary documents to obtain the right to work in the UK, leaving us financially strained and without any assistance. During those days at home, I engaged myself in knitting and crocheting, creating numerous children's dresses, jumpers, hats, and toys. However, despite my efforts, I couldn't sell any of my creations due to a lack of resources for advertising. At a certain point, our financial situation became dire, and we could no longer afford our pay the rent. We made the difficult decision to move to a shared house with people of a different nationality. Adapting to their house rules was challenging, but we managed somehow. Andrew's earnings were divided to cover rent, bills, Oyster card top-ups, and food expenses.

I vividly recall a day when I stood before empty cupboards, my heart sinking at the sight of nothing to cook. Andrew was on his way home from work, undoubtedly tired and hungry, expecting a warm meal. The only small relief was knowing that Emma had enough powdered milk to get by. Desperation, however, led me to a shameful act—I stole a handful of rice from our housemates, praying they wouldn't notice. I cooked the rice, hoping it would be enough.

The next morning, I was met with a harsh reality. All the kitchen cabinets, except mine, were chained and locked. The weight of my actions hit me hard. Overwhelmed with guilt and shame, I approached our housemates, apologized sincerely for taking the rice, and promised to replace it with a new bag. This incident taught me a valuable lesson: in life, we can't have everything, but we can find contentment in what we already possess. During those challenging moments, we relied solely on each other, and that was enough. We held onto hope and confidence that everything would eventually be okay.

I remember my grandmother's words echoing in my mind: "The rich will become even richer, and the poor will become even poorer." She always reminded me, "No matter how wealthy you become, never forget where you came from and what you've endured. Always extend a helping hand to those around you. It's not your fault if you're rich, but it is your fault if you don't share a loaf of bread when someone goes to bed hungry."

These words have stayed with me, guiding me through life's ups and downs. They remind me of the importance of empathy, generosity, and staying grounded, no matter the circumstances.

In my mind, I kept telling myself that one day, when I have money, I will always assist the poor and those in need. When I help someone, I won't seek praise or boast in front of the world. There won't be a video on Facebook aiming for a thousand likes. Instead, I'll find joy in my soul and experience the fullness of giving.

Observing the world around me, especially in stores and shops, I notice people filling their shopping carts without restraint or consideration. Everyone chases after brand names, expensive perfumes, luxurious bags, costly clothing, extravagant cars, exotic vacations, and all manner of pricey foods. Some wear expensive watches, forgetting that time itself is far more precious. Many have lost sight of the fact that one day, we'll leave this earth, leaving behind our homes, cars, and wealth.

Until that moment arrives, let us be good people—fair, helpful, respectful, and loving toward everyone. Let's find joy in life's little things, live in the present, and respect each other. Today, whether rich or poor, we don't know what tomorrow holds. On this earth, we are all equal, regardless of our wealth, skin colour, nationality, or social status.

Threads of Hope

It has been an incredibly challenging time. Nearly four years had passed since we arrived in London, and we hadn't had the opportunity to return home. I deeply missed my mother, my grandmother, my brother, and the familiar comfort of our house. Emma was almost three years old, and our family had only seen her through photographs. Despite the hardships, what mattered most was our happiness; we were grateful to God for our health and our wonderful little girl. Whenever we faced financial difficulties, Andrew always reassured me.

"Don't worry; everything will be fine. I know that one day we'll have our house with a big garden, just like we dreamed. I promise you," Andrew would say, his voice filled with unwavering confidence.

"I know; everything will be okay. I trust you, and I know we'll make it. All that matters is that we're together, and we have our beautiful little girl," I reply, drawing strength from his optimism.

Eventually, we managed to obtain all the necessary documents to live and work in the UK, and Andrew found a good job. His increased income allowed us to move into a larger shared house, which we rented with other Romanian families. In our new home, I met our neighbour, Lily, and we quickly became friends. Lily was also married and had a little boy named Daniel. Emma loved playing with Daniel, and their laughter filled our days with joy. I always thanked God for sending Lily into my life when I needed someone I could trust, especially during those lonely moments.

Meanwhile, Andrew's mother decided to visit us, eager to finally meet her granddaughter, Emma. She planned her trip to

London to coincide with Christmas, hoping to celebrate the holiday together as a family. Additionally, she wanted to encourage us to get legally married and celebrate the occasion with her.

Given our financial constraints and the impracticality of returning to Romania for a traditional wedding with our families and friends, we opted for a civil ceremony at the local council. Although Andrew hadn't formally proposed, I was thrilled at the prospect of becoming his wife. It felt like the perfect moment for us to take this step.

By a fortunate coincidence, I managed to book the ceremony for December 13, 2013—the only available date during that period. It seemed like everything was falling into place, and we were excited to embark on this new chapter of our lives together.

In a fleeting moment of uncertainty, I asked myself what my heart truly desired and realized that something was missing—like the last piece of a puzzle that I couldn't quite place. Instead of looking inward and questioning what I truly wanted and how to change it, I meticulously planned every detail with the funds we had. This moment had been a lifelong dream, and I wanted it to be a memorable day. Marriage, after all, isn't just a piece of paper; it requires love, respect, trust, understanding, friendship, and loyalty to endure.

"You're already my wife! Remember when you signed the paper, and as witnesses to our wedding, the film stars Christian Slater and Patricia Arquette were there," Andrew said with a playful smile.

"I remember, but this time, we're legally getting married," I replied, feeling a mix of excitement and nervousness.

Coincidentally or not, on the day of the ceremony, I encountered a series of hilarious obstacles. It felt as though the universe was placing various barriers in my path, subtly hinting that something was missing. However, I didn't pay too much attention to these signs.

Despite the challenges, I pressed on, determined to make the day special. As we stood together, ready to exchange vows, I realized that the obstacles we faced only made the moment more meaningful. It wasn't just about the ceremony or the legalities; it was about the journey we had taken together and the love that had brought us to this point.

First, my friend Lily thoughtfully arranged an appointment for me at the beauty salon to style my hair for the ceremony. My naturally silky and soft hair proved to be quite a challenge for the hairstylist, who seemed inexperienced and struggled to manage it properly. With only an hour left until the ceremony, my hair was a complete mess. I returned home from the salon on the verge of tears—I had envisioned a special look, not my usual style. Thankfully, Andrew's mother came to the rescue and managed to fix my hair quickly, although it wasn't exactly what I had hoped for.

The second amusing incident involved my dress. I had ordered a stunning white dress online, but it arrived just one hour before the ceremony. Knowing the delivery was late, I had already bought another dress from a store. Unfortunately, I disliked the store-bought dress. When the online order finally arrived, I tried it on, only to find it was too small and too short. Removing the dress risked ruining the hairstyle Andrew's mother had created. Faced with this dilemma, I decided to wear the short little dress.

The third amusing incident happened as I made my way to the town hall for the ceremony. I quickly realized that my shoes were one size too big as if my feet had miraculously shrunk overnight. Wearing silky tights only made things worse, causing my shoes to slip off with every step. I had to walk very slowly, fearing I might lose a shoe on the stairs—much like Cinderella. In my dreams, I had always imagined wearing a dress like Cinderella on my wedding day, not losing my shoes like she did.

Additionally, we didn't have the budget for golden rings. Instead, I found titanium rings on eBay for a total of £20. Unfortunately, the sizes were too big.

Despite these little mishaps, the ceremony was intimate and beautiful. We'll always treasure the emotions we felt as we exchanged our vows. Even though we couldn't afford an expensive dress, fancy shoes, or golden rings as I had always dreamed of, I was genuinely happy and grateful for the simple things we had.

We were thrilled that everyone we invited attended the ceremony, except for George. When Andrew invited him, George assured us he would be there, but he didn't show up. He claimed his car had broken down and he needed to go to the mechanic. I couldn't understand why he couldn't come up with a more believable excuse. Any other reason would have sufficed, but he chose the oddest explanation.

The ceremony itself was held in a charming little town hall adorned with delicate flowers and soft lighting that created a warm and welcoming atmosphere. As we stood there, surrounded by our closest friends and family, the love and support in the room were palpable. The officiant's words were heartfelt, and as we exchanged our vows, I felt a deep sense of connection and commitment to Andrew.

After the ceremony, we had a modest reception with homemade food and simple decorations. The laughter and joy shared among our guests made the day even more special. Despite the challenges and unexpected events, the day was filled with love, happiness, and unforgettable memories.

That evening, after the ceremony, as if by magic, George's car was suddenly fixed. Without any prior plans, he decided to leave for Romania, to the village where we grew up, to celebrate Christmas. Coincidence or not, on the day I civilly married Andrew in London, George chose to return to the place where he had left me five years ago.

When Andrew's mother arrived in London, Emma quickly formed a strong bond with her grandmother. After the Christmas holidays, when Andrew's mother returned to Romania, Emma felt quite sad. She had spent two wonderful weeks with her grandmother, and their bond was truly special. I also realized that Andrew's mother wasn't just a caring grandmother; she was a wonderful friend. While she was with us, our home felt warm and positive, easing our longing for the places where we were born and raised. However, after her departure, we all felt that longing even more.

During those two weeks, our home was filled with laughter and stories from the past. Andrew's mother shared tales of her childhood, and we reminisced about our own memories from Romania. The aroma of traditional Romanian dishes filled the house, bringing a sense of comfort and nostalgia. Emma loved helping her grandmother in the kitchen, learning family recipes that had been passed down through generations.

The bond between Emma and her grandmother grew stronger each day. They spent hours playing games, reading stories, and exploring the local parks. It was heartwarming to see Emma so happy and connected to her roots. Andrew's mother also became a source of support and wisdom for me. We had long conversations about life, family, and the challenges we faced. Her presence brought a sense of stability and reassurance.

A Home Away from Home

A year after the ceremony, we finally managed to afford our first family holiday with Emma, who was almost four years old. After five years of living in London, I returned to Romania with my family. When I left home and came to London, I never imagined that I would return five years later with a little girl. I was overjoyed to introduce her to the whole family.

Grandma was ecstatic when she saw us. She told me that seeing us had rejuvenated her by twenty years. She had feared she might never meet her great-granddaughter. My mom also cried when she met Emma for the first time. She hugged her tightly and admired her, calling her a shining diamond, the most beautiful little girl. I felt like the luckiest mother in the world.

Reuniting with my brother and his family was another highlight. My brother, Charlie, had married Katie, and they had a two-year-old daughter named Sophie. It was the first time I met Katie and my beautiful niece Sophie in person. Until then, I had only seen them on Facebook. Charlie had also only seen Emma online and in pictures. The joy of finally being together in person was indescribable.

Our holiday was filled with laughter, love, and cherished moments. We visited familiar places, shared stories, and created new memories. Emma bonded with her great-grandmother, grandmother, uncle, aunt, and cousin, forming connections that would last a lifetime. The warmth and love from our family made the trip unforgettable.

After visiting everyone in my family, we went to see Andrew's oldest brother, Lucas, and his wife, Gabrielle. We also visited

Andrew's grandparents and his father. When we met Andrew's grandmother, she was crying tears of happiness. Andrew's grandmother had three sons, all grandsons and great-grandsons, and Emma was her only great-granddaughter. Her joy was palpable as she held Emma, her eyes sparkling with tears of happiness.

"Do you remember when I told you that Andrew is mine?" I asked Andrew's father.

"Of course, I remember!" he replied with a warm smile. "You were very confident when you told me. I'm glad you're happy, and my son has a lovely family."

After two weeks of holiday, we returned to London, fully recharged. Despite having our family, friends, and our house in Romania, London had become more than a place—it was a feeling, a sense of belonging. In this vibrant city, dreams could transform into reality. London offered countless opportunities for career success and the promise of a better future for Emma.

London, the capital of the United Kingdom, stands as one of the most cosmopolitan metropolises in the world and, without a doubt, the largest in Britain. It is a city where history intertwines with modernity, creating a vibrant tapestry of culture, commerce, and creativity. London is more than just a financial hub—it's a melting pot of cultures, languages, and traditions. Here, you can meet people from all corners of the globe, and the opportunities for learning and research are boundless. London offers hundreds of thousands of jobs across diverse fields. For me, it was about discovering these possibilities and evolving within this dynamic city—a place where dreams flourish, and connections deepen.

The city's iconic landmarks, from the historic Tower of London to the modern Shard, symbolize its rich heritage and forward-thinking spirit. The bustling markets, serene parks, and world-class museums add to its charm, making it a place where every day brings new experiences and adventures. The diversity of London's neighbourhoods, each with its unique character and community, made us feel at home. Whether it was the vibrant streets of Camden, the elegant avenues of Kensington, or the artistic vibe of Shoreditch, there was always something new to explore and enjoy.

Living in London also meant access to excellent education and healthcare, ensuring a bright future for Emma. The city's schools and universities are among the best in the world, offering endless opportunities for learning and growth. The healthcare system, with its state-of-the-art facilities and dedicated professionals, provided us with peace of mind.

The Missing Piece

When Emma started school, I took a part-time job at a coffee shop. However, my aspirations extended beyond that—I dreamed of becoming an accountant, a playful suggestion my father had made when I was little, calling me his "little accountant." When I discovered the opportunity to study in London, the dreams I had nurtured for years began to take shape. I was overjoyed; I wanted to provide Emma with a brighter future. So, I enrolled in university to study Business Management.

I can still picture the exact moment I decided to enrol in college. I was with my friend Lily, and for the first time, we dared to take our dreams seriously—dreams we had only whispered about until then. Together, we walked nervously into the college admission interview, our hearts racing with equal parts fear and excitement.

Our English was far from perfect, and the academic vocabulary felt like a foreign world to us. The first question we faced was simple yet confusing: *"Do you want to enrol in university or college?"* Lily and I glanced at each other, bewildered. In Romania, "college" meant high school, while "university" was what we called *faculty*. We had no idea which option we were supposed to choose.

I leaned closer to Lily and whispered, "Where do we enrol?" Without missing a beat, she answered, "At the faculty." We both burst into nervous laughter, our embarrassment spilling out in giggles we couldn't control.

Luckily, the student advisor was Romanian. She immediately understood our confusion, her smile kind rather than mocking. She gently explained the difference, putting us at ease. What could have been a humiliating mistake turned into a lighthearted moment, one that Lily and I still laugh about years later. That day marked the beginning of a new chapter in my life—a leap toward something bigger, filled with hope, fear, and the comfort of sharing the journey with a true friend.

As time passed, life in London began to feel less like a struggle and more like a homecoming. Our financial situation gradually improved, and our circle of loved ones grew wider. My brother Charlie eventually joined us in London, as did Andrew's brothers, Michael and James, each bringing their families. With them came three wonderful women—Katie, Christina, and Sarah—who became more than sisters-in-law; they became my friends, my confidantes, my allies in this new chapter. Together, we built a network of support, a kind of chosen family that kept us grounded in a city that could otherwise feel overwhelming.

Andrew, in particular, found joy in our family gatherings, especially the fishing trips and camping weekends. Those excursions became his moments of pure contentment—surrounded by nature, laughter, and the people he loved most. One trip remains etched in my memory. Emma stayed behind with my brother so she could spend the day with her cousin Sophie, which gave us, the adults, a rare chance at adventure.

The day began with radiant sunshine as we pitched our tent by the lake, but soon the sky darkened, and a sudden storm unleashed its fury. Rain pelted down in icy sheets, thunder roared overhead, lightning split the sky, and wind whipped so hard it nearly tore our tent apart. For a moment, it felt as though the storm might wash us away.

When the chaos finally subsided, we debated whether to pack up and leave, but it was already late, and our car was trapped in the locked parking lot until morning. With no choice but to stay, we lit a fire to chase away the chill, huddling close as flames crackled against the night.

That evening stretched into something magical. We gathered in the large tent—two compartments with a narrow hallway—telling stories of ghosts, witches, and vampires. Every creak of the branches, every flicker of shadow outside the tent deepened the tension. To make matters even more surreal, the fishing spot was near a zoo, and through the darkness we could hear lions roaring in the distance. The sound was so close, so powerful, it felt as though the beasts were circling us in the night.

We didn't sleep at all. Instead, we laughed, screamed, and whispered until dawn broke, our fear dissolving into warmth and camaraderie. That stormy night became one of those rare, unforgettable memories—the kind that binds people together forever.

Every fishing trip brought extraordinary moments and pure enjoyment. I found myself in friendly competition with Andrew and Emma—who could catch the most fish? The stakes were high: the winner would receive a surprise. Whenever we reeled in a fish, we handed the fishing rod to Emma, cheering her on to victory. Her joy was contagious, and she transformed into a true little fisherman.

With Andrew and Emma by my side, I experienced the most beautiful moments of my life. Our family became my pride and joy. Watching our daughter grow has been a multifaceted journey—filled with joy, impact, and occasional stress—but above all, it has been the most meaningful part of our lives. We consider ourselves the luckiest parents in the world because we have an incredible daughter. As Angela Schwind wisely said, "While we try to teach our children all about life, our children teach us what life is all about."

Even though we had everything and were happy, something was missing. It was a nagging feeling I didn't want to confront, so I pushed all the problems to the back of my mind. Amidst all the beauty in our lives, there was an emptiness I refused to acknowledge. I didn't want to think about it, let alone seek solutions, before it was too late.

Despite our seemingly perfect life, there was an undercurrent of unease that I couldn't shake off. The laughter and joy we shared masked a void that grew deeper with each passing day. I often found myself lost in thought, wondering what it was that eluded us. The more I tried to ignore it, the more persistent it became, like a shadow that followed me everywhere.

I immersed myself in daily routines, hoping the feeling would fade away. But in quiet moments, when the house was still, and the world outside seemed distant, the emptiness would resurface, demanding my attention. I knew I had to face it eventually, but the fear of what I might uncover held me back. The thought of disrupting our happiness was too daunting, so I continued to push it aside, hoping that, somehow, things would resolve themselves before it was too late.

A Family's Odyssey

After months of careful planning and saving, we finally had enough money for a holiday. The destination: Turkey.

"This is our chance," Andrew said, his eyes shining with excitement. "We've never had the opportunity to go on a proper vacation until now."

I felt a surge of joy. "I can't believe it! I need to pack everything we'll need. Emma will be over the moon—I can't wait to see her face when we get there!"

A thrill of disbelief coursed through me. After all our hard work, we could finally afford a holiday, and it felt as though our dreams were starting to take shape. An exotic vacation had always seemed distant, almost impossible, but now it was within reach. Every effort, every late night and extra hour, had led to this moment.

I glanced at Andrew and felt a wave of gratitude. He had fought tirelessly for our family, a father and partner who carried responsibility with quiet strength. Even though at times there had been moments of distance between us, I couldn't help but admire him for everything he had done. As the old saying goes, "A man who fights hard for his family deserves all the respect in the world"—and I respected him more than words could capture.

There were moments when I wished Andrew would be more romantic, pamper me, give me compliments now and then, and help with household chores. But we were both so focused on our jobs, university courses, projects, and spending time with Emma. When I first met Andrew, he was more romantic, more active, and a bit wild. However, I consoled myself, thinking that perhaps he had become more mature and was no longer the reckless, impulsive guy who lived in the moment.

Despite these changes, our shared goal of providing a better life for Emma kept us united. This holiday was a testament to our hard work and dedication, and I hoped it would rekindle some of the spark that had dimmed over the years.

When we arrived in Turkey, it felt like stepping into another world—a place straight out of a storybook. The breathtaking beauty of the landscapes resembled scenes from fairy tales. As I gazed at the azure sea and basked in the sun's warmth, I knew we were about to embark on an unforgettable holiday.

In Turkey, our days unfolded like a kaleidoscope of experiences. Each sunrise brought the promise of discovery, and we embraced it wholeheartedly. We immersed ourselves in the rich cultural tapestry of Turkey. From bustling bazaars to ancient rituals, every encounter felt like turning the pages of a forgotten legend. The locals welcomed us with open arms, their laughter echoing through narrow alleys. Their zest for life was contagious, and we found ourselves dancing to their rhythm.

We soared above the azure coastline, our hearts racing as the wind carried us higher. The world below transformed into a miniature mosaic—a patchwork of cliffs, beaches, and turquoise waves. The Mediterranean sun embraced us, leaving warm imprints on our skin. We sprawled on sandy shores, our toes digging into golden grains, and whispered secrets to the waves.

Every moment in Turkey was magical, from the vibrant markets to the serene beaches. It was a journey of discovery and connection, where every experience added a new layer to our story. This holiday was not just a break from routine; it was a celebration of life, love, and the beauty of the world around us.

We rented bicycles, which became our trusty steeds, carrying us through cobbled streets and olive groves. We pedalled past ancient ruins, our laughter echoing off the timeworn stones.

As twilight painted the sky in hues of orange and pink, we gathered at seaside restaurants. Candlelight flickered, and we feasted on meze platters, fresh seafood, and laughter. Emma's eyes sparkled with delight. We savoured baklava dripping with honey, sipped strong Turkish coffee, and devoured kebabs that melted on our tongues. Each meal was a celebration of taste and tradition.

The hotel pool became Emma's enchanted realm. She splashed, giggled, and swam like a mermaid. Her joy was infectious, and we revelled in her happiness.

Our Turkish odyssey wove its magic—threads of adventure, love, and wonder. As we returned to London, our hearts carried the sun-kissed memories. We felt happier, more joyful, and incredibly motivated to resume work and school. Time flowed gracefully; our days were infused with energy, and we found contentment in the smallest details.

Woven in Time

Over time, I learned to appreciate things for their intrinsic meaning rather than their mere representation. A truly valuable person is one whose actions align with their words. Some individuals are born lucky, while others are born fighters. We realized that we were a blend of both—fortunate and resilient. The world around us merely observed, and other people's opinions held little sway. Yet, deep within my heart, there lingered a sense that the final piece of my puzzle remained elusive. Or perhaps it was never lost; it was simply waiting for me to find it in the warmth of shared moments.

After all these years, I believed George had left the past behind, but it wasn't that simple. One day, he extended an invitation—an invitation that would unravel memories and weave new threads into our lives. Dinner at a restaurant, followed by a venture to a club—the prospect of reconnecting with George made Andrew cheerful. It had been some time since we'd spent time together, and we decided to accept this meeting. Besides, we needed an outing. We hadn't been out to a restaurant in a very long time. Firstly, because Emma was little, and secondly, because we didn't have much money and were working tirelessly. Hence, it was a good opportunity for us to go out. Emma, my little princess, stayed at my brother's house, playing joyfully with her cousin Sophie.

And there we were, stepping into the restaurant, its walls adorned with mirrors. George stood there; his gaze fixed on me—a reflection within a reflection. Our eyes met through the mirrors, and he smiled—a knowing smile that bridged the years we had been apart. In that suspended moment, I chose silence, allowing him to believe that I hadn't noticed. Andrew sat across from me, and beside him was George—the ex-boyfriend turned brother-in-law. Life's intricate dance had woven our paths together, and I wondered why fate revelled in such coincidences.

Questions swirled in my mind like autumn leaves caught in a gentle breeze. Why did George still carry fragments of our shared history? How had our paths diverged and converged again? And why did life insist on these intricate knots? Maybe the missing piece of my puzzle lay there in the mirrored gaze of an old flame.

As we settled into our seats, the ambience of the restaurant enveloped us. The soft clinking of glasses, the murmur of conversations, and the warm glow of candlelight created an intimate atmosphere. I glanced at Andrew, who was engrossed in a conversation with George and felt a pang of nostalgia mixed with curiosity.

Throughout the evening, I found myself stealing glances at George, each time catching a glimpse of the past we once shared. The memories were bittersweet, a reminder of a different time and place. Yet, amidst the laughter and the shared stories, I realized that the present held its own beauty and significance.

Perhaps the missing piece of my puzzle was not about rekindling old flames but about embracing the journey that had brought us here. It was about finding peace in the present and cherishing the connections that had shaped our lives. As the night drew to a close, I felt a sense of closure and a renewed appreciation for the path we had travelled.

Life, it seemed, was a master weaver, intertwining our stories, stitching together chance encounters and deliberate choices. As the evening unfolded, I realized that sometimes the past doesn't fade— it merely takes on new hues, casting shadows and light on our present. We dined, laughed, and reminisced; three souls bound by shared memories and unspoken words. The mirrors reflected not just our images but the layers of time—the echoes of what was and what could have been.

As we left the restaurant, I glanced back at George. His eyes held secrets, and I wondered if he, too, pondered the threads that tied us together. Life's coincidences—bittersweet and mysterious—remained our silent companions. In the mirror of moments, we find fragments of ourselves.

In my mind, I wondered: How is it possible that after all these years, lingering feelings from the past still persist? Why hasn't he married, settled down, and dreamt of a brighter future?

As I observed the way he looked at me, I realized that I secretly relished his gaze—it didn't intrude; it bolstered me. Even though I knew it wasn't right, his eyes bestowed upon me a newfound self-assurance. Accepting and seeking his gaze through the mirrors felt both thrilling and guilt laden. *"My mirror staring back at me,"* I thought, recalling Justin Timberlake's lyrics. In that reflection, I glimpsed beauty and vulnerability intertwined—a mosaic of memories and unspoken desires.

I found myself questioning the nature of our connection. How could something that seemed so distant still hold such power? His eyes, filled with unspoken words, made me feel seen in a way I hadn't felt in years. It was as if the mirrors around us were not just reflecting our images but also the complexities of our emotions.

The thrill of his gaze was intoxicating, yet it came with a heavy dose of guilt. I knew it wasn't right to seek validation from someone other than Andrew, but in that moment, it felt like a lifeline. The mirrors became a conduit for our silent communication, each glance a whisper of what once was and what could never be.

In that reflection, I saw a version of myself that was both beautiful and vulnerable—a reminder of the past and a testament to the present. It was a fleeting moment, but it left an indelible mark on my heart, a mosaic of memories and unspoken desires that would linger long after the evening had ended.

As we arrived at the club, Andrew ordered some drinks, and George entrusted me with the key to his car, asking me to keep it safe in my bag. We settled onto a plush couch, the air thick with anticipation and the promise of a memorable night.

After a while, George wandered through the club, his eyes scanning the crowd for a potential new flame. Meanwhile, I swayed on the dance floor with Andrew, our bodies moving in sync with the rhythm of the music. Time seemed to blur, and the room pulsed with energy, the vibrant lights casting a kaleidoscope of colours around us.

George returned, his shirt slightly unbuttoned, fingers fumbling to secure the buttons. Moments later, he approached me, his invitation to dance both daring and magnetic. As he took my hand, his gaze bore into mine, igniting a silent challenge. The dance floor became our battleground—a game of desire and restraint.

The music enveloped us, and we moved together, each step a blend of familiarity and tension. The crowd around us faded into the background as we danced, lost in our own world. George's touch was electric, and the unspoken words between us added a layer of intensity to the moment.

I stole glances at his chest, where a tattoo peeked from beneath the fabric. My fingers brushed against the buttons of his shirt, a subtle exploration. His smile held secrets, and he analysed my every move as if deciphering a cryptic code. I wanted to button up his shirt to conceal his exposed chest. Then, he whispered in my ear words that blurred the lines between past and present, temptation and consequence. The music enveloped us, and I wondered if this dance was merely a prelude—an awaiting memory etched into the fabric of time. With each passing second, guilt weighed heavier as we continued dancing. "In the dim light of desire, we danced," I thought, stepping into the night, where the past and the present swirled in a silent rhythm.

"Instead of undressing me, you're dressing me up," George said, his voice tinged with amusement.

"A real man always ensures an impeccable appearance in any situation. If you leave your shirt unbuttoned like that, I doubt you'll catch any lady's eye," I replied, trying to maintain a semblance of control.

"Believe me, I'm not seeking their attention. I only want…" he began, his voice trailing off as he leaned closer.

"Shhh…"

I stopped dancing and made my way over to Andrew. George, now with his shirt buttoned up, headed to the bar for a refill. When he returned, he handed me another drink. Andrew eyed us with a hint of suspicion and mentioned his plan to chat with the lady sitting solo at the bar. Maybe, just maybe, she'd join our group and share a drink with George. As Andrew engaged in conversation with her, George shot me a sly wink, inviting me to dance. When I turned him down, George leaned in and whispered:

"Whatever I do, I'll come back to you," George said, his voice low and intense.

"Maybe because I have the key to your car," I replied, trying to keep the mood light.

"You have more than one key, not just the key to my car!" he declared, his eyes locking onto mine.

"I only have one key from you; I lost the other one," I told him, my voice barely above a whisper.

"Is that why my heart is locked?" George asked, his tone softening, a hint of vulnerability in his eyes.

In that moment, memories flooded back—when George gifted me a teddy bear during our time together. The bear wore a silver necklace with a tiny key pendant, and George entrusted me with its care, saying it held the key to his heart. And then there was Andrew, who once left his keys on my table. I gestured toward them through the window, and when he returned to retrieve them, he echoed the same sentiment: "Whatever I do, I'll come back to you." Life, it seemed, wove these coincidences into our shared story.

As I reminisced about our past, George approached, enveloped me from behind, and pulled me toward the dance floor, disregarding the fact that I had just declined his invitation. The warmth of his touch and the familiarity of his presence stirred a whirlwind of emotions within me.

"Why do you look at me that way and not say anything?" he asked, his lips brushing against my ear, sending shivers down my spine.

I met his gaze, perplexed by his behaviour. "I don't understand why you're acting like this," I replied, my voice tinged with confusion. "What do you want from me? Why do you keep dredging up the past?"

His confession caught me off guard. "I want you to be mine," he confessed, his voice low and earnest. "I can't help it. I know it's not right, but I can't stop."

The intensity of his words hung in the air, mingling with the music and the dim lights of the club. It was a moment of raw honesty, a glimpse into the depths of his feelings that left me both flattered and conflicted. The dance floor, once a place of carefree movement, now felt like a stage for our unresolved emotions.

His lips grazed my cheek, and the scent of his cologne intoxicated me. I tried to be strong, to resist him, to show no trace of attraction. I wanted to prove that I had changed, that I wasn't the same innocent girl from before. But instead of being strong, I responded provocatively, humming the lyrics of the song playing in the speakers: *"Ride it, just lose control. Ride it, come touch my soul"* ("Ride It" by Jay Sean).

At that moment, I should have gone to Andrew, taken his hand, and danced with him. But he was engrossed in conversation with the lady sitting alone at the bar. Perhaps, fuelled by jealousy toward Andrew, I responded provocatively to George. Or maybe, and most likely, George made me feel beautiful and special in those moments while Andrew exchanged glances and engaged in discussions with someone else.

"I'll probably get mad if you stop looking at me the way you used to," I confided to George. "It's become a habit—ever since we've known each other, you've had this particular way of looking at me."

"Because, since I've known you, you've been the most special person to me," George smiled, his eyes locking onto mine with an intensity that made my heart race.

The club's vibrant lights and pulsating music faded into the background as we stood there, caught in a moment that felt both timeless and fleeting. George's words hung in the air, a reminder of the deep connection we once shared. It was a connection that, despite the years and the changes in our lives, still held a powerful grip on my heart.

As I looked into his eyes, I felt a whirlwind of emotions—nostalgia, longing, and a hint of guilt. The past and present collided, creating a complex tapestry of feelings that I struggled to untangle. In that instant, I realized that some bonds are never truly broken; they merely evolve, taking on new forms and meanings.

I met his gaze, my tone firm. "But don't expect from me what I embodied in the past. That part of me no longer exists."

"You haven't changed at all," he replied, his eyes searching mine for a hint of the girl he once knew.

Just then, Andrew joined us, asking if we wanted to step outside for a cigarette. I grabbed my purse, and we made our way to the designated smoking area. Andrew paused briefly at the men's room, leaving us waiting outside. As we stood there, I noticed the lady from the bar sitting in a corner, puffing on her cigarette. Earlier, when Andrew had spoken to her and invited her to join us, it became evident that her interest lay with Andrew rather than George. Despite George's attempts at conversation and humour, she patiently awaited Andrew's return from indoors.

"Your girlfriend doesn't mind if you make inappropriate jokes with other ladies?" she inquired, her eyes fixed on George.

George's annoyance was palpable. "She's my sister-in-law, not my girlfriend," he retorted. "The man you spoke with at the bar five minutes ago, is he's her husband and my brother."

The lady raised an eyebrow, clearly sceptical. "Are you sure she's your sister-in-law? The way you look at her says something else."

"Of course, I'm sure. She's special!" George's reply was firm, his voice carrying a note of finality.

The tension in the air was palpable as we waited for Andrew. George's declaration hung between us, a reminder of the complicated web of relationships and emotions that bound us together. It was a moment of clarity where the past and present collided, revealing the depth of our connections and the unspoken feelings that lingered just beneath the surface.

When Andrew stepped outside, he took my hand. The lady, visibly upset and disappointed, left without another word. I couldn't fathom what she had inferred from her conversation with Andrew, but she disappeared, and I never saw her again.

Half an hour later, we exited the club and climbed into George's car. As he drove us to his house, George searched for a song he wanted to hear. Just before reaching home, we made a brief stop at a late-night store to buy some drinks. Andrew went inside, leaving us waiting in the car.

I sat in the back seat; my eyes fixed on the windshield. As the music began to play, George turned towards me, his face dangerously close. He held my gaze for a few seconds, a soft smile playing on his lips. The music enveloped us, rendering me immobile. I gazed deeply into his eyes, barely breathing.

In that charged moment, he leaned in even closer, his lips delicately brushing against mine. He kissed me gently, and I felt my resolve begin to waver. Slowly and silently, I regained my composure and retreated to the back of the car, pressing myself against the seat. The lyrics of the song echoed softly in our minds: *"Turning and returning to some secret place inside."* (Berlin, Take My Breath Away).

When Andrew returned to the car, the song had ended. Confusion and overwhelming guilt washed over me. Why had I let him kiss me? Why did my heart race so wildly? The song continued to play in my mind as I urged myself to stay strong and avoid any foolish mistakes.

Andrew's subtle yet insistent signs were impossible to ignore. His deliberate and magnetic gestures demanded my attention. Amidst this emotional turmoil, I questioned my feelings. Did I truly love Andrew, or were George's lingering signs still entangled in my thoughts?

My grandmother's wisdom echoed in my mind: "Never give false hope to a man." Yet, my actions betrayed me. Through my gestures, I had unwittingly fed George's hopes instead of rejecting him outright. I had been utterly mistaken, and the weight of it settled upon me, leaving me feeling miserable. Now, guilt gnawed at my insides. I was married—bound by vows and promises to someone else. Yet, in that stolen kiss, I had betrayed it all. The weight of my actions pressed down, threatening to suffocate me.

As Andrew spoke, his voice a soft melody, I wondered if he sensed my turmoil. Did he know that I was unravelling, torn between loyalty and desire? His eyes held questions, and I couldn't meet them. "We can't undo what happened," I whispered to myself, "but we can choose what comes next."

Upon arriving home, I kept to myself, the events of the evening swirling in my mind. As we entered the house, George led us into the kitchen, suggesting we find something to eat. Andrew discovered a plate of grilled meat in the fridge, and we began our meal.

In the kitchen stood a highchair reminiscent of a pub stool, and I perched on it. George's eyes widened when he saw me there. He approached, gently nudging me off the highchair and onto the kitchen countertop. His smile was both playful and possessive as he declared it his chair, off-limits to anyone else. Then, with a surprising twist, he took his place between my legs on the highchair.

Andrew watched us, his expression a blend of amusement and confusion. We were like children squabbling over a prized toy—a dance of territorial claims.

George lived with Michael and his family, and our noisy commotion had woken everyone up. George was perched on the highchair between my legs, and I politely asked him to move so I could get down from the kitchen counter. Just then, my sister-in-law, Christina, walked into the kitchen. She looked a bit confused at first but quickly understood—we were arguing like two unruly children.

After a few minutes, George finally moved, allowing me to step down. I followed Christina to another room, where we prepared a bed for a few precious hours of sleep next to Andrew. He was utterly exhausted, his fatigue evident in every line on his face. As soon as the bed was ready, Andrew collapsed onto it, surrendering to sleep.

Christina beckoned me back into the kitchen, where we shared a cigarette and caught up on lost time. It had been a while since we last saw each other. As I re-entered the kitchen, George was still there, shirtless and bored, perched on his highchair. I tried not to admire his tattoos, avoiding direct eye contact. His silent, provocative gaze created a tension I couldn't ignore.

Christina lit her cigarette, but her son appeared at the door. She quickly handed me her cigarette and rushed to her son's bedroom to put him back to sleep. By coincidence or fate, I found myself alone in the kitchen with George.

I smoked half of the cigarette before deciding it was time to go to bed and sleep next to Andrew. Just as I was about to say good night to George, he suddenly grabbed my hand and gently pushed me against the wall, then turned off the light. A lamp in the hallway cast a purple glow through the slightly open kitchen door. His eyes and smile were captivating as he held me firmly. The cold wall pressed against my back, my heart racing, and I whispered in his ear as he gently touched my neck with his lips.

"That's a mistake; it's a sin! Let me go, please," I pleaded.

"I want to commit this sin; then I will pray to God for forgiveness for the rest of my life. I've been trying for so many years to commit this sin, and I can't stop now. Please don't stop me! It's a sin if you do stop me! I want you. I miss you."

"You've had too much to drink. Tomorrow, you'll forget everything, and if you don't forget, you'll feel guilty. I already feel guilty," I said.

"You have no idea how many times I've gotten drunk to forget everything about us, but I couldn't. I won't forget anything! I feel you. Please tell me you haven't forgotten anything about our past. I'll forget everything if you're able to forget."

He whispered every word in my ear, and with each touch, I became lost in his embrace, allowing his lips to find mine. When our mouths met, time seemed to stand still. It was a sin, yet I kissed him back. His hold tightened as he kissed me tenderly, his hands tracing the contours of my skin.

"Let me go, please! If anyone walks in, what will happen? Think of Emma and Andrew!" I pleaded.

"Tell me if you desire me as much as I crave you. At least for a few hours. I want you to be mine again."

"I don't want to be an unfaithful wife! I feel so guilty. I belong to Andrew now!" I said.

"Please don't feel guilty about what just happened; it's my fault," he said.

"It's my fault, too."

He touched my lips again softly, then stepped back and let me go.

I went to bed next to Andrew, but I couldn't sleep at all. Millions of thoughts swirled in my mind. I replayed his kiss, the feel of his lips, the contours of his body—each touch lingering. Guilt consumed me, threatening to spill over into tears. I longed to forget, to erase every moment.

I had committed a colossal mistake, an unforgivable sin. How could I meet Andrew's gaze after what had transpired? His words echoed in my mind: "If someone's hands touch you, forget about me!" But disappointment cut deeper than any blade. I didn't want to disappoint or hurt Andrew. Even though Andrew wasn't the most romantic or attentive to me, he deserved love and respect, not betrayal.

Why had I faltered? The greatest battle raged within me—the war between mind and heart. It's easy to be unfaithful; the challenge lies in remaining loyal. That night, I wasn't strong; I failed. Rihanna's haunting lyrics, *"I don't wanna be a murderer,"* echoed through my guilt-stricken soul.

Between Two Flames

It happened again, and I allowed it, but nothing in life can be programmed. Everything that must happen will happen. I couldn't control anything. It all unfolded rapidly, as if preordained. I couldn't explain to myself what I felt when he kissed me, and I couldn't confide in anyone to seek answers. We all deserve a friend who listens without judgment. Trust eluded me. I'm not perfect; I make mistakes, too, yet I value those who stand by me, even when they witness my flaws. Everyone knows me, but only part of me. I no longer recognize myself. Why do I transform in his presence? Why do we forget everything when our eyes meet? Why do unquenchable flames burn within us, defying even holy water? Who cursed me? Why is this happening? Why do I still care about him, defying indifference?

Dear heart,

I write this letter to you, beginning with a question: If you love Andrew, why do you still flinch at the sound of George's voice? Are you still entangled in thoughts of him? You must resist listening, fight, and bury those memories. Forget that you once loved him. Instead, focus on Andrew and Emma. Recall the pain when he left, how he disregarded you, not even bothering to call. Don't be foolish. You're submerging deeper, and I, dear heart, cannot mend your mistakes again. I cannot erase the traces, discard my thoughts, or tear out the pages.

I'll discipline you, training you to silence. I refuse to let you ruin my life. Instead, I'll confine you to a castle—a facade of beauty from the outside, but within, only ruins await. Hush now, naive heart! Your selfishness blinds you. Why won't you let me forget the past? "Don't stop; the past will trip you up. Right now, it is enough. Just keep moving."- "Flames" by David Guetta and Sia.

The heart accumulates experiences over time—feelings left unspoken and voids no one can fill. Life guides us to our destiny, and what will happen happens—with or without our consent. When the heart desires, the mind remains silent. As Hozier sings in "Take Me to Church," *"Take me to church, I'll worship like a dog at the shrine of your lies. I'll confess my sins, and you can sharpen your knife."*

The following day, I struggled to appear normal, as if nothing had happened. After our morning coffee, I left with Andrew for our home, yearning to be far from George and avoid any encounter. Upon arriving home, I engaged in a serious conversation with Andrew.

"I saw how you were dancing in the club with George, and I noticed the way you looked at each other. You were like two magnets," Andrew told me.

"That's not true!" I replied, at a loss for words.

"Every time you two meet, something has to happen. I'm tired of all the coincidences between you two. Why don't you talk to him? Maybe you'd be better off together!" added Andrew.

"Do you hear yourself? Please don't think like that! I love you, and I want to be with you. You're my family. You and Emma are everything to me!"

"And George is your family. He's your brother-in-law. Maybe you stay with me because you want to be near him," Andrew said.

"Stop! Enough! Refrain from uttering another word. After all these years spent together, can you truly grasp the weight of your words? I implore you to think twice before making such statements," I told him.

I was deeply upset, overwhelmed with guilt and disappointment in myself. The weight of my mistake pressed heavily on my chest, making it hard to breathe. Andrew was confused, too, his eyes searching mine for answers. I had made a mistake, but I needed to show Andrew that he was the only one I loved. Yes, it was a huge mistake, but everyone makes mistakes. No one's perfect; I'm only human. When it comes to my family, I am capable of anything, and I want to ensure that Andrew and Emma are happy. If they're happy, so am I. As the song goes from 'Just Give Me a Reason' by Pink - *"Just a second, we're not broken, just bent."*

When you truly love someone, you can't cheat or betray them. What was happening with me and my feelings? I felt guilty every time I looked at Andrew. His familiar scent, the warmth of his embrace, and the sound of his voice all reminded me of my betrayal. I kept repeating in my mind how guilty I was, and I swore to myself that I would never make that mistake again. I just wanted to be happy with Andrew and overcome any situation. The taste of regret lingered on my lips, and the memory of George's touch haunted me, but I was determined to move forward and rebuild the trust I had shattered.

Just when I thought I'd put my mind and heart in order, George called me.

"What are you doing? Are you okay?" he asked.

"Yes, I'm fine," I replied.

"I didn't forget what happened that night. I remember every beat of your heart. I tried to forget, but I can't," he added.

"Try harder and forget everything! Is that why you called me?" I asked him.

"No! Yes! No! Hmm... I'm calling to ask you something. You have to help me! Please come with me to view a shop for rent. I want to move my store to your area because I'll have more customers there. If you come with me, I'll appear more serious. If I go alone, they'll think I'm not serious and that I won't pay the rent on time or something like that."

"I can't go with you! Andrew won't agree! I will talk to him. If he allows me to go, I'll go," I told him.

"He won't let you come with me. Come without him knowing. Please! I'll come tomorrow, pick you up from home, and after half an hour, I'll take you back home."

"I'll think about it, and I will text you later. Everything you say seems suspicious. If you're alone, can't you rent the shop? Who knows what you're up to!"

"Please trust me!" George pleaded.

I was torn, unsure whether to go with him or not. I didn't want to do anything that could upset Andrew again. I was tired of feeling guilty about all the poor decisions I had made. I didn't want to regret my choices later. But in the evening, George texted, "What's up?" He continued, "I'll come tomorrow and pick you up. We'll go together to view that shop, and then we need to talk! Please listen carefully to the song I'm sending you now. You have my heart; I want it back."

After reading the message, I felt a surge of determination. We needed to talk seriously and put an end to this dangerous game. I blamed him, but deep down, I knew I had accepted his game. We had to acknowledge that we were no longer children; we were adults with responsibilities. Later, I played the song he sent me: *"We belong together. Won't you believe in my song?"* - from the song 'Lady' by Kenny Rogers.

While listening to the song, tears welled up in my eyes. I didn't want that to happen. The confusion inside me was overwhelming, and I didn't want him to suffer because of my indecision. I couldn't bear the weight of being everything to him. My heart belonged to Andrew, and he needed to understand that nothing could alter that truth. As the song played once more, his message arrived: "I know what I'm doing is wrong, but I miss you. I yearn to wake up and see you every morning, even though I realize it's impossible. I promise to try and build my own family, but I want you to remember that once, with all my heart, I loved you, and you were meant to be mine." After a few minutes, I replied: "One day, you'll find happiness too."

I drifted off to sleep beside Andrew, my thoughts consumed by George. As I lay there, I rehearsed the words I would say to George—words meant to encourage him to release the grip of the past and seek his own happiness. Simultaneously, I wondered if he, too, struggled to banish thoughts of me. Our minds, it seems, always know what our hearts secretly harbour. Love defies the rational musings of the mind; it resides in the realm of feelings. Caught in this seemingly endless cycle, I clung to hope that a resolution would come soon. My deepest desire was to build a contented and blessed family with Andrew. Three things I vowed never to sacrifice: my family, my heart, and my dignity.

Shadows of the Past

After I calmed down, it felt like a fresh beginning. **The change in mood made the house feel different**—the air seemed lighter, carrying the faint scent of jasmine from the garden. I decided to prepare dinner, **and as I worked,** the rhythmic chopping of vegetables and the sizzle of onions in the pan grounded me. **Meanwhile,** the anticipation of seeing Andrew was almost overwhelming, a warm flutter in my chest.

Everything that had transpired that day made me yearn for Andrew—to hold him close and ensure that everything would be alright from now on. **In that moment,** I believed I had made peace with the past, and a sense of freedom washed over me like a gentle breeze on a hot day. Guilt lingered, **yet at the same time,** I felt unshackled—much like when the police removed handcuffs from my wrists, and in that same moment, they released the handcuffs from my heart.

However, just when I thought everything was perfect and I revelled in my happiness with Andrew and Emma, fate threw another unbelievable coincidence our way—one that shook the very foundation of my marriage. At the intersection of patience and strength, a new challenge emerged, testing the resilience of our bond.

One day, I decided to go shopping alone, leaving Andrew at home with Emma. My goal was to save time and return quickly to prepare something special. I rushed through the supermarket, the fluorescent lights casting a harsh glow on the aisles as I hurriedly filled my cart. The anticipation of surprising Andrew with a special dinner kept me moving swiftly.

However, on my way back home, the bus encountered infernal traffic due to a marathon event. The streets were packed with runners, their determined faces a blur as they passed by. The bus crawled along, and my frustration grew with each passing minute. By the time I finally arrived home, I was half an hour late.

Andrew had called me while I was still at the store, but I didn't hear the phone. When I stepped through the door, I was met with his anger, his eyes blazing.

"Where have you been? Were you with George? Why are you late? Did you meet with him?" Andrew's questions came rapid-fire; his voice edged with suspicion.

"I didn't meet with George! What's wrong with you?" I replied, my own frustration bubbling to the surface.

"I know you met with George. Tell me where you've been! George called me and said he'd be here in ten minutes."

"Believe me, I swear I did not meet with George!" I insisted, my heart pounding.

"Then why is he coming here? Why is he in this area, and why did you return so late from shopping? Wasn't one hour enough for you two?" Andrew's voice was accusatory, each word a dagger.

"Ask him when he arrives—why is he coming here?" I said, my voice trembling with a mix of anger and desperation.

I didn't know what was going on, but Andrew was visibly angry. When George arrived, Andrew tried to stay calm and went straight into the garden to smoke a cigarette. George had come to our area to view another shop available for rent, and then he came over to see us. Andrew sensed that something wasn't right between me and George, but he remained composed and waited for George to leave so we could continue our discussion.

"I'm sure that you met with George. This isn't just a coincidence. You came back late from shopping because you met him," Andrew said, his voice tight with suspicion.

"It's just a coincidence!" I replied, trying to keep my voice steady.

"I've seen the way you look at each other. I'm not stupid! Every time he's around you, you're someone else. You guys have a big secret. Sooner or later, I'll find out everything," Andrew added, his eyes narrowing.

"I have nothing to hide!" I replied calmly, though my heart was racing.

"I don't even know for sure if Emma's my daughter," Andrew said, his voice trembling with emotion.

"Let's do a DNA test! After all these years together, how can you have doubts about our daughter?" I replied, my voice breaking.

"You don't love me! You love George! Why did you always love him? Why didn't you choose him? You both act like two stupid kids when you're together. Do you think I haven't seen it?" Andrew's voice was filled with hurt and anger.

"I chose you because I love you, but it seems you're not happy anymore. You don't believe a word I say," I said, desperate to make him understand.

"Because you don't know what you want to achieve in your life. You are very confused. You're not happy," he added, his voice softening slightly.

"I do know, but right now, all I want is for Emma to be happy because I can't be anymore!" I replied, tears welling up in my eyes.

Not long ago, George asked me why I chose Andrew, and now Andrew is asking me why I didn't choose George. Fate and destiny have played cruel tricks on me. In those moments, I wondered if it might be better to go far away with Emma and grant Andrew his freedom. Guilt consumed me—I believed I had disrupted his life, and I even considered that he might be happier without me.

Everything I had done for our family seemed insignificant. All my gestures of tenderness and affection toward Andrew felt like mere illusions. If he even doubted that he might not be Emma's father, it was already too much. All these years together with Andrew felt wasted. Nothing was true; none of the goodness I tried to bring forth was visible.

I was at rock bottom, profoundly saddened by the realization that my relationship with Andrew would become increasingly impossible, colder with each passing day. Eventually, after the words spoken earlier or later, we would part ways. I will never forget what he said, and he won't forget the coincidences that unfolded between me and George.

The weight of these thoughts pressed down on me, making it hard to breathe. I could feel the cold tiles beneath my feet, grounding me in the harsh reality of my situation. The house, once filled with warmth and laughter, now felt like a prison of my own making. The scent of dinner still lingered in the air, a cruel reminder of the life I was desperately trying to hold together.

As I looked at Emma playing innocently with her toys, my heart ached. I wanted to protect her from the storm brewing between her parents. The thought of leaving Andrew, of tearing our family apart, was unbearable. Yet, the guilt and doubt gnawed at me, whispering that perhaps this was the only way to find peace.

I contemplated quitting, but I noticed who was watching. I couldn't give up. I had to fight to fix everything for Emma. If my path demands that I walk through hell, I will stride as if I own the place. What doesn't kill me makes me stronger. Every flower grows through dirt, yet I am no longer as fragile as a flower. I'm fragile like a bomb. From now on, if someone causes me to stumble, I'll make it appear as though I'm dancing. *"This world can hurt you; it cuts you deep and leaves a scar. Things fall apart, but nothing breaks quite like a heart"* - from "Nothing Breaks Like a Heart" by Miley Cyrus.

For nearly a week, Andrew didn't speak to me. The silence between us was heavy, filled with unspoken accusations and lingering doubts. He no longer trusted me, and no matter how hard I tried to explain, he remained sceptical. I allowed time to work its magic, unsure of what to say or do. Amidst countless compliments, promises, and vows I've encountered in life, the most profound truth emerged from silence itself. There are no falsehoods in silence; it reveals what words cannot.

Each day, I went through the motions, the weight of Andrew's distrust pressing down on me. The house felt colder, and the once warm and inviting spaces now seemed distant and unwelcoming. I focused on Emma, her innocent laughter and bright eyes a beacon of hope in the midst of my turmoil. I cooked her favourite meals, read her bedtime stories, and held her close, drawing strength from her presence.

At night, when the house was quiet and the world outside was still, I would lie awake, staring at the ceiling. The darkness seemed to amplify my thoughts, each one a sharp reminder of the precarious state of my marriage. I replayed conversations in my mind, searching for the moment when everything had started to unravel.

Despite the pain and uncertainty, I resolved to keep fighting. I would not let this break me. I would find a way to rebuild the trust that had been shattered, to mend the fractures in our relationship. For Emma, for Andrew, and for myself, I would keep moving forward, one step at a time.

Perhaps time alone doesn't always heal wounds. Maybe, in the end, it's the quiet moments and love that hold the power to mend. The soft glow of the evening sun filtered through the curtains, casting a warm, golden hue across the room. I sat in the quiet, the only sound the gentle ticking of the clock on the wall.

Lara Fabian's poignant lyrics *from "Je t'aime"* echoed in my mind: *"Je t'ai volé ce sang qu'on n'aurait pas dû partager."* These words resonated deeply, stirring emotions I had tried to bury. The melody wrapped around me like a comforting embrace; each notes a reminder of the love and pain intertwined in my heart.

In those moments of solitude, I realized that healing comes not just from the passage of time but from the tender moments of connection and understanding. The quiet evenings spent in reflection, the gentle touch of a loved one's hand, the unspoken words that convey more than any conversation ever could.

As I sat there, bathed in the soft light, I felt a sense of peace wash over me. The wounds were still there, but they seemed less raw, less overwhelming. I knew that the journey to healing was far from over, but in that moment, I felt a glimmer of hope. Love, in its quiet and persistent way, had the power to mend what time alone could not.

Andrew chose to believe that the episode with George was merely a cosmic coincidence, and together, we navigated our way back to happiness. When we were upset, I yearned for his kiss, missed the warmth of his touch, and longed for an embrace. His reassuring smile was a beacon of comfort. Even though Andrew wasn't the most romantic or affectionate, even though he didn't shower me with compliments, I couldn't bear to be estranged, upset, and silent. With each passing second of silence, my heart withered a little.

One evening, as we sat in the living room, the soft glow of the fireplace casting flickering shadows on the walls, I turned to him. "Andrew, I miss you," I said, my voice barely above a whisper.

He looked at me, his eyes softening. "I miss you too," he replied, reaching out to take my hand. "I hate it when we're like this."

"I know," I said, squeezing his hand. "I need you to know that you're my everything. I can't stand the thought of us being apart."

He sighed, pulling me into his arms. "I believe you. It's just… sometimes, it's hard to forget."

"I understand," I murmured against his chest, feeling the steady rhythm of his heartbeat. "But we have to try. We have to move forward."

They say that people meant for each other will always find their way back. Sometimes, two souls must break apart to recognize their irrevocable need for one another. Andrew occupies a space in my heart like no other; to me, he was my universe. As Jennifer Rush aptly sang, *"Cause I am your lady, and you are my man."*

Wagered Hearts

A few weeks later, George entered a new relationship, but it proved short-lived. Coincidentally or not, his girlfriend happened to be a childhood friend of mine who had harboured feelings for Raul. George discovered her talking on the phone with another man, leading to their breakup. A few months later, he embarked on a fresh romance and swiftly married his new partner—just two months into their relationship. Unbeknownst to us, he tied the knot without sending a wedding invitation. It was only a week after their wedding that Andrew's mother informed us of George's marital status.

Initially, I believed George had finally found happiness, but after a mere three weeks of marriage, he faced divorce. Single once more, he reached out to me after some time.

"You gave me back my heart, but I don't know how to take care of it. Because of you, I got married, and because I didn't marry for love, I ended up divorced. At least I tried. No one truly loves me, and I no longer trust any woman. I'll never get married again!" he said, his voice filled with bitterness.

"Don't blame me! It's not my fault that you're fleeing from love as if it were a marathon. For a while now, you've only believed in abandonment. You've wagered your heart like a token, and yet you wonder why you keep losing," I replied, trying to keep my voice steady.

"I've bet my heart, and I've lost it. I no longer possess a heart. Love is beyond my reach. I harbour hatred for everyone, even you!" he said, his eyes dark with anger.

"Hate may have its logic, but love defies reason. Hate weighs heavily; perhaps it's time to release it," I suggested gently.

"Anyway, you don't care how I feel," he said, his voice dropping to a whisper.

"I do care, but my hands are tied. I am holding Andrew's hand," I replied, feeling the weight of my words.

I recall my grandmother's words: "Hate has logic, but love doesn't." When I first laid eyes on Andrew and fell deeply in love, those words echoed within me. The memory of our first meeting is still vivid—the way his eyes lit up when he smiled, the warmth of his hand when he first held mine. Similarly, when George left, the ache was familiar. I had lost my heart, convinced I'd never love again. The nights were long and filled with tears, the days a blur of going through the motions. Yet, somehow, Andrew's presence stitched the broken pieces back together. His patience, his unwavering support, and the way he made me laugh when I thought I'd forgotten how.

Coincidence or not, George experienced what I had long ago—wagering his heart and losing it. The difference? I wasn't the one who hurt him. When he wounded me, I had no confidence in my pain; I was alone. The loneliness was suffocating, a constant reminder of my vulnerability. Perhaps, someday, he'll find love again. I hope he does because everyone deserves a second chance at happiness.

Journey of Contrasts

After a string of girlfriends, George crossed paths with Alice. This time, he seemed genuinely content, and he proudly introduced her to our circle. Alice possessed an alluring beauty, yet her demeanour stood in stark contrast to his. While he blazed like fire, she flowed like water—discreet, peaceful, and calm. She was the light to his darkness. Watching them together, I felt a pang of envy mixed with relief. Envy for the ease with which they seemed to fit together and relief that perhaps George had finally found someone who could balance his intensity.

As I observed them, I couldn't help but reflect on my own journey. The ups and downs, the moments of doubt and the reaffirmations of love. Andrew occupies a space in my heart like no other; to me, he was my universe. Despite the challenges, despite the moments of uncertainty, our love had endured. And for that, I was profoundly grateful.

Their personalities clashed. George's enigmatic temperament often left us puzzled, while Alice's quiet strength radiated serenity. He craved attention, always seeking the spotlight, while she preferred the shadows. Their union was an intriguing paradox—a dance between fire and water, darkness and light.

I befriended Alice, and our visits grew more frequent. One day, as they came over to our home, George pulled me aside. I stood in the garden, the scent of blooming roses mingling with the fresh-cut grass next to Andrew, while Alice chatted and played with Emma.

"Talk to her, teach her to be like you!" George asked me, his voice tinged with desperation.

"No! She can't do that. It's not a good idea, and Alice will be upset," Andrew interjected, his tone firm.

"But how am I?" I asked George, genuinely curious.

"I don't know; don't get me wrong. You're always cheerful and happy, and you know how to keep a good mood around you. Alice is too quiet and calm," George explained, his eyes pleading.

I took a deep breath, feeling the weight of his request. "If you love her now, don't just love her petals. Love her spines, too. She's the one who loves the parts of you that no one else knew how to."

George looked at me, a mixture of frustration and understanding in his eyes. "I just want her to be happy," he said softly.

"She is happy, George. She just shows it differently," I replied, hoping he would understand.

As we stood there, the evening sun casting long shadows across the garden, I realized that love, in all its forms, requires acceptance. George and Alice were a testament to that—a union of opposites, each bringing out the best in the other.

I found myself at a loss for words. Alice possessed a unique charm, and her love for George was evident. They made a beautiful couple. Andrew seemed mildly surprised when George requested that I talk to Alice and guide her to be more like me, yet he remained silent. Perhaps Andrew sensed that George sought someone who mirrored my behaviour and appearance.

A few minutes later, as I prepared a meal, the aroma of garlic and herbs filling the kitchen, George entered and asked for an empty glass. The clinking of dishes and the hum of the stove created a comforting backdrop to our conversation.

"Do you recall what I promised you long ago?" I inquired, turning to face him. "You'll search for me in another person, but you'll never find me."

George's eyes narrowed, a flicker of frustration crossing his face. "You're a witch," he retorted, his tone accusing.

I shook my head, a small smile playing on my lips. "No, it's merely a coincidence," I countered, my voice calm and steady.

He sighed, running a hand through his hair. "It's just... I want what we had. I want that connection."

"You can't recreate the past, George. You have to find your own path with Alice," I said gently, handing him the glass.

As he left the kitchen, I returned to my cooking, the conversation lingering in my mind. Love, I realized, is not about finding someone who mirrors you but about embracing the differences and growing together. George and Alice had their own unique journey, and I hoped he would come to see the beauty in that.

Wheels of Freedom

After a while, I managed to buy my first car. It was a Volkswagen Passat. I was overjoyed, my heart racing with excitement as I held the keys in my hand for the first time. It was a small and affordable car, but to me, it felt like a ticket to freedom and new adventures. I was eager to learn how to drive. Even though I had a driving license, I hadn't had the chance to drive much beyond my lessons with the instructor.

The car was a huge help, especially when I needed to do the shopping—I no longer had to carry heavy bags, struggling with each step. Instead, I could load everything into the trunk and drive home with ease. On weekends, taking Emma out for a walk was no longer a struggle with the bus. We could just hop in the car and go wherever we wanted, the wind in our hair and a sense of boundless possibilities ahead of us. The simple act of driving brought so much joy and convenience into my life, making everyday tasks feel like small adventures.

Our first road trip was unforgettable. We decided to drive to the countryside, a place we had always wanted to explore. The journey was filled with laughter, music, and the thrill of the open road. The scenic views of rolling hills and quaint villages were breathtaking. We stopped at a charming little café for lunch, savouring the moment and the freedom that the car had brought into our lives. That trip marked the beginning of many more adventures, each one adding to the tapestry of memories we were creating together.

One of the most heartwarming moments during our small road trips happened when we found a quiet, secluded spot by a lake. We decided to take a break and enjoy the serene surroundings. As we sat by the water, Emma curled up next to me, resting her head on my lap. The gentle sound of the water, the rustling leaves, and the warmth of the sun created a perfect moment of peace and contentment. Emma looked up at me with her big, trusting eyes, and I felt an overwhelming sense of gratitude for having her by my side. It was at that moment that I realized how much joy and companionship she brought into my life. The bond we shared felt stronger than ever, and I knew that that trip was just the beginning of many more beautiful memories to come.

Festive Fragility

After some time, we embarked on a holiday together, spending more time with Andrew side by side. The tension that once hung between us dissipated, leaving everything in a state of calm. Andrew and I, together—nothing felt righter, even if there was something missing. We clung to our dreams, refusing to surrender. In my mind, our world was encased in a crystal ball, and we vowed not to let anyone shatter it.

Yet, my heart whispered secrets. It reminded me that a missing piece still eluded my puzzle. I couldn't shake the feeling that something was missing. It was like a faint whisper in the back of my mind, a reminder that our perfect picture had an invisible crack. Still, I held onto hope, believing that with time, we would find the missing piece. Andrew and I were like a beautifully plated dish but without the essential seasoning. Everything looked perfect, but the taste was incomplete. Despite this, whenever I stood next to Andrew, I repeated my silent mantra: "Andrew is mine, now and forever." Our beautiful family was a testament to that devotion. Each day, I reminded myself of our love, of the family we had built together. And though the whispers of doubt lingered, I chose to focus on the present, on the joy of being with Andrew and Emma.

Our decision to spend the holiday together involved an ensemble: me, Andrew, Emma, George, and Alice. We journeyed to the village where I had grown up. Andrew's mother had recently acquired a new house there, and our plan was to celebrate Christmas as a united family. The situation felt both amusing and slightly awkward. I hoped my mother-in-law wouldn't make any uncomfortable remarks. Andrew's mother, usually brimming with cheer and boundless energy, never hesitated to speak her mind directly.

It was inevitable that my mother-in-law would notice that something wasn't quite right between George and me. When we arrived, George and I were bickering like two children. For instance, during the room selection process, we both insisted on the same bedroom, and neither of us wanted to back down.

"I chose this room because it's painted in pink. I plan to unpack my luggage here," I said firmly, standing my ground.

"Every time I visit my mother, I sleep in this room," George retorted, his voice rising.

"However, since you've never been here when I was, you'll have to give up your claim. As far as I know, the green-painted room is yours. Your mother mentioned that you have clothes in the wardrobe and many belongings stored there," I countered, trying to keep my tone calm.

"I've changed my mind, and from now on, this will be my room," George declared, crossing his arms defiantly.

As Andrew and his mother observed us, Andrew grew visibly angry. I decided to stop fighting with George, but our argument left its mark. However, my mother-in-law didn't say anything. Andrew eventually got used to the coincidences between George and me, and his anger subsided.

The next day, my mother-in-law, Alice, and I were preparing the shopping list and contemplating what to cook for Christmas. The kitchen was filled with the aroma of freshly brewed coffee and the soft hum of holiday music playing in the background. Alice, always calm and quiet, sat at the table, her hands folded neatly in her lap.

My mother-in-law directed more questions toward me regarding our shopping and menu choices, her voice lively and animated.

At that moment, George noticed and seemed a bit jealous. I was the one deciding the menu, and Alice readily agreed to everything without complaint.

"Why are you only talking to her? Why don't you ask Alice for her opinion? Maybe she doesn't like everything you plan to cook," George interjected, his tone sharp.

"I've already asked her. She agrees with everything. It's not just us who decide," His mother replied, trying to keep the peace.

"It means you can't see or hear well. What's wrong with you?" George snapped, his frustration evident.

They were on the verge of an argument, but my mother-in-law wisely decided to end the conversation. "Let's not argue about this. We're here to enjoy the holidays together," she said, her voice soothing.

I couldn't fathom why George reacted that way. Perhaps he was jealous that my mother-in-law might favour me, even though she had known me for a long time. Later, when I stepped outside for a cigarette, the crisp winter air biting at my skin, George followed and decided to tease me.

"Remember the time you came over to my house to write the shopping list for my birthday party?" he began, a mischievous glint in his eye. "Instead of focusing on the list, we got completely sidetracked."

The memory brings a smile to my face. "Yes, I remember. We ended up talking about everything except the shopping list."

George chuckled, the tension between us easing. "Those were simpler times."

"Indeed," I agreed, taking a drag from my cigarette. "But we're here now, and we have to make the best of it."

George laughed, shaking his head. "It's enough if you'll be there," he said, his tone softening. "And it's nice to know that you were there." He started singing the song "It's nice to know that you were there" from "Boracay" by Adrian Sina and Sandra N.

After finalizing the shopping list and setting up our cooking plans, my mother-in-law suggested we go shopping together. Since Alice wasn't driving, she asked me to accompany her as the designated driver. Our destination was the nearest town with a supermarket. Meanwhile, Andrew and George had their own tasks, and Alice stayed with Emma. As we drove, my mother-in-law started a conversation, her voice tinged with a mix of curiosity and concern.

"George is quite perplexing. I struggle to understand him," she began, her eyes reflecting a deep-seated confusion. "While I appreciate Alice's reserved nature, it's easier for me to talk to you. We've known each other for a long time, and our rapport is like that of friends. It's interesting—you changed your lover but not your mother-in-law," she said with a wry smile.

"Life is full of coincidences," I replied, trying to keep my tone light, though I felt a knot forming in my stomach.

"Whether by chance or design, there's a connection between you and George," she continued, her voice growing more serious. "Having lived a full life, I've developed an intuition for detecting hidden truths. You and George started something long ago, yet it remains unfinished," she added, her gaze piercing as if trying to read my thoughts.

"It's all water under the bridge now," I said, attempting to dismiss the topic, though my heart raced.

"I'm attuned to my children's emotions, and I notice the way George looks at you. Even when he tries to ignore you, his eyes tell a different story," she observed, her tone softening with a hint of sadness.

"I hadn't noticed; it didn't concern me," I said, though I could feel my cheeks flush.

"Regardless of your feelings, tread carefully. Andrew and George are capable of anything. I don't want my children to become enemies," she warned, her voice filled with maternal protectiveness.

"My sole concern is Andrew and Emma," I said firmly, though doubt lingered in my mind.

"Love can be hauntingly powerful. When the devil falls in love, they'll descend to the depths of hell for their beloved," she said, her words echoing with a haunting truth.

"Whom are you referring to?" I asked, my curiosity piqued.

"Both Andrew and George. Love transforms them into similar beings," she replied, her eyes reflecting a deep understanding.

"In this case, I am the devil! If necessary, I'll journey to hell for Andrew," I declared, my voice filled with determination.

"Beware of playing with fire; you might get burned! Your eyes betray feelings for George—you're not adept at deception," she cautioned, her voice a mix of concern and resignation.

"I'm fully aware of the situation. I recognize the boundaries and obstacles," I said, though my heart ached with the complexity of it all.

"True, but the heart operates independently," she concluded, her words hanging in the air like an unspoken truth.

In that moment, as the conversation hung in the air like a delicate thread, I made my choice. I allowed her to have the last word, knowing that silence could be more powerful than any retort. The truth weighed heavily on my tongue—I couldn't deny it, nor could I confess. Instead, I smiled, a mask of calm resolve.

"How can I get burned when I am the flame?" I mused silently. The words echoed in my mind, a defiant mantra. I had faced infernos before, emerged unscathed, and returned with newfound strength. Hellfire was no match for my determination.

Andrew and Emma—the pillars of my existence—were my compass. Their well-being fuelled my purpose. I would traverse any abyss, confront any adversary, to shield them. Family wasn't just blood; it was an unbreakable bond, fierce and primal. So, like a lioness defending her cubs, I stood ready. The flames licked at my heels, but I remained unyielding. For Andrew, for Emma, I would defy even the infernal depths.

During the discussion, my rudimentary driving skills were put to the test. My attention was divided between manoeuvring the vehicle to avoid any accidents and processing every word she uttered, which seemed to pierce through me like arrows. My palms were damp on the steering wheel as I struggled to maintain composure and silence. Despite her laughter, she seized the opportunity to express her every thought. I remained resolute, aiming to appear as credible as possible and successfully pass her test.

"Long ago, during your initial visit with George, he confided that you were his best friend. Sceptical, I dismissed his claim. However, when I later spoke to him, he candidly revealed his deep affection for you. Now, as his sister-in-law, I observe that his regard for you remains unchanged from the past. It finally makes sense to me why George was absent from your wedding ceremony and why he didn't extend an invitation to his own wedding," she said, her voice tinged with a mix of curiosity and accusation.

"We, unfortunately, couldn't attend his wedding due to various reasons: Andrew's work commitments, Emma's lack of school holidays, and my university exams. Our busy schedules prevented us from taking a holiday, which is why George likely omitted our invitation, knowing we couldn't participate. The situation unfolded spontaneously, and George's wedding was unplanned," I explained, trying to keep my voice steady despite the rising tension.

"You insist on and maintain these excuses, but I am certain it is not merely a simple coincidence. Furthermore, despite your meticulously planned wedding ceremony and the invitation sent to him a month in advance, George declined to participate," she added, her eyes narrowing as she scrutinized my reaction.

While we were shopping together, our conversation continued. She was acutely aware that George's feelings for me extended beyond mere friendship or sister-in-law status. Her concern was that our relationship might inadvertently hurt Andrew, and she emphasized the importance of my commitment to family. Although I may have passed her scrutiny, George's subtle gestures conveyed a different message. Our conversation motivated me to maintain distance from George, but it seemed inevitable.

Upon returning home from our shopping excursion, we dove into a joyful, shared cooking adventure. The kitchen was alive with warmth, laughter, and the comforting aroma of fresh ingredients. Our mission: to prepare a feast of traditional dishes for our Christmas dinner. Andrew worked diligently, chopping vegetables with precise, rhythmic movements for the soup and carefully preparing the cabbage rolls (sarmale). His focus was steady, yet there was a quiet charm in the way he moved, a subtle intimacy that made my heart flutter.

I, in turn, devoted myself to crafting a classic lemon layer cake, affectionately known as 'Snow White,' letting the zest of citrus perfume the air. Emma, our little princess, played nearby with the dough, giggling as flour dusted her cheeks and tiny hands left sweet fingerprints on every surface. Her laughter rang through the room, a delicate melody that made the kitchen feel like the heart of our home.

Meanwhile, my mother-in-law and Alice worked side by side on the cozonac, the traditional sweet bread, their hands moving in perfect harmony as they kneaded and braided, exchanging smiles and quiet conversation. The room was a tapestry of sights, scents, and sounds—a symphony of domestic bliss.

George, meanwhile, busied himself with seasoning the turkey for the oven. As he sprinkled aromatic spices over the bird, he glanced at me, eyes quietly seeking guidance on flavour combinations and measurements. There was an unspoken weight in his gaze, a silent plea that made it impossible to maintain distance or avoid engagement. Each brief exchange felt like a subtle test of my composure, a reminder of the delicate balance I had to uphold amid the warmth, festivity, and undercurrent of unspoken tension.

Despite the festive atmosphere, an undercurrent of tension lingered. I could feel George's gaze on me, a mix of longing and unspoken words. My mother-in-law's earlier warnings echoed in my mind, urging me to tread carefully. Yet, in the warmth of the kitchen, surrounded by family, it was hard to keep my guard up.

As the aroma of our cooking filled the house, I found solace in the familiar tasks. The rhythmic motions of baking and cooking provided a temporary escape from the complexities of my emotions. For Andrew and Emma, I would navigate this intricate web of relationships, ensuring that our family remained intact.

At one point, Andrew came over to me, took me in his arms, and kissed me while George moved closer to Alice. My mother-in-law wasn't paying attention when Andrew approached. Seeing George seasoning the turkey next to me, she thought for a moment that George was kissing me. Her eyes widened in shock, and she started shouting, "What are you doing there?"

The room fell silent, everyone frozen in place. My heart pounded as I turned to see her face, a mix of confusion and anger. Just as quickly, her expression shifted when she realized it was Andrew. She began to laugh, though it was tinged with embarrassment. "I didn't see Andrew come over to you," she stammered, trying to explain her outburst.

We all looked at her in astonishment, the tension in the room palpable. Trying to stifle our laughter, we exchanged glances, each of us wondering how she could have thought that George was kissing me. The moment hung in the air, a strange mix of relief and lingering unease.

During a brief break, I stepped outside for a cigarette. George followed, and in those fleeting moments, we exchanged words.

"You must keep your distance from me," I said abruptly. "Your mother noticed something amiss between us, and she told me about her thoughts during our shopping today."

"She was probably just curious about your opinion. After all, I haven't done anything wrong. Am I not allowed to speak with you? Let her believe what she wants," he replied, a hint of defiance in his voice.

"This isn't right. Don't look at me, and don't bother asking questions. From now on, if you need answers, consult your mother or Alice," I insisted, trying to maintain a firm tone.

"Fine! I'll never speak to you again! Go away! Leave me alone! I have no desire to see you anymore. You're ugly and unkind. I'll even tell Santa not to visit you," he retorted, clearly amused by the situation.

"Well, Santa visits me because I've been a good girl. As for you, perhaps he'll skip you this year due to your naughtiness," I shot back, trying to keep the mood light despite the tension.

George thought I was joking. His laughter echoed in the cold winter air as he playfully urged me to leave. The snowball he held in his hand was a mischievous weapon, and he tossed it at me with a smile. Then, without hesitation, he retreated into the warmth of the house. However, after our conversation, George maintained a cautious distance, but his gaze betrayed a spark of interest.

Once I finished preparing the cake, its enticing aroma filled the kitchen, drawing George in like a moth to a flame. He took a slow, deliberate bite, and his expression transformed. His eyes widened, savouring the flavours dancing on his tongue. "This," he declared, "is the best lemon cake I've ever eaten."

At that moment, his vigilant mother raised an eyebrow, her gaze shifting between George and the cake. She studied him, assessing his sincerity. But George wasn't joking; he was lost in the delight of my creation, his thoughts spilling out unfiltered.

"You must make this cake again for New Year's Eve," he insisted, his voice a mix of admiration and urgency. His request was both a heartfelt compliment and a plea, a testament to the impact of my baking.

Snowbound Secrets

On Christmas Eve, our home was adorned with twinkling lights, and the scent of pine needles hung in the air. Children gathered at our doorstep, their voices rising in harmonious carols. And then, as if summoned by the magic of the season, Santa Claus himself appeared.

Emma, wide-eyed and filled with wonder, knew deep down that this wasn't the real Santa Claus. But oh, how her heart danced when she saw him! Santa bestowed upon her a trove of gifts, and each of us discovered a carefully wrapped surprise beneath the tree. As Brenda Lee's lyrics echoed through the room—"You will get a sentimental feeling when you hear voices singing"—we revelled in the joy of the moment.

Yet beyond the tinsel and laughter, my thoughts wandered to Andrew. Six years together, countless serendipitous encounters, and still I wondered: Does he still love me? I studied Andrew, searching for answers in the lines etched on his face. Is he happy? The question echoed relentlessly within me: "Is Andrew happy with me?"

Threads of time wove around us, altering our paths, yet the heart remained resolute. I vividly recalled the day I first glimpsed Andrew, just two days before Christmas. There he stood with Evelin, and I couldn't help but wonder: Would he be happier if he had stayed with her? Or perhaps happiness lay in the arms of another. Maybe, just maybe, he would have been happier never crossing my path at all. The haunting refrain of "Fairytale of New York" played in my mind: *"I could have been someone. Well, so could anyone. You took my dreams from me when I first found you."*

After the flurry of unwrapping gifts, I sought solace in the garden's cool night air. A cigarette between my fingers, I grappled with a million thoughts. In the war of my mind, silence waged its own battle—an enemy that gnawed at my peace.

And then Andrew joined me outside. His arms enveloped me, lips brushing against mine. For a fleeting moment, I banished the doubts, but my heart whispered otherwise. Something was amiss—I sensed it, even if I didn't fully acknowledge it.

Life had taught me a lesson etched in permanence: When everyone else departs, family remains. In my musings, I trusted myself, yet reality left me adrift. The smile I wore felt borrowed, and true joy had become a distant memory. An emptiness nestled in my chest, and I grappled with loneliness—the kind that defied understanding, even from my own self.

Guilt clung to me like a shadow, a persistent companion. I replayed the refrain in my mind: I must find a way. Those dark days had swallowed me whole, leaving behind fragments of the person I once was. This new version of myself—hollow-eyed and disenchanted—felt like a betrayal. Despite having everything, an elusive void gnawed at my soul. My life had veered off course, diverging from the dreams I once had. Dissatisfaction simmered within, urging me to transform. Consciously, I vowed to seek the missing piece of the puzzle, to mend what had fractured.

George's interference had worn thin, like a frayed thread threatening to unravel my path. I aimed for indifference toward his gestures, determined to shield my heart. My desire? To find happiness alongside Andrew, to feel genuinely loved. That peculiar feeling—the doubt that Andrew was only with me because of Emma—no longer held sway. Instead, it felt as though Andrew was bound by circumstance to remain by my side. A thousand unanswered questions swirled within me, yet one truth remained: I had to keep striving for improvement. The entire path need not reveal itself; taking those first steps mattered. Right now, my hopes stretched wide, and it all began with me.

On Christmas Day, we embarked on a visit to my grandmother's and my mother's homes. George expressed a desire to see my grandmother as well, and he decided to accompany us. Years ago, George and my grandmother shared a warm rapport; she affectionately referred to him as "Charlie's brother." You see, my brother Charlie and George had been inseparable friends. My grandmother was well aware of the special connection that once existed between George and me, and she genuinely held him in high regard. Whenever they conversed, she offered him sage advice and reminded him to look after me.

As we arrived at my grandmother's house, her joy at seeing us was palpable. Her hearing wasn't as sharp as it used to be, and George addressed her loudly:

"Grandma, do you recognize me?" asked George.

"Of course, I recognize you! You're Charlie's 'brother.' You two were such good friends. It's been far too long since I last saw you. Where have you been all these years?"

"I've wandered to distant realms."

"It warms my heart that you haven't forgotten your roots. Are you well? Happy? And is this lovely lady your wife?"

"She's my future wife!" George replied, somewhat unsure.

"Well… I wish you both happiness and healthy children! May you have all the best in life. May your days be filled with joy."

The way my grandmother regarded Alice spoke volumes. There was no warmth in her gaze, yet she maintained a stoic silence. And then it struck me: my grandmother favoured George over Andrew. Her interactions with Andrew were frosty, and she feigned deafness even when he spoke loudly enough for her to hear.

When I found myself alone with my grandmother, she leaned in, her eyes searching mine. She wanted more details about Alice. I obliged, explaining that Andrew was now my husband and George's marital choices were of little consequence to me as long as he found happiness.

"Grandma," I began, "life continues its course. We've both built our families—I have a daughter now. The past no longer holds sway. I'm content, and I believe George is too."

"If it were as simple as you say," she countered, "he wouldn't have come here. Do you truly think he missed me?" Her gaze pierced through me, demanding honesty.

"He came because memories linger here," I replied, my voice faltering. I grappled with the truth—the tangled threads of love and longing that tied us all together, woven across time and choices.

In the twilight of her eighty-fifth year, my grandmother's mind remained as sharp as the edge of a blade. She had never swallowed a pill, relying instead on soothing herbal teas to ease her ailments. Her legs occasionally protested with a dull ache, but her memory stood unwavering, and her understanding of love remained intact. I found no words to counter her wisdom; instead, I enveloped her in an embrace, silently wishing her health and longevity. Conversations with her felt like a sanctuary, and somehow, she heard even the unspoken whispers of my heart.

My grandmother, the beacon of my life, had weathered storms and hardships. Yet, she clung to hope with a tenacity that defied adversity. She was my unwavering pillar of support, guiding me through the labyrinth of existence. Despite life's challenges, she held onto the belief that things would improve—a testament to her resilience and unwavering spirit.

When she was young, she found herself taken in by a wealthy family, only to become their servant. Her formal education lasted just four years, during which she learned to read and write. But her true education came from the countless books she devoured on her own. School was a luxury she couldn't afford; instead, she toiled on the family farm from an early age.

Marriage brought three children—two daughters and a son—into her life. Unfortunately, her husband's struggle with alcohol left her largely responsible for raising the children. She worked tirelessly on their small farm, managing all the household chores independently.

Over time, she separated from her husband, and as a result, I never had the chance to meet my grandfather. I'd glimpsed him only in a few faded photographs. Her son—the one who tragically took his own life—remained a stranger to me. On his wedding day, just as everyone awaited the groom's arrival, he made that fateful decision. The exact reasons behind it remained a haunting mystery. My grandmother carried this immense pain in her heart. Losing a child is a lifelong trauma for any mother. Yet, despite her heartache, she never gave up. She fought and worked tirelessly on her modest farm throughout her life.

As a child, I cherished those cold winter evenings spent sitting with my grandmother, captivated by her stories. She wove her tales with care, and I listened with wide-eyed eagerness. I can still taste the sweetness she'd share—hidden treats tucked away in the pantry, doled out when I'd ask, "Grandma, do you have something sweet?"

Our bond ran deep throughout my childhood. She wasn't just a storyteller; she was my guide. Her lessons echoed through the years: faith in God, the compass for all possibilities.

Weekdays followed a predictable rhythm. School from 8 a.m. to 2 p.m., Monday to Friday. Saturdays meant a trip to the market, where we stocked up on animal feed for our modest farm. But Sundays held a different purpose—a day devoted to prayer. Mornings found us at the church, and afternoons were for rest or for me to play with other village children.

In the warmth of summer vacations, I made occasional visits to my paternal grandmother. However, her affection for us grandchildren felt diluted. With eleven children of her own and a multitude of grandchildren, she juggled a bustling household during those breaks. Her time was divided among many, leaving little room for individual attention.

In stark contrast, my maternal grandmother had only three grandchildren—my brother, my cousin, and me. Her love was more concentrated, like a sunbeam focused through a magnifying glass. It created a special bond that remains etched in my memories—a tapestry woven with care, warmth, and shared moments.

As we left my grandmother's house, George and Alice made their way to the pub, eager to reconnect with old friends. Meanwhile, Andrew, Emma, and I paid a visit to Andrew's uncle.

Hours later, Andrew's uncle received a call—a distressing one. George had become intoxicated and was embroiled in an argument, dangerously close to a physical altercation. Concerned, we all piled into the car and rushed to the pub to assess the situation. When we arrived, Alice looked terrified, her eyes on the verge of tears. I reassured her that everything would be alright and asked her to stay in the car with Emma while I stepped inside to talk to George.

Inside the dimly lit pub, I found George—a mix of inebriation and shame. His words slurred, and he pleaded, "Please leave! Go home! I don't want you to witness me like this. I'm a drunken fool. Take Alice and go home."

But I stood my ground. "I can't go home without you," I insisted. "You're coming with me now. Please listen and don't upset me."

George's defiance flared. "I'm not going home," he declared. "Andrew and my uncle are here. I want to confront them all—I'll break their legs. Tonight, there'll be a war."

I shook my head. "I don't believe that. We're all going home. The war ends here."

I took his hand, and together, we stepped outside into the cool night air. It was surreal—George actually listening to me. His steps were unsteady, and he clung to my hand to keep from stumbling. As we approached the car, he pleaded with me once more to go home, but before I could respond, he tripped, and I caught him in my arms. Slowly, he hugged me, his touch gentle.

"I'm fine now," he murmured. "Your perfume—it brought me back."

"You're not fine yet," I insisted. "You can barely stand. Tomorrow is when you'll truly be okay. You need to come home and rest."

His eyes held a desperate plea. "If you kiss me now, I'll be perfectly and completely fine."

I sighed. "Try standing on your own without that kiss. Alice is watching! She's in the car with Emma. And Andrew and your uncle will be out of the pub any moment now. Why did you drink so much? What's going on with you? Why the argument with your friend?"

"Please don't judge me," George whispered. "I drank to forget everything. Funny, isn't it? I drank to forget everything about you, yet here you are, holding me."

George remained silent, his gaze intense. After a few minutes, Andrew and his uncle emerged from the pub. George's friend—the one he'd argued with—looked sheepish and apologized to Andrew. It had all been a misunderstanding, and the tension dissipated. We headed back home, the night still echoing with unspoken words and fragile emotions.

As we drove home, I followed behind the wheel of my car while Andrew drove George's vehicle. Our plan was to arrive home simultaneously, but I ended up getting there first. Just as I stepped inside, my phone rang—it was Alice. Her voice trembled with fear as she urgently asked me to return. Leaving Emma with my mother-in-law, I quickly hopped back into the car. When I reached George's car, I parked mine and rushed over to assess the situation.

Alice recounted what had happened: an intoxicated driver had veered into their lane. Andrew had stopped their car, waiting for the reckless driver to pass. Instead, the driver pulled up alongside them, hurling profanities. George stepped out of the car, and tempers flared. Andrew tried to defuse the situation, but the driver shoved George, sending him sprawling into the snow.

By the time I arrived, the drunk driver had fled, and the altercation had subsided. Andrew and his uncle were helping George into the car. Seeing that everything was under control, I felt a wave of relief. Andrew asked me to drive George's car home while he would take ours to drop off his uncle. Alice stayed with Andrew, acting as a lifeline since he'd left his phone at home.

As I drove, George remained silent, and I wondered if he'd dozed off in the back seat, out of sight. When we finally reached our destination, he asked if we were home. As I opened the car door to help him out, he unexpectedly grabbed my hand and pulled me back inside. Suddenly, I found myself on top of him, his grip firm, preventing my escape.

"Let me hold you, even if just for a moment!" he pleaded.

"Stop! Your mother must have heard the car pull up, and she'll be out any second to investigate," I said.

"Mom is busy putting Emma to bed. It's late, and Emma needs her rest," George replied.

"Enough! Let's go inside. You're drunk, and you need to sleep."

I stepped out of the car, and he embraced me. But his unsteady footing caused me to lose balance, and we both tumbled into the snow. As I regained my composure, George rolled over and sat atop me. His gaze held mine, and he playfully scooped up some snow, pressing it against my lips. I blew the snow away, leaving my lips cold and wet.

"Leave me alone. I'm freezing because of you. My lips are like ice," I said.

"Shhh... don't shout. Maybe my mom will hear us. Let me warm your lips!"

His touch ignited a tempest within me—a whirlwind of confusion, desire, and trepidation. The snow cradled us, its icy embrace mirroring the frostiness of my thoughts. His lips, warm against mine, whispered secrets I dared not acknowledge.

"Did you feel something?" he murmured, his breath mingling with mine. "Butterflies in your stomach?"

I scoffed, pushing against his chest. "I felt nothing. Let me go!"

His laughter danced in the frigid air. "That means your lips are still frozen," he teased, pulling me closer.

At that moment, I wanted to unravel—to unravel him, to understand why he stirred emotions I'd buried deep. But reality intervened. I slapped him, the sting echoing through the quiet night. His grin widened, eyes challenging me. Annoyed, I pushed back, sprinting toward the house, my heart pounding.

Yet he caught me effortlessly, lifting me into his arms. Snowflakes clung to my hair, and I struggled, half-panicked. He set me down gently, our breaths visible in the moonlight. We slipped, falling once more, and pain shot through his hand and back. Still, he laughed—a reckless, maddening sound.

"Why?" I gasped, frustration and longing warring within me. "Why all this?"

His gaze held mine, unyielding. "Because life is too short for restraint," he said. "Because sometimes, even chaos feels like freedom."

I couldn't fathom his madness or why I allowed it. Everything unfolded rapidly, leaving me unable to react. Did I like his kiss? Fear overwhelmed any other emotion. Guilt, shame, betrayal—I felt them all, tangled in a chaotic web. But beneath it all, undeniable and terrifying, were the butterflies in my stomach—a silent rebellion against reason.

And so, we remained there, entwined in snow and secrets, two souls teetering on the edge of something neither of us could name.

As we trudged into the house, snow clinging to our clothes, my mother-in-law awaited us. She raised an eyebrow, curious about the situation, but George bypassed her, heading straight to his room and collapsing onto the bed. I attempted to explain, but my phone buzzed—Alice was calling urgently. They were stuck not far from home; their car's wheels had skidded on icy snow, and the back wheel was lodged in a ditch.

Five minutes later, I reached Andrew and Alice. The scene was comical—Andrew couldn't contain his laughter. I hopped into the car while Andrew and Alice pushed. After a few attempts, we freed the wheel from the ditch and made our way back home. That night, we stayed up late, sharing stories—everyone except George.

The next morning, over coffee with Alice and my mother-in-law, Alice displayed a hint of jealousy. Surprised, she commented:

"I'm amazed! He ignored my plea to return home, yet he listened to you and left the pub immediately. Why does he listen to your words and not mine?" Alice said.

"Perhaps he knew Emma was waiting in the car, and he wanted to ensure we were heading home. He needed to be certain," I replied.

"Likely," Alice conceded.

"They've known each other for years. She knows how to persuade him," my mother-in-law chimed in.

The tension in the room was palpable—a delicate balance between truth and deception. My mother-in-law's gaze lingered on me, assessing our explanations. Had she seen through our hastily woven tale? Andrew, too, pressed for answers, his eyes narrowing.

I replayed my conversation with George—the raw vulnerability in his voice as he'd asked me to leave, ashamed of his drunken state. The memory hung heavy, like snow-laden branches threatening to break.

And then George joined us for coffee, his demeanour a mix of contrition and defiance. His eyes, bloodshot from last night's excesses, bore into mine.

"Have you caught a cold?" he asked, concern etching his features. "Is your nose running? Do you need medicine, hot tea, or anything?"

I hesitated, caught off guard. "No, I'm okay. I'm fine!"

George smirked, triumphant. "See? I told you!" His words hung in the air, a fragile bridge spanning the chasm of our shared secrets.

His mother's gaze bore into us—a strange smile playing on her lips. The room felt smaller, suffocating, as if the walls held secrets we dared not utter. When it was just her, George, and me, she broke the silence:

"I know everything. Last night, I saw the two of you playing in the snow... I watched you on the surveillance cameras."

George's response was nonchalant, a smile tugging at his lips. "Yes, I playfully tossed her into the snow, but she was worried about getting cold."

The room seemed to hold its breath. His mother's eyes narrowed. "I think you both should go to church and pray for your sins. You're both guilty in front of God."

George's defiance flared. "Who told you that loving someone is a great sin?" he retorted, then abruptly left, ending the conversation.

I stood there, speechless. Guilt weighed heavily on my chest, an anchor pulling me down. I had no explanation for my actions, no defence against her judgment. And yet, she didn't say anything more—she kept secret everything she had seen and knew.

The snowflakes whispered secrets as they settled on our shoulders, and the world transformed into a hushed wonderland. George's laughter echoed through the crisp air, and I wondered if the snowflakes carried our shared secrets—a clandestine language only we understood.

Andrew, oblivious or perhaps wilfully blind, focused on Emma. His eyes softened when she giggled, and he cradled her tiny hands in his. But when I sought his gaze, it slipped away like snow melting through my fingers. His absence weighed on me—an ache that intensified with each stolen glance exchanged with George.

And George—the enigma wrapped in a snow-kissed scarf. His touch ignited sparks, and I wondered if he, too, felt the fragile thread connecting us. We navigated treacherous paths, both literal and metaphorical, our footsteps leaving imprints in the snow. His lips against mine held promises and peril.

His mother's knowing smile haunted me. Had she glimpsed our stolen moments? Did she see the frost-kissed edges of our hearts? Her words—pray for your sins—echoed in the quiet of my room. But what sins? The stolen kisses? The longing that twisted like ivy around my soul?

As the holiday drew to an end, I clung to those memories—the warmth of George's hand and the taste of snow on his lips. And when we returned to London, I carried the weight of guilt and desire, wondering if love, too, could be both fragile and unyielding—a delicate balance between sin and salvation.

Dreams and Discoveries

Back in London, Andrew began his new job, and Emma and I embarked on our school journey. I secured a part-time job as a waitress in a cosy little café. During the hours when Emma was at school, I spent my time earning a bit of money. The pay wasn't great, but I felt a sense of pride and accomplishment knowing I could contribute financially. Each shift, I found solace in the routine and the brief interactions with customers. It was a small step towards regaining my independence and self-worth, even if just for a few hours each day. Despite the modest earnings, the job gave me a glimmer of hope and a sense of purpose.

Life seemed promising, and we diligently pursued our dreams. Amid our forward-looking efforts, we also revelled in the present. Emma, a pint-sized scientist, perpetually curious, asked "why" and "how" about everything. Her boundless creativity infused our days with purpose. She spun intricate tales of magical creatures, brave heroines, and daring adventures, her mind a treasure trove of fantastical wonders.

Emma's adventures were as diverse as her imagination. She'd explore the hidden corners of our garden, convinced they held secret portals to magical realms. Armed with a makeshift wand (usually a stick), she'd cast spells on imaginary creatures and whisper enchantments to the wind.

One sunny afternoon, she declared herself an intrepid explorer and embarked on a quest to find the legendary "Golden Acorn." Armed with a treasure map drawn on a crumpled piece of paper, she followed clues—like "where the daffodils bloom" and "beneath the old oak"—leading her deeper into the woods. Her determination was unwavering, even when faced with nettles and thorny bushes. Alas, the "Golden Acorn" turned out to be a shiny pebble, but Emma celebrated her discovery, nonetheless.

In winter, she transformed our living room into an Arctic expedition base. Blankets became igloos, and couch cushions served as icebergs. Emma donned her explorer hat (a woolly beanie) and set off on a daring mission to rescue the "Frozen Penguins" (stuffed animals) from the clutches of the "Snow Monster" (our friendly cat named Bubu). Her bravery knew no bounds!

And then there was the time she decided to be a pirate. Armed with a cardboard cutlass and an eyepatch (made from an old sock), she commandeered our sofa, which became her pirate ship—the "S.S. Adventure." She sailed the high seas (living room carpet) in search of buried treasure (chocolate coins). Her crew (stuffed animals) followed her every command. Arrr, matey!

These were just glimpses of Emma's enchanting adventures. Each day brought new quests, new characters, and new wonders. She taught me that magic exists in the ordinary, waiting for curious hearts to discover it.

At just five years old, Emma's intelligence shone brightly. Each school day, she approached with enthusiasm, soaking up knowledge like a sponge. Her popularity was undeniable; friends flocked to her, teachers admired her, and classmates cherished her presence. As her mother, I swelled with pride, thanking the heavens for this precious gift.

A child's giftedness and talent extend beyond mere grades. It's about perceiving the world differently and wholeheartedly embracing their unique ways of learning. Education serves as our passport to the future, and those who prepare today will own tomorrow. Yet, we often worry about a child's future, forgetting that they are someone today. Each child is a miracle, irreplaceable in this world. Instead of pushing our children toward distant goals, we should allow them to thrive where they are.

Taking our children seriously means valuing them for who they are right now. To motivate them, we must consistently express our belief in their abilities, trust their judgment, and assure them of their importance. Listening to their words is equally crucial.

Every child is a universe unto themselves—a constellation of dreams, quirks, and potential. Their giftedness extends far beyond the confines of report cards and standardized tests. It's about seeing the world through their eyes, understanding their idiosyncrasies, and celebrating their individuality.

Imagine a classroom where each child learns differently. Some thrive on visual cues, while others absorb knowledge through hands-on experiences. There are auditory learners who soak up information through conversations and kinaesthetic learners who need movement to grasp concepts. As educators and parents, our role is to recognize these diverse learning styles and tailor our approach. We must provide a rich tapestry of teaching methods, allowing each child to find their unique path to understanding.

Education isn't just about textbooks and syllabi. It's about igniting curiosity, fostering creativity, and nurturing passions. When we encourage children to explore their interests—whether it's painting, coding, or gardening—we open doors to hidden talents. Let's create spaces where a child's love for astronomy is as valued as their proficiency in mathematics. Let's celebrate the budding poet, the young scientist, and the aspiring chef with equal enthusiasm.

Children are natural questioners. Their "whys" and "how's" are the seeds of innovation. Instead of stifling their curiosity, let's water it. Encourage them to ask, explore, and seek answers. When a child wonders why the sky is blue or how plants grow, we should celebrate their inquisitiveness. Who knows? The next groundbreaking scientist or philosopher might be brewing within those innocent queries.

Children speak volumes through their words, expressions, and silences. When they share their dreams, fears, and aspirations, we must listen intently. Sometimes, their whispers reveal hidden talents. Perhaps the quiet girl in the corner has a gift for storytelling waiting to be nurtured. Children speak volumes through their laughter, their tears, and their whispered dreams. Be their confidante. When they share their fears, their hopes, or their latest invention, listen with your heart. Sometimes, their words reveal hidden talents. The boy who stammers might be crafting poetry in his mind. The girl who doodles during math class could be the next Picasso.

Our belief in a child's abilities becomes their inner anthem. When we say, "You can do it," we infuse courage. When we trust their judgment, we empower them. Let's be their cheerleaders, standing on the sidelines as they explore their passions. Whether it's building robots, playing chess, or dancing ballet, our unwavering support matters.

Your belief in your child's abilities is their secret superpower. Whispering encouragement in their ears. Applaud their efforts, whether they win the spelling bee or build a wobbly tower of blocks. Trust their judgment. When they choose a book, a hobby, or a friend, respect their choices. They're learning autonomy—the art of steering their own ship.

Let's celebrate the uniqueness of every child—their quirks, their dreams, and their infinite potential. For within their small hands lies the promise of a brighter tomorrow.

Fragile Ties

Over time, Andrew and I received the joyous news: Alice was pregnant, and George was about to embrace fatherhood. Their happiness permeated our lives, and we celebrated alongside them. When their daughter, Beatrice, arrived, George's elation knew no bounds. I believed he had finally discovered contentment, that life was steering him toward positivity. But reality had other plans—George remained unsatisfied.

As Beatrice blossomed, George and Alice made a life-altering choice: they relocated permanently to Romania. Yet, once settled there, their relationship began to unravel. They faced the painful truth—they were breaking up.

Alice confided in me, her voice laden with hurt. George had betrayed her, spending scant time at home with her and Beatrice. Instead of nurturing their family, he vanished for days, lost in his own world. His alcohol consumption escalated, and their once-strong bond frayed.

At the end of our conversation, Alice implored me to talk to George, hoping he'd listen and find his way back. She confessed her willingness to forgive—for Beatrice's sake, so their daughter could grow up with both parents. The weight of their shared history hung heavy in the air, and I wondered if George would heed her plea.

Alice's revelations hung in the air like a storm cloud, casting shadows over our once-hopeful world. George's transformation was a seismic shift—an erosion of the man I thought I knew. Instead of improving, he'd crumbled, indifference etching lines on his face, erasing the light from his eyes. I grappled with the urge to confront him, to shake him awake from this apathy, but doubt gnawed at my resolve. Was I the right messenger for life's harsh lessons? And deep down, I feared that change was elusive, a mirage shimmering on the horizon.

I remembered my own metamorphosis—the girl who once wore virtue like a cloak, now dancing on the precipice of right and wrong. George followed my footsteps, tracing the same treacherous path. His heart, once a vessel of warmth, now echoed with emptiness—a cavern carved by the blades of betrayal.

Life revelled in irony, weaving threads of coincidence. George hungered for the spotlight, craving every gaze upon him. Love, for him, wasn't a fleeting emotion; it was a desperate plea to fill the void within—a void that seemed to widen with each passing day.

And then, fate intervened. My mother-in-law, a sage with eyes that held lifetimes of wisdom, implored me to bridge the chasm between George and Alice. She had tried, her words falling like rain on parched soil, yet he remained deaf to her entreaties. But this wasn't an ordinary rift; it was a fracture that threatened a child's destiny—a fragile thread connecting Beatrice to a fractured family.

Summoning courage, I prepared my speech—a fragile bridge across the abyss. The phone trembled in my hand as I dialled his number, each digit echoing my uncertainty. Would my words be enough to mend hearts and rewrite their shared future?

"It's been a while," I began, my voice steady despite the turmoil within. "How's life in Romania?"

"Honestly," George's voice crackled through the line, "it's not great here. I want to return to London. Chaos surrounds me, but I'm hanging in there."

I pressed on, determined to unravel the tangled threads of their broken relationship. "What happened? Why did you break up with Alice? Do you miss Beatrice?"

His sigh carried the weight of regret. "I miss her, but Alice and I couldn't get along anymore. We argued constantly. Breaking up was for the best. Beatrice doesn't need to witness our fights. But it's hard—I can't set a wrong example of love for her."

"Every couple argues," I countered gently. "Nobody's perfect. Beatrice needs both her parents. You know what it's like growing up without them."

"But Beatrice isn't the only child without a father," George's voice wavered. "I'll be there for her from a distance, visit often, and life will continue. I can't stay with a woman I don't love, even if we have a child."

"Why agree to have a child if you don't love her?" I probed, my heart pounding.

"I thought things would work out," he confessed, vulnerability seeping through the cracks.

"If you want everything to be okay," I insisted, "you must stay with your family. Don't go with other women! It won't be okay if you keep drinking excessively and coming home after three days. What's going on with you?"

"Even you're judging me," George snapped, irritation flaring.

"What's going on isn't happening because of me," I retorted, my frustration boiling over. "Everything happens because of you. Don't blame me for all your wrong decisions. You've sunk into alcohol, you've changed, and I don't recognize you anymore. Buy yourself another life; nothing's enough for you now!"

"You're right!" His admission hung in the charged silence. "I've made a lot of mistakes and wrong decisions. I feel like a monster, and I'll change when I'm able to love again."

"Don't just think about yourself," I implored. "Think about Beatrice's future." The words hung there, fragile as gossamer, waiting for George to grasp their significance.

In the aftermath of our conversation, hope hung by a fragile thread. Alice's heart yearned for change, but George remained ensnared in a cycle of fleeting connections. New girlfriends paraded through his life—some hidden in shadows, others exposed to the harsh light of scrutiny.

Yet, fate wove its intricate pattern. After two months, George wearied of the hollow love and the false attention. He returned to Alice, seeking solace in familiar arms. She forgave him, her joy palpable as they rekindled their fractured bond. But love, it seemed, was a delicate equation—one they struggled to balance.

Their relationship remained a tempest, fierce and unpredictable. Storms brewed, and calm eluded them. Still, they clung to their roles as parents, committed to Beatrice's well-being even from a distance. Their love story, though marred, held a chapter of resilience—a testament to the ties that bound them, frayed yet unbroken.

In the intricate dance of human connection, we often find ourselves entangled in beds that don't belong to us. The allure of physical intimacy is potent, yet true happiness remains elusive for those who carry a conscience. In this twenty-first-century landscape, sex flows freely, but love exacts its toll—a currency of vulnerability and sacrifice.

Once, honour and respect stood tall, pillars of virtue. Now, they've faded into the background, overshadowed by a pursuit of relationships devoid of obligations. Love, it seems, has become a game—a high-stakes gamble where survival hinges on strategic moves, and emotional recklessness leads to inevitable defeat.

Some men betray their partners, seeking solace in the arms of younger women. Meanwhile, some women resist infidelity, fearing exposure and the unravelling of their carefully constructed lives. Our contemporary world measures a person's worth by attire, and material wealth often outweighs the significance of family bonds and friendships.

Within the walls of homes, maintaining harmony and equilibrium has become a Herculean task. Temptations swirl like eddies in a river, threatening to erode the foundations of commitment. Yet, a rare few persist with unwavering purpose. These families stand united, weathering storms, prioritizing their children's well-being, and treasuring every shared moment.

While many families chase financial gain, a precious handful is built on the bedrock of authentic love. It's here that imperfections are embraced, mistakes forgiven, and vulnerabilities accepted. For in the crucible of genuine love, we find our truest selves—the flawed, resilient, and infinitely hopeful beings who dare to believe that even amidst chaos, there exists a path to lasting happiness.

As I reflect on my own marriage, the years have woven a tapestry of arguments and shared moments with Andrew. When two strong-willed souls coexist, love doesn't exempt us from contradictions; it merely amplifies them. Our disagreements span the spectrum—from food preferences to clothing choices and musical tastes to holiday destinations. We've debated where to travel, which car to buy, and even the merits of various restaurants. And while we haven't yet sparred over the taste of water, who's to say what the future holds?

An ideal wife doesn't harbour illusions of an ideal husband. Instead, a perfect marriage emerges from the crucible of imperfection. We—flawed, stubborn, and fiercely committed—refuse to surrender, even when challenges threaten to unravel our bond. Marriage, like a blacksmith's forge, tempers us. It weakens our rough edges, revealing both our best and worst qualities. It transforms us in ways we couldn't have fathomed, leading to growth that transcends mere biology.

Within this sacred union, mutual trust becomes our sanctuary. Each partner stands guard over the other's solitude, a silent sentinel against the storms of life. Without understanding and empathy, cohabitation would be impossible—a house divided against itself. The space between us becomes hallowed ground, where love thrives, forgiveness blooms, and shared dreams take root.

And so, we cling to our promises—the whispered vows exchanged under moonlit skies, the unwavering commitment etched into our hearts. As long as love persists, as long as respect remains our compass, nothing can dismantle the bond between our two imperfect hearts.

Reunion

After nearly a year of living in Romania, George made the heart-wrenching decision to return to London. His reunion with Alice was bittersweet; they dreamed of saving enough money to renovate their modest house. Years ago, George had left me behind, seeking financial stability and a home in London. Now, he left Alice once more, chasing the same elusive goal.

One day, George reached out to Andrew, his big brother. His voice trembled over the phone as he explained his situation. "Could I stay with you for a couple of weeks?" he asked. "I need to find a job, settle in, and then I'll rent my own place." Andrew hesitated, torn between loyalty and practicality, but in the end, he accepted to help his brother. Even if, for the next two weeks, while Emma attended school and Andrew worked, I would be at home with George—an unexpected twist in our lives. Andrew tried to suppress the gnawing jealousy that surfaced. He knew George's presence would test our marriage and strain our household dynamics. But he agreed, driven by memories of shared secrets and childhood adventures.

A week later, George landed in London. The day before leaving Romania, George called me and asked if I could pick him up from the airport. I had taken the day off from my job in the cafe shop to go to the airport for George, knowing he had no money, and I wanted to help him. I didn't act the way he did when I came to London.

He stepped off the plane, clutching a battered suitcase, his smile weary. His transformation was striking—noticeably thinner, eyes haunted, like an entirely different person. When we got home, I concealed my surprise, casually offering coffee and food as though nothing had shifted.

After a few hours, George decided to join me on a trip to the grocery store. Together, we stepped out into the world, the supermarket aisles filled with unspoken questions. Silence hung between us, laden with memories and words left unsaid.

Upon returning home, I realized I had no key to unlock the door. George's laughter rang through the air—a blend of amusement and mild panic.

"What's our plan now?" he asked, mischief dancing in his eyes. "Are we just going to stand here until Andrew gets back in the evening?"

"Stop laughing!" I retorted. "I have a hunch that the garden door might be unlocked. Let's approach our neighbours and ask if we can pass through their gardens. Then, we'll navigate our way over the fence and into our own backyard."

George raised an eyebrow. "Are you sure the garden door is unlocked?"

"Not entirely," I admitted. "But it seems like our only option."

"Did you lose the key?" George inquired. "Or did you leave it at home?"

"I think I lost it," I replied. "We'll find out for sure once we're inside."

"How is it that you always manage to lose your keys?" George asked. "A long time ago, I gave you a special key, and you lost it."

"I threw away that key," I replied.

Our mission ended in success. Our kind neighbour graciously allowed us passage through their garden, and our backyard door opened effortlessly—it had been unlocked all along. And, as if fate played a gentle jest, the key sat innocently on the table. It turns out I hadn't lost it after all.

In the end, our mission was successful. Our kind neighbour allowed us passage through their garden, and our backyard door yielded easily—it was unlocked all along. And as if fate were playing a gentle joke on us, the key sat innocently on the table. I hadn't lost it after all.

As we hauled the shopping bags from the car into the house, George's laughter returned. He wove tales and shared jokes, and for a fleeting moment, our worries dissolved. Perhaps, in life's unexpected turns, laughter served as the key that unlocked our unspoken words.

"I've just arrived in London," George quipped, mischief dancing in his eyes, "and already I'm exploring the neighbourhood, leaping fences through gardens. Let's hope you won't misplace the keys again during my stay."

"My mistake," I replied matter-of-factly. "I didn't lose the key; I simply left it at home."

"But the house key," George teased, "you left it on the table. The other key, though—you tossed it away."

"That other key?" I trailed off. "It no longer exists."

As we stood there, I made a silent promise to myself: this conversation would end, the past left undisturbed. Indifference became my armour, shielding me from memories I wished to bury. I longed to tell him not to resurrect old stories, but coincidences had their way of breathing life into forgotten moments.

Inwardly, I wrestled with the curious timing: how could I forget the key at home precisely when George arrived? It felt like fate's gentle nudge, a forgotten melody echoing through time. And then, like a bittersweet refrain, memories resurfaced scenes of Andrew leaving his key at my place, promising that wherever life took him, he'd find his way back to me. Sometimes, the echoes of lost keys held more weight than the keys themselves.

For two weeks, George tirelessly scoured job listings, making countless phone calls. Meanwhile, I buried myself in university assessments, our conversations sparse but meaningful. In the kitchen, amidst simmering pots and sizzling pans, George would join me, lending a hand. He shared stories about Beatrice, his daughter—how he missed her and connected through video calls on Messenger. Even during playful moments with Emma, Beatrice's memory lingered.

As the fortnight slipped away, George's job hunt remained fruitless. He and Andrew had a conversation, leading to an unexpected decision: George would stay with us until the summer holidays. Andrew, harbouring a hint of jealousy over my prolonged time with George, accepted the arrangement. The tension between the brothers was palpable, yet I refrained from meddling. Their unbreakable bond held sway, even as my marriage teetered on the edge.

In the quiet corners of Andrew's mind, shadows danced—a symphony of doubts and fears that defied my every effort. Trust, elusive as a fleeting wisp of smoke, slipped through our fingers like sand. Our conversations, once tender exchanges, now spiralled into heated arguments fuelled by unspoken grievances.

Love, I discovered, was not enough to shield us from the tempests that raged within. Coincidences conspired against our peace, weaving intricate patterns of chaos. I trod carefully, balancing on the tightrope between hope and despair, hoping that amidst the complexities, our hearts would find solace.

Life, I realized, was not a linear path but a spiral—a journey that looped back upon itself, revisiting concepts we thought we had mastered. In those revisits, we unearthed deeper truths, like buried treasures waiting to be discovered.

Strength, I observed, rarely emerged from an easy past. Resilient souls bore scars—etched reminders of battles fought, storms weathered, and trials endured. These scars were not signs of weakness; they were badges of endurance, testaments to the unwavering resolve that carried them through. And so, I held onto hope, tracing the contours of our shared vulnerabilities. Perhaps in those scars, we would find our solace—a fragile sanctuary amidst life's relentless currents.

Curiously, humans adapt to the absence of happiness. When joy graces our lives, we tiptoe toward it as if afraid it might vanish like a wisp of smoke. Perhaps it's the knowledge that happiness is ephemeral—a delicate bloom that could wither at any moment.

But let us take a lesson from the spiral—the intricate dance of life's twists and turns. It leads us back to wisdom, revealing hidden truths in its cyclical journey. Amidst vulnerability, we find strength—the kind that emerges from scars and resilience. And so, let us savour happiness without reservation, knowing that even if it fades, its essence lingers—a sweet memory etched into our souls.

Torn Between Love and Deception

Balancing studies, work, and taking care of Emma felt like being trapped in a relentless whirlwind. This hectic pace left me with little time to reflect on my relationship with Andrew, which had deteriorated significantly. Our communication dwindled, and even simple embraces became rare. We hardly managed to share a meal together, especially since Andrew's late arrivals became routine. His reasons and excuses were increasingly hard to believe or accept. Often, Emma and I would sit by the window, our dinner waiting, playing a game to stave off boredom. Our challenge? Guessing the colour of the passing cars on the street.

During that time, Andrew had a coworker with whom he got along quite well, and they became friends. However, that colleague wasn't exactly a positive influence. He consumed a significant amount of alcohol, and this negative environment led Andrew to excessive drinking. As a result, he would come home late, and even worse, he would drive under the influence of alcohol.

Countless times, I begged Andrew to cut ties with that colleague, consider changing his workplace, and limit their interactions. But he remained stubborn. He'd dismiss my concerns, insisting that I didn't truly understand the guy, labelling me irrational, and accusing me of weaving imaginary tales. Frustrated, I decided to meet this friend personally. I accepted the invitation to Andrew's friend's child's birthday party.

There, I discovered that Andrew's buddy was married with two kids, yet despite his responsibilities, he indulged in excessive alcohol consumption. The 4-year-old's party felt more like a nightclub—Jack Daniels bottles emptied within minutes, and the adult guests were drunk. Andrew revelled in the spotlight while I sat alone at the table, unnoticed. Envious glances from other women followed me, their silence a testament to their discomfort. They perceived me as aloof, and our interactions remained strained.

That night, I pleaded with Andrew for hours to leave the party, but only after he'd drunk excessively did, he finally agree to head home.

After that evening's heated argument with Andrew, I vowed never to meet his friend again. However, Andrew's persistence wore me down, and I eventually agreed to go fishing with them. Andrew assured me that his friend wasn't a bad influence and asked for another chance for me to get to know him. Reluctantly, I accepted.

George, who worked with his brothers Andrew, James, and Michael, was too tired to join us for fishing. He didn't like Andrew's friend either. In fact, George, James, and Michael had all advised Andrew to end his friendship with this person, believing it to be unhealthy. Unfortunately, Andrew didn't heed their advice.

I took charge of purchasing and packing everything we needed for our fishing trip. Carrying all the essentials was crucial since we planned to spend the night in a tent. Once everything was ready, we set off for the fishing location. The scenery was breathtaking— serene and enveloped in lush greenery. At least the surroundings provided a sense of calm and an open playground for Emma.

Upon arrival, we met Andrew's friend and his family. I focused on setting up the tent and preparing the grill while Andrew busied himself with the fishing equipment, bait, and alcohol. Despite their silly jokes, I concentrated on my tasks and maintained my self-control. Conversation with Andrew's friend's wife was limited; she remained quiet, amusedly listening to their chat.

After a long, exhausting day, I decided to unwind by the fire, even though the sound of their jokes was beginning to grate on my nerves. Andrew's friend—whom I couldn't stand—seemed to take perverse pleasure in provoking me. I stared into the flames, trying to find some peace, inhaling the crisp, slightly chilly evening air. Emma, tired from running around the campsite all day, seemed content and happy, which brought a small, fleeting smile to my face. At least one of us was finding joy in this chaos.

As night fell, I made my way into the tent to prepare for sleep alongside Emma. The cold air outside was biting, signalling that it was time for her to rest. Inside, the atmosphere was warm and soothing, a stark contrast to the disarray outside. Just as I was about to drift off, I heard the sound of a car engine. My heart sank. Andrew and his friend had decided to abandon fishing, drive under the influence, and search for a nearby club to have fun. Earlier, Andrew's friend had boasted about knowing the area and mentioned an interesting club where they could find beautiful women for a night of adventure. At first, I thought he was joking, but it turned out he wasn't.

A wave of frustration and disappointment washed over me. I felt a knot tighten in my stomach as I realized how reckless and irresponsible they were being. I glanced at Emma, peacefully asleep, and felt a surge of protectiveness. The thought of Andrew putting himself and others in danger made my blood boil. I lay there, torn between anger and worry, hoping they would come to their senses before it was too late.

They waited until we were settled in the tent before heading off to the club, recklessly driving while drunk. They abandoned us in the forest, leaving me feeling vulnerable and exposed despite the presence of other fishermen around the lake. Fear gnawed at me as

I desperately tried to call Andrew, but his phone was off. My mind spiralled with terrifying scenarios, each one worse than the last, fearing he might have an accident in his drunken state.

That night, sleep was a distant dream. I stayed by the fire, my eyes wide open, heart pounding with anxiety. I kept calling Andrew, but each unanswered ring only deepened my dread. The forest, usually a place of solace, felt like a prison of uncertainty and fear.

It wasn't until around 5 a.m. that they finally returned. Their excuse was flimsy—they claimed the gate had closed at midnight, preventing them from re-entering the lake area. I knew it was a lie; there was a 24/7 gatekeeper. But I was too exhausted, too emotionally drained to argue. The betrayal cut deep, leaving a scar that would take time to heal. I was heartbroken, realizing how fragile trust can be. 'This world can hurt you; it cuts you deep and leaves a scar, things fall apart, but nothing breaks like a heart.' – Miley Cyrus, from 'Nothing Breaks Like a Heart.'

In the morning, when Emma woke up, I was overwhelmed with sadness, but I tried my best to hide it from her. I methodically packed up the tent and all our belongings, each task a small distraction from the turmoil inside me. After two hours, we were ready to leave, but Andrew was still engrossed in fishing, showing no sign of wanting to head home.

As the minutes turned into hours, my patience wore thin. Anxiety gnawed at me, and I felt on the verge of a breakdown. Finally, after what felt like an eternity, we set off for home.

The drive was silent and tense. We didn't exchange a single word. My only focus was on getting Emma and myself home safely. Andrew, clearly intoxicated and possibly under the influence of drugs, acted as if nothing had happened. He seemed to genuinely believe that I had bought his story about the gate being closed, preventing their return. He probably thought I believed they had just gone to find an open store to buy more alcohol.

The betrayal and the fear from the night before lingered, making the journey home feel even longer. I was heartbroken and exhausted, realizing how fragile our situation had become.

Regardless, all I wanted was to get home and never see or hear about Andrew's friend again. When we finally arrived, I confronted Andrew with a heavy heart. I asked him to cut all ties with his friend, hoping he would understand the depth of my pain. Then, I retreated to Emma's room, feeling utterly alone, disappointed, frustrated, unattractive, and unwanted. It felt like I was teetering on the edge of madness, but I had to stay strong for Emma. The weight of my emotions was almost unbearable, and I felt like I was drowning in a sea of despair.

The next day, after Andrew and George left for work, I took Emma to school. Once I was home alone, the silence was deafening. I couldn't shake the feeling that something was terribly wrong. My mind raced with suspicions, and I didn't trust Andrew for a second, especially when he was with his friend. Instead of focusing on my projects and courses, I found myself spiralling into a frenzy, scouring the internet for ways to spy on Andrew. I needed to uncover the truth—why he wouldn't sever ties with his friend. The fear of betrayal consumed me, and I felt like I was losing control of my life.

After a few hours of searching, I found a solution: an app called Spy Era. With its help, I could monitor Andrew's every move. All I had to do was find the right moment to install it on his phone. Once installed, I could record his conversations, track his GPS location, and even capture photos from home while he was away. The app wasn't overly expensive, but it required precise settings to function correctly. I doubted my ability to pull it off, especially considering I had to install it on Andrew's phone discreetly.

That day, I meticulously planned each step, purchased the app, and waited for the opportune moment to put my plan into action. Nothing in the world is more dangerous than a disappointed, jealous, and deceived woman. She can transform into the ultimate spy when she senses that something is amiss.

In the evening, George arrived home on time, but Andrew was late. He stumbled in three hours later, reeking of alcohol. None of us sat together for dinner that evening. Emma's room had already become my sanctuary, the place where I spent most of my time.

When Andrew arrived, being drunk, I fell asleep immediately, and I seized the moment to put my plan into action. I took his phone and, without worrying that he would wake up, installed the app following the given instructions. I didn't even know if it would work, but I had to try.

As I watched the app load, my heart pounded with a mix of fear and determination. The betrayal I felt fuelled my resolve. I needed to know the truth, no matter the cost. The night was long, and sleep was elusive, but I felt a strange sense of empowerment. For the first time in a long while, I felt like I was taking control of my life again, even if it was through desperate measures.

A Spy in My Own Life

For an entire month, I was consumed by a whirlwind of emotions. The thrill of playing a clandestine spy was intoxicating, yet it was laced with a gnawing guilt that I couldn't shake off. Every time the application hummed with activity, my heart raced with a mix of excitement and dread. I meticulously tracked every move Andrew made, feeling a strange blend of power and helplessness. Deep down, I knew I was treading on forbidden ground, that my actions were ethically questionable. Yet, I couldn't tear myself away. My insatiable curiosity drove me to uncover the truth, and uncover it, I did.

The revelation hit me like a tidal wave. Andrew, along with his friend and two others, had been dismissed from their jobs due to alcohol-induced workplace incidents. The shock of this discovery was compounded by a sense of betrayal. But there was more—Andrew had a new job; one he hadn't shared with me. The sting of being kept in the dark was sharp and painful. Without the app, I'd have remained blissfully ignorant, as no one volunteered this information.

As I pieced together Andrew's daily routine, a picture of his double life emerged. He would clock in at his new workplace, then slip out to pubs and restaurants for leisure, only to return in the evening to clock out. His daily habits included alcohol consumption and drug use with his friend. The more I uncovered, the deeper my heart sank. And there was more—Andrew's escapades involved watching explicit content and connecting with women on a dating app. I even recorded conversations and stories with these women, listening in on every phone call and reading every message Andrew exchanged. Each revelation was a dagger to my heart, leaving me reeling with a mix of anger, sadness, and confusion.

At home, we maintained a facade of normalcy, but it was a fragile one. If Andrew returned from work sober, he'd claim fatigue and avoid conversation, his eyes never quite meeting mine. His phone messages were promptly deleted as if erasing any evidence of his life with his best friend. Each deletion felt like a slap; a reminder of the secrets he kept from me.

I bore this burden alone, my heart heavy with the weight of secrets. Even my friend, Lyli, remained unaware. Fear gnawed at me—what if she persuaded me to cease my surveillance? The thought of losing my only lifeline to the truth was unbearable.

Despite my moral compass pointing elsewhere, I couldn't bring myself to halt this covert operation. The truth had its hooks in me, and I clung to it, even as it tore at my conscience. I trembled with pain as I listened to the recordings or read the messages. My heart ached, and I felt like I was losing my sanity, yet I couldn't confide in anyone—at least not yet. I felt like the lowest woman, the ugliest. Regret gnawed at me, especially for my involvement in all the episodes with George. The desire for revenge simmered within me, but I maintained my composure. For Emma's sake, I needed to unravel the cause and find a solution. I yearned to understand how to fix it.

Every night, as I lay in bed, the weight of my actions pressed down on me. The guilt was suffocating, but the need to know the truth was stronger. I felt like I was walking a tightrope, balancing between my need for answers and the fear of what those answers might reveal. The emotional toll was immense, but I couldn't stop. Not until I had the full picture, not until I understood why Andrew had become this stranger in our home.

One evening, while waiting for Andrew, who was predictably late, I received a shocking call from him. He had been in an accident. Driving under the influence, he had crashed his car into a tree. In a panic, he fled the scene, leaving behind a severely damaged front wheel that barely turned. Despite this, he managed to drive home, the damaged wheel leaving tire marks on the road from the accident scene to our house. Miraculously, he arrived home unscathed, but the car was very damaged.

Determined to confront him, I waited for him to calm down and arrange for the car repairs. Once he was settled, we had our conversation.

"I knew everything you were doing," I started, my voice trembling with a mix of hurt and frustration. "I knew about your new job, how you only clocked in and out. I knew your supervisor was friends with you and your best friend. I knew about your drinking and your drug use. I knew that after excessive alcohol consumption, you'd take drugs to appear fresh when you came home. I knew you were lying to me."

Andrew's face contorted with anger and disbelief. "How do you know?" he retorted, his voice rising. "Did your boyfriend George tell you? Or did my friend betray me?"

"No one told me," I replied, my voice breaking. "So, you admit it? That's your concern—finding out who told me? Instead of caring that you lied and hurt me?"

"Tell me who told you!" Andrew continued to shout; his eyes wild with desperation.

"I found out myself!" I shouted back, tears streaming down my face. The room seemed to close in around us, the weight of our words hanging heavy in the air.

At that moment, I showed him the recordings, the photos, and everything I had gathered. All the evidence from my month-long stint as a spy—I handed it all over, letting him listen and read. My hands trembled as I watched his face, searching for any sign of remorse or understanding.

"In my eyes, you can never be who you once were," I began, my voice quivering with a mix of anger and sorrow. "To me, you've become a stranger—I no longer recognize you. If this is the life you desire, continue doing what brings you happiness. Even without asking for forgiveness, I will grant it—not for my sake or yours, but for Emma's."

Tears welled up in my eyes, blurring my vision as I continued. "I view it as a regrettable episode, and I hope you'll sever ties with your friend. You underestimated me, but I'm not as naive as you thought." My voice broke, and I could feel the weight of my words hanging in the air between us.

Then I went to Emma's room. There, I felt alone but safe. The silence of the room enveloped me, and I sank to the floor, hugging my knees to my chest. The soft, thick rug beneath me was a comfort, its texture grounding me at the moment. Emma's innocent presence was a comfort I clung to desperately.

The following day, Andrew sought out a new job, distancing himself from his friend. He attempted to engage in conversation with me, hoping to mend our fractured relationship and move beyond the events that had transpired. Although I had verbally forgiven him, I required time to heal. We went through the motions, trying to recapture the initial spark, but everything felt different. Over three months had passed since I'd last received a hug from him. The strain in our relationship was palpable, and I grappled with uncertainty about how to repair it or if I even possessed the strength to do so. Approaching him became an arduous task. Each time he drew near, I couldn't shake the memories of the messages I'd read and the recordings that exposed his drinking and deceit.

In the following period, I immersed myself in my studies. I stopped working at the coffee shop to be able to focus more on my studies. Even though I was only working a few hours, it was exhausting, and I no longer had free time to study and work on my projects. The constant rush and the physical demands of the job left me drained. When Emma was at school, it was the only time I could study. Those quiet hours became precious moments of solitude and concentration, where I could immerse myself in my books and assignments.

When Emma was at home, my responsibilities multiplied. I had to take care of her, cook, feed her, bathe her, and look after her, as well as clean the house. Each task, though done with love, chipped away at the time and energy I had left for my studies. I would often find myself staying up late into the night, trying to squeeze in some study time after Emma had gone to bed. The fatigue was overwhelming, and I felt a constant tug-of-war between my duties as a parent and my academic aspirations. Despite the challenges, I knew that focusing on my studies was the best decision for both of us in the long run.

My relationship with Andrew hadn't completely deteriorated, but it remained unrepaired. Everything hung in the balance, and neither of us made significant efforts to mend it. We simply lived from moment to moment, taking things as they came.

The Price of Success

After several months of relentless hard work, I finally graduated from university with first-class honours. The achievement was nothing short of a dream come true—I had always aspired to become an accountant, and now that goal was within my grasp. My elation knew no bounds; it felt like I was walking on air.

Receiving my final grades was a moment of pure validation. All the late nights, the sacrifices, and the unwavering dedication had paid off. It wasn't just about the numbers on a piece of paper; it was about the immense pride and confidence that surged through me. With this newfound determination, I made a pivotal decision to pursue further studies and enrolled in a master's program, specifically an MBA. This decision marked a significant turning point in my life.

There were quite a few challenges I faced during my studies. Balancing academic responsibilities with personal life was one of the toughest. The pressure to maintain high grades often meant sacrificing social activities and personal time. There were moments of self-doubt, especially during intense exam periods or when tackling complex assignments.

Time management was another significant hurdle. Juggling multiple deadlines and ensuring I stayed on top of my coursework required meticulous planning and discipline. There were also financial pressures, as managing tuition fees and living expenses added an extra layer of stress.

Despite these challenges, each obstacle taught me valuable lessons in resilience, perseverance, and prioritization. Overcoming them made the achievement of graduating with first-class honours even more rewarding.

For the first time, I felt genuine pride in myself. The pursuit of knowledge and the opportunity to evolve my career became my driving force. Continuing my studies was not just a dream; it was the path to creating new opportunities and shaping my professional future. The journey ahead was filled with promise, and I was ready to embrace it with open arms and an eager heart.

While I was studying, I began to practice accounting. I started closing financial years for family members and a few friends, but the transition from theory to practice was quite different. I didn't give up; instead, I continued to practice and learn something new every day.

I vividly remember a moment when I wasn't sure about a calculation for Andrew's financial year-end, specifically related to his self-assessment account. Faced with this uncertainty, I decided to seek help from an accountant. Upon reaching the accountant's office, I explained the situation. He pointed out what was amiss, but then he dropped a bombshell: he demanded £150.00 for a mere 5-minute consultation. It felt like a nightmare, especially since he refused to return my documents until I paid him. I had only £50.00 in my pocket, which had to last me the entire week.

Feeling desperate, I called Lily and asked her for a loan, but she was also strapped for cash. Fortunately, Lily had an acquaintance who lent her some money, allowing her to help me out. Fuelled by frustration, I managed to gather the necessary funds and returned to the accountant's office. I paid him for the information, which shouldn't have cost so much, and retrieved my documents.

The experience was a harsh lesson in the realities of the professional world. It taught me the importance of perseverance and resourcefulness. Despite the frustration and financial strain, I emerged more determined than ever to master my craft and help others without exploiting them. This incident became a pivotal moment in my journey, reinforcing my commitment to ethical practices in my future career.

At that moment, I expressed my gratitude for his service and made a promise to both him and myself: "One day, I will become an accountant. I aspire to attract your clients and assist them without imposing hefty fees for basic information." The greatest professional satisfaction in any job is being appreciated for the work you do and seeing satisfied clients. No one becomes wealthy overnight, but with hard work and patience, fulfilment—both professionally and financially—will eventually come.

Additionally, I expressed my heartfelt gratitude to Lily for her financial assistance. I truly don't know how I would have managed without her unwavering support.

Lily, my steadfast companion, embodies the warmth of a sunbeam on a chilly morning. Her goodness radiates effortlessly, touching everyone fortunate enough to cross her path. Married and a devoted mother, she juggles life's responsibilities with grace, never missing a beat.

Her kindness is like a gentle breeze, soothing hearts and lifting spirits. And oh, the laughter we've shared! It's a symphony of joy echoing through our memories. Secrets whispered in hushed tones, woven into the fabric of our friendship—each one a precious gem entrusted to her care.

Lily's unwavering support during my toughest times has been a beacon of hope. Her ability to find light in the darkest moments and her unwavering belief in me have been my pillars of strength. Every challenge faced, and every triumph celebrated has been made sweeter by her presence. She is not just a friend; she is family, and her impact on my life is immeasurable.

Lily's attentive ear absorbs my worries, fears, and dreams. She stands unwavering, a lighthouse in my stormy seas. Never once has she betrayed my trust; her loyalty is an unbreakable bond. When darkness threatened to engulf me, she held my hand, whispering, "You've got this."

She believed in me when doubt clouded my vision. Her unwavering faith fuelled my determination. And now, as I stride confidently toward my career goals, I owe a debt of gratitude to Lily—the beacon of unwavering support and the keeper of our shared laughter. So here's to Lily: the one who stood by me when the world felt heavy, the one who laughed with me until tears blurred our vision, the one who knew that success wasn't just about numbers on a balance sheet—it was about the fire in my eyes, the grit in my soul. "Lily, my friend, my confidante, my cheerleader—thank you for being my guiding star".

A Moment of Solitude, A Lifetime of Triumph

After years of study and countless battles, I refused to surrender. I found myself preparing for the graduation ceremony. My dad wasn't there to watch me with pride, and Andrew, too, was absent—he cited work commitments. So, there I stood, alone. It was my moment, and I resolved to savour it regardless.

The auditorium buzzed with anticipation. Rows of empty seats stretched before me, each one a reminder of the absence I felt. The stage, adorned with flowers and diplomas, beckoned like a beacon. I adjusted my gown, the fabric rustling against my skin—a tangible reminder of my journey.

As the ceremony commenced, speeches echoed through the hall. Professors praised our resilience, our late-night study sessions, and our unwavering commitment. But when they called my name, it was a solitary echo—an applause that hung in the air, waiting for an audience.

I stepped onto the stage, diploma in hand. The dean's smile was kind, but it couldn't fill the void. I glanced at the empty seat, imagining my dad's proud face. He was with me in spirit, I told myself. And so, I smiled—a bittersweet curve of lips—and accepted my hard-earned degree.

The weight of the moment pressed down on me, a mix of triumph and melancholy. Each step towards the stage felt like a journey through time, every stride echoing the struggles and victories that had led me here. The absence of my dad and Andrew was a stark contrast to the joy of the occasion, a reminder of the sacrifices made along the way.

As I stood there, diploma in hand, the applause seemed distant, almost surreal. The faces in the crowd blurred, but the empty seat stood out sharply, a poignant symbol of what was missing. Yet, in that moment, I felt a surge of pride and resilience. This was my achievement, a testament to my perseverance and strength.

The dean's congratulatory handshake was warm, but it was the imagined presence of my dad that brought a tear to my eye. I could almost hear his voice, feel his pride. It was a bittersweet victory, one that I would cherish forever. With a deep breath, I stepped off the stage, ready to face the future with the same determination that had brought me here.

Later, outside the auditorium, I stood on the steps. The sun dipped low, casting long shadows. A breeze tousled my hair, and I closed my eyes, inhaling the moment. Yes, I was alone, but I was also triumphant. The diploma in my hand was more than paper; it was a testament to my resilience, my late-night battles, and my refusal to yield.

Whispers of the Open Road

Shortly after my graduation ceremony, we bought a new car and decided to embark on a summer holiday. Our ambitious itinerary featured a three-week road trip from London to Romania, with captivating stops along the way—the sun-kissed shores of the French Riviera (Côte d'Azur) and the enchanting canals of Venice, Italy. From Romania, we would make our way back to London.

The idea for this adventure sprouted spontaneously, fuelled by wanderlust and the allure of open roads. We invited George to join us, and he eagerly accepted. After nearly a week of meticulous planning, everything was neatly packed—the car, our dreams, and our shared excitement. We stood ready to set off, our hearts brimming with anticipation. This journey also presented an opportunity for Andrew and me to spend time together and work on mending our relationship.

The road stretched before us like a ribbon of possibility. Our journey would be more than just miles covered; it would be a symphony of laughter, discovery, and familiarity. With maps in hand and the wind whispering promises, we stepped into the sun-drenched canvas of our summer adventure.

The French Riviera—Côte d'Azur—was our siren song. Azure waters, palm-fringed promenades, and the scent of lavender awaited us. Nice, with its pebble beaches and vibrant markets, welcomed us like an old friend. We strolled along the Promenade des Anglais, our toes dipping into the Mediterranean. Our dad tried socca, a local chickpea pancake. Its crispy edges and savoury centre danced on our taste buds—a flavour memory we'd carry forever.

Monaco, a pocket-sized kingdom, dazzled us with its opulence. The Monte Carlo Casino stood like a jewel, its grandeur defying reason. We didn't gamble, but we did people-watch—imagining the high-stakes dramas unfolding behind those gilded doors. Monaco, a playground for the wealthy, unfolded before us like a dream. The sun glinted off sleek surfaces—the polished armour of opulence. And there we were, our humble Toyota SUV, battle-scarred from the journey, nestled among the automotive aristocracy.

Maserati's purred like contented cats, their curves sculpted by desire. Lamborghinis, vibrant and unapologetic, flaunted their angular prowess. Our Toyota, with its mud-splattered flanks, stood like a curious interloper—an unexpected guest at a glittering soirée. Monaco, with its yachts and casinos, had welcomed us all—the high rollers and the road warriors alike. And as we drove away, our Toyota's tyres crunching gravel, we left a piece of our story behind—a dusty imprint on the glamorous canvas of the French Riviera.

Our road trip hugged the coastline, each curve revealing a new vista. Antibes, with its Picasso Museum and ancient ramparts, whispered secrets of artists and pirates. Cannes, synonymous with film glamour, teased us with glimpses of red carpets and starlit nights.

And then there was Saint-Tropez. Oh, Saint-Tropez! Its harbour cradled yachts that seemed to defy gravity. We sipped chilled rosé at a waterfront café, our eyes tracing the horizon where the sea met the sky. Andrew declared he'd return someday on his own yacht. We laughed, but secretly, we all had hidden dreams of our own.

Venice—the final jewel in our crown—beckoned across the Adriatic. The Grand Canal unfolded like a Renaissance painting, and we marvelled at the audacity of a city built on water. As we stepped onto the cobbled streets, Venice enveloped us—the scent of salt, the echo of footsteps, the promise of hidden alleys. We lost ourselves in the labyrinth, stumbling upon quiet squares and crumbling facades. I bought a carnival mask, and we posed for photos, our laughter echoing off ancient walls.

Our road trip had become a symphony of memories—a crescendo of laughter, discovery, and friendship. We returned to London, our hearts full, our passports stamped with stories. I knew that the French Riviera had woven itself into our souls—a sun-soaked tapestry of adventure, love, and the promise of more journeys to come.

Unfortunately, our vacation turned into a series of unfortunate events. Despite the beautiful azure waters and palm-fringed promenades, our experiences were overshadowed by frustration and exhaustion. Our mud-splattered Toyota stood out like an uninvited guest at a glamorous party, a stark reminder of our misadventures.

We visited all the locations I mentioned, but the trip was far from what I had hoped for. The final blow came when George, whom we had invited to join us, betrayed Alice by bringing another woman along. With just two phone calls, he arranged for a much younger, less sophisticated companion to join us. Alice, with her beauty and grace, was in a league of her own, making the contrast even more glaring.

This new woman had little to offer beyond her physical appearance, and her fashion sense was appalling. I couldn't understand how George could engage with her, but it wasn't my place to judge. What infuriated me was the impact on Emma. I didn't want her to witness such behaviour or see George with anyone other than Alice. I wanted her to see him as a good uncle, a loving husband, and a caring father. However, I couldn't control his decisions, especially since Andrew also agreed to let her join us.

Despite our lack of organization, we managed to book accommodations through Airbnb. However, the GPS often led us astray, showing alternate routes and different destinations. Our time was wasted searching for places to stay, setting up, and then collapsing from exhaustion before moving on. Our first lodging was a two-room flat on the seventh floor of a building without an elevator, only spiral stairs. We struggled to haul our luggage up, each step feeling like a marathon. Fortunately, we didn't stay there more than one night, taking only the essentials from the car.

The second accommodation was a luxurious flat, a brief respite from our troubles. However, we had to cook for ourselves as no nearby restaurants were open due to our late arrival. We scoured the map for a supermarket, and Andrew and George set off to find one. They returned two hours later, having lost their way, their faces etched with frustration and fatigue. The whole ordeal left us drained, both physically and emotionally.

When they finally arrived, we explained that we had been concerned and had gone to the street corner to search for them. That's when the biggest argument erupted. Our well-intentioned words ignited a storm. George and Andrew scolded us for going out at night, especially with a young child, insisting that it was a dangerous area and that we should have stayed indoors. Their anger flared, fuelled by their own disorientation from being lost. The tension was palpable, and the evening, which could have been a moment of relief, turned into another exhausting ordeal.

We quickly ate something, and I took Emma and Andrew to bed. Too tired to argue, I took Emma and Andrew to bed. The tension hung heavy in the air, and I regretted not realizing the risks earlier. In one way or another, they were right. I should have realized that it was dangerous to venture out alone at night in a completely unfamiliar location. Perhaps in those moments, we worried more about them than about our own safety. I had driven most of the way, my nerves frayed, and I wanted nothing more than peace.

That night, we went to bed, while in the other room, George and that woman continued their argument. George was drinking, and after a few hours, the argument escalated. The roots of their dispute ran deep, and I lay still, hoping Emma wouldn't wake up. George's voice rose, punctuated by the sound of a slap and the desperate tug of hair. I couldn't fathom the complexities of their relationship, nor did I want to. All I could do was lie there, praying for calm to descend upon our troubled night. I couldn't intervene; there was nothing I could do.

The next morning, George and the woman behaved as if nothing had happened. They were deeply in love, oblivious to the events of the previous night. I couldn't fathom how George, the man I thought I knew, could raise his hand against a woman. And Andrew, too, seemed like a stranger. Time had changed us, but not for the better.

Lost in my thoughts, we hurriedly prepared to set out. I insisted on driving again, seeking the comfort of familiarity behind the wheel. As we headed toward our third destination, I gazed at the passing landscapes. The scenery around us was breathtaking, yet our hearts harboured turmoil.

From location to location, everything remained the same. After their passionate moments of love and loud kisses, George and the woman would quickly descend into arguments. Almost every evening, they quarrelled, and George's temper flared. Their voices echoed, demanding attention as if they craved the spotlight. They constantly hurled insults at each other and exchanged foul language.

I couldn't believe that George could be like that. There was a side of George I had never known. That woman had turned him into a clown.

I felt a heavy sadness that Emma had to witness their circus, their heated disputes. Andrew, misreading my emotions, believed I was jealous of George spending time with the woman instead of me. But the truth was, I no longer had any feelings. I didn't feel jealousy, love, sympathy, or attraction. Perhaps a touch of pity, but otherwise, George's actions didn't affect me in any way.

Instead, I longed to spend more time with Andrew—to converse more, embrace, walk hand in hand, exchange compliments, smile, and find happiness. However, we were constantly interrupted by circumstances and the entire situation, which, rather than relaxing us, only added to our tension. The tension hung over us, preventing any enjoyment of the sun, the sand, or the world around us.

While there were beautiful moments during this vacation, most of the time, we were on edge, exhausted, and worn thin. My heart soared when we finally returned to London and to our home. The familiar streets, the comforting hum of the city, and the warmth of our own space felt like a balm to my weary soul. It was in those moments, back in our sanctuary, that I realized how much I had missed the simple, untroubled times.

In Her Footsteps

After that unforgettable vacation, George decided to move to Germany for a better-paying job. His departure brought me a sense of peace, and I hoped that Andrew would no longer harbour any jealousy or suspicion about George and me. Perhaps our relationship would improve.

Andrew continued working in a different location, far from his closest friend, but not for long. After numerous apologies and irrelevant excuses, Andrew declared that the job where his best friend worked paid better than his current position, and he needed to return to work with him. I had nothing more to say or argue; no matter what I did, he proceeded as he pleased.

I hoped that history wouldn't repeat itself, that he wouldn't come home late, and that he would refrain from drinking. I longed for a peaceful life. I had promised myself not to harm myself anymore and not to spy on him ever again. I didn't want to lose my sanity and sink into despair. "If he loves me, he will make things right," I whispered to myself, trying to encourage my own heart.

As the days passed, I clung to the hope that Andrew would change, that our lives would find a new rhythm of harmony and trust. The weight of uncertainty was heavy, but I held on to the belief that love could mend what was broken. Each night, as I lay in bed, I imagined a future where we laughed together, shared our dreams, and found solace in each other's arms. The fear of disappointment loomed large but so did the flicker of hope that kept my heart beating.

During that difficult period, as if things weren't already challenging enough, my mother called me one day with a trembling voice to tell me that my grandmother had passed away. I was stunned, feeling my heart shatter at my mother's words. I couldn't believe it. My grandmother, who had raised me, supported me and served as my guide, mentor, and educator, passed away at the age of 98. Although she was indeed elderly, I was never prepared to face the reality of living without her.

The news hit me like a tidal wave, leaving me gasping for air. Memories of her flooded my mind—her warm smile, the way she used to hold my hand, and the countless stories she shared with me. She was the cornerstone of our family, the one who held us all together with her unwavering love and wisdom. Losing her felt like losing a part of myself.

Unfortunately, I did not have the money to travel to Romania to attend her funeral. I felt so down. All the money I had, I sent to my mum to cover the funeral expenses. I was left with the image of her when she was alive, from the last time I visited her and said our final 'goodbye' before I left. I feel guilty that I couldn't be there to accompany her on her final journey.

The guilt weighed heavily on my heart. I longed to be there, to say a proper farewell, to honour her memory in person. Instead, I found myself alone, thousands of miles away, grappling with the pain and sorrow. I tried to find solace in the memories we shared, but the ache of not being able to be there for her final moments was overwhelming. I felt like I had let her down, even though I knew she would have understood.

A Tribute to Grandmother

In the quiet moments of dawn, I hear your voice.
A whisper in the wind, a gentle choice.
You raised me with love, your wisdom so grand.
Guiding me through life, holding my hand.

Your smile, a beacon, in the darkest night.
Your stories, a treasure, filling me with light.
You taught me to be strong, to stand tall and true.
In every step I take, I carry a piece of you.

The day you left; my world turned grey.
A tidal wave of sorrow, sweeping me away.
I remember your warmth, your tender embrace.
The love in your eyes, the lines on your face.

Though I couldn't be there, to say my last goodbye.
My heart was with you, as the angels took you high.
I sent my love, across the miles so far,
Hoping it reached you, like a shooting star.

You were the cornerstone, the heart of our home.
With you, I never felt alone.
Your legacy lives on, in the lessons you gave,
In the strength you instilled, in the courage you made.

Thank you, dear Grandmother, for all that you taught,
For the love that you gave, for the battles you fought.
You are my guide, my mentor, my friend,
In my heart, your memory will never end.

Rest now, in peace, in the heavens above,
Wrapped in eternal, unending love.
Though I miss you dearly, I know you're near,
In every whisper of the wind, I feel you here.

Your laughter echoes in the halls of my mind,
A melody of joy, so gentle and kind.
The recipes you shared, the songs you would sing,
Are now cherished memories, a beautiful thing.

You taught me to dream, to reach for the stars,
To find beauty in life, even in scars.
Your hands, though aged, were strong and sure,
A testament to a life lived pure.

I see you in the flowers, in the morning dew,
In the golden sunsets, in skies so blue.
Your spirit lives on, in nature's embrace,
In every kind act, in every warm face.

Though distance kept us apart at the end,
Your love was a bridge, that would never bend.
I carry your lessons, your wisdom, your grace,
In every challenge, in every new place.

Thank you, Grandmother, for being my light,
For guiding me through, both day and night.
Your legacy is love, pure and true,
And I promise to live, always honouring you.

Shattered Bonds

Over the next two years, my life spiralled into a relentless nightmare. My relationship with Andrew deteriorated beyond repair, worsening with each passing day. He frequently came home late from work, and minor car accidents due to his alcohol-induced driving became alarmingly common. His fishing trips with his best friend and other anglers turned into a regular escape, leaving me and Emma increasingly isolated. The time he spent with us dwindled to almost nothing. Only when he was drunk would he approach me, attempting to express love, but I couldn't bear him in that state.

On his days off, he would stand still and silent at home, glued to the TV, watching movie after movie without uttering a word to me. In desperate attempts to connect, I would drink with him, hoping to bridge the growing chasm between us. But every time we consumed alcohol together, it ended in bitter arguments. The insults and curses became a daily torment. When I tried to talk to him, he would demean me, calling me names and belittling my university degree. He constantly reproached me for not contributing anything valuable to our family, claiming he was the sole provider. He even criticized me for eating the food he provided for ten years, labelling me as worthless. He believed I stayed with him just to be close to George. He'd tell me that he tolerated me only because of Emma, and when he was calm, he'd apologize. There was no peace between us anymore. When I needed advice or a kind word, he was absent. I was absolutely alone in every situation when I needed him.

The emotional toll was immense. Each day felt like a battle, and I was losing myself in the process. The man I once loved had become a stranger, and the home that was supposed to be my sanctuary felt like a prison. The constant tension and fear of the next argument left me walking on eggshells. I longed for the days when we were happy, but those memories felt like a distant dream. The loneliness was suffocating, and the emotional scars ran deep. I felt trapped in a cycle of despair with no end in sight. The weight of his words and actions crushed my spirit, leaving me feeling utterly broken and hopeless.

I couldn't fathom why he behaved the way he did. He made me feel guilty for things I hadn't even done, and I started to believe I was truly worthless. My confidence was shattered. I couldn't understand why he only saw my flaws and never acknowledged anything good in me. Despite all the time we spent together and everything we went through, he never saw anything positive in me; he viewed me as an enemy, a traitor. I was emotionally and physically drained. Even when I cooked, I couldn't get anything right; I thought he wouldn't like it anyway. Cleaning the house was no longer the same—I used to keep everything spotless, but after what happened, I couldn't even bring myself to vacuum. I cleaned because it had to be done for Emma, but it felt like I was working in vain.

Since I was with Andrew, I stopped going to beauty salons. I cut my own hair at home and occasionally managed to do my nails. Occasionally, I managed to do my nails, but it was never quite the same as a professional manicure. I refrained from spending money on my personal needs; every penny we had went toward bills, rent, and food.

My wardrobe was sparse. I wore the same few outfits repeatedly, avoiding any unnecessary expenses. Unlike other women, I didn't have a collection of bags, dresses, or shoes. My social life was non-existent; I didn't go to clubs or pubs. My days were consumed with taking care of Emma, ensuring she was safe and well-cared for.

I vividly remember the mornings, dropping Emma off at school and then sprinting for 15 minutes to get to work just to save on bus fare. After a long day at work, I would rush back to pick her up from school. It was a relentless cycle, but I did it all for her and for us, for a better future.

Also, I vividly remember the days when fixing my teeth was a luxury I couldn't afford. As a child, I had a terrible fall from a swing, breaking my front tooth in half. The dentist did what they could, but the repairs were made with cheap, visibly yellow materials. This made me incredibly self-conscious, and I often found myself covering my mouth with my hand when speaking to others, trying to hide my embarrassment.

One day, while biting into a crisp apple, the filling came loose and fell out. I was left with a noticeable gap and had to endure this until I could save enough money to get it fixed. Finally, I managed to visit a specialized dentist who transformed my smile. My teeth were now white, beautiful, and perfectly straight. Despite the years of embarrassment and the yellow filling, I never lost hope. I didn't blame anyone for my situation; instead, I focused on saving money for our daily needs, ensuring we never lacked the essentials. This experience taught me resilience and the importance of hope, even in the face of adversity.

I couldn't fathom why he treated me so unfairly and accused me without cause. His words echoed in my mind daily: "I've been feeding you for ten years," as if he had rescued me from the streets or an orphanage. He never listened to my side of the story. I sent him countless messages, sharing my pain, but he never replied. Each day felt like an eternity, waiting for a call or even a single message that never came.

Sometimes, Andrew would try to show remorse, his voice trembling as he claimed he spoke out of anger and frustration. Yet, I couldn't understand why he was so upset. I simply asked him to drink less, spend more time with us, give up his friend, and stop going fishing every weekend—especially since he rarely caught any fish; he just sat there with his fishing rod and beer, staring blankly at the water.

He often told me he couldn't imagine life without me, that if we ever separated, he'd be "nothing without me," and that I meant everything to him. But these were just words. Deep down, I wanted to believe him. I knew he wasn't like that—I wanted to forgive him. Yet, I began to resent myself for being unable to forgive him, and I started treating him the same way he treated me.

I grew quieter by the day, retreating into a shell of silence. But during our arguments, I would lash out, hurling insults and curses at him. Each harsh word that left my mouth only made me feel more miserable. Emma often witnessed our fights, her innocent eyes wide with confusion and fear. I felt immeasurably guilty, knowing that I was failing to provide her with the peaceful, loving home she deserved.

I longed to show Emma peace, love, romance, hugs, calmness, respect, and communication. I wanted her to see a home filled with warmth and understanding. But all she saw was conflict, arguments, or prolonged silence. The weight of my failures pressed heavily on my heart, and I wondered if I would ever be able to break free from this cycle of pain and resentment.

I remember Emma's birthday vividly. She invited her school friends, and we ordered a delicious cake that was decorated with her favourite characters. The house was adorned with colourful balloons, and the table was laden with sweets and treats that sparkled under the lights. I cooked and prepared meat for the grill, the aroma filling the air with a sense of festivity. I had meticulously organized everything to ensure Emma's happiness, down to the smallest detail.

Andrew's brothers, Michael with Christina, James, and Sarah, were also there, bringing laughter and warmth to the gathering. Andrew's close friend, who had always been a part of our family celebrations, couldn't miss the occasion. Despite the joy around me, I felt a pang of sadness. I was upset, but I reluctantly accepted it; there was no other choice. All I wanted was peace and for Emma to be happy. Seeing her smile as she blew out the candles made all the effort worthwhile.

I remember how I repeatedly reminded Andrew not to drink too much alcohol because Emma's school friends were present, and I didn't want them to see him drunk. We had two girls staying overnight, and I wanted us to set a good example. Andrew promised he wouldn't drink excessively and wouldn't get drunk. But as the evening wore on, Andrew continued to drink, ignoring my pleas, and didn't care that he was embarrassing Emma in front of her friends. He drank until he fell asleep with his head on the table after the guests had left. Again, I was disappointed, but I continued to hope that things would improve.

During the party, whenever I spoke to Andrew or asked him something, his friend immediately answered, interrupted me, and defended him. And if I called Andrew for help, his friend would interject, saying, "My wife has no right to tell me what to do; women should keep quiet." I simply despised that man. His presence cast a shadow over the celebration, making it hard to focus on the joy of the day.

At one point, I confronted him, and both Christina and Sarah came to my defence. Their support was a small comfort in an otherwise frustrating situation. But arguing with that man was futile; he lived by misguided principles, and in his world, women were insignificant. His dismissive attitude and condescending remarks only fuelled my anger. Eventually, I let go of the argument and focused on ensuring Emma's happiness rather than lecturing a valueless person.

Despite the turmoil, I found solace in the moments of joy that Emma experienced. Her laughter as she played with her friends, the excitement in her eyes as she opened her presents, and the pure delight on her face, as she blew out the candles on her cake made all the effort worthwhile. Those precious moments were a reminder of why I worked so hard to make her birthday special, even in the face of adversity.

The following day, I tried to talk to Andrew about how he had broken his promise and gotten drunk. My heart was heavy with disappointment. However, instead of listening, he told me to be quiet, stop rambling, and stop thinking everything revolved around me. He said, "You're not the centre of the universe." His words cut deep, and I fell silent, feeling a lump in my throat. There was nothing more to say. The words felt pointless, and the actions had already occurred. If it wasn't about me, about us, then who was it about? Who mattered more? It had become a habit not to recognize Andrew anymore, yet deep down, I clung to a fragile hope that things would improve. Sometimes, in moments of sheer frustration, I felt like packing my bags and leaving, just going far away. But I didn't. I stayed, hoping for a miracle.

Even with my brother Charlie, I couldn't have a meaningful conversation or rely on him. He was in a similar situation as

Andrew. Alcohol had become a destructive habit for him. Sometimes, he turned into someone unrecognizable, and it broke my heart. My sister-in-law Katie and my niece Sophie were experiencing similar struggles, just like Emma and me. Everything around me felt like a continuous fall, and I couldn't find anything to hold onto, to stay grounded. Emma was my beacon of hope. Her innocent smile and unwavering love were my lifeline. She was my source of energy, and I desperately wanted to make a change for her sake. I wanted to create a better world for her, one where she wouldn't have to face the same struggles.

Sometimes, I managed to have deep conversations with Andrew. During these moments, we would promise each other that everything would be resolved, and life would return to normal. Occasionally, I'd find solace in these promises, hoping that perhaps it had been just an ugly episode. I was prepared to forgive and fight for us, believing that our love could overcome any obstacle. What I craved was a little more attention, a few embraces, maybe even a stolen kiss now and then—I longed to feel like a cherished woman beside him. But instead, I felt insignificant, unwanted, and unattractive.

I couldn't help but retreat into myself. Too many disappointments had accumulated in my heart. Even the smallest ones weighed heavily. Each unfulfilled promise and every moment of neglect added to my growing sense of despair. I couldn't bear being accused of something I hadn't done, and the loneliness of being unheard gnawed at me. The silence between us became a chasm, and I felt myself slipping further away, like a ship lost at sea, drifting aimlessly without a compass. My unmet needs and unspoken words were the waves that threatened to pull me under. Our relationship felt like a garden left untended, where once vibrant flowers of love and trust had withered, replaced by thorns of resentment and sorrow.

Every night before falling asleep, I found myself lost in thought, trying to unravel the mystery of what had destroyed our relationship. I questioned myself endlessly, wondering how guilty I was in the grand scheme of things. Despite my introspection, I couldn't pinpoint any fault in myself. It seemed like the root of our problems lay in Andrew's lack of trust in me. His constant suspicion cast a shadow over everything we had.

Then there were the episodes with George. Those moments replayed in my mind, but George had long since moved on to his own world. He was with Alice now, and they were eagerly awaiting the arrival of their second child. This time, they were expecting a boy. George had found stability working in Germany, while Alice stayed in Romania with her parents, caring for their daughter Beatrice and preparing for the new baby. Their lives were intertwined in a way that mine no longer was.

George and Alice were in their own bubble, navigating their own joys and challenges. Whether they were happy or sad, it no longer had any bearing on my life. Our connections had faded, and the past was firmly behind us. I realized that dwelling on what had been would not change the present. The past was the past, and it was time for me to find the best way to solve our problems and finally be happy.

The Quiet Victory

During one of the most challenging periods of my life, I applied for British citizenship and successfully obtained my passport. When I attended the naturalization ceremony to pledge my commitment as a responsible citizen, I stood alone, much like when I graduated. There was no one to accompany me, but I felt my late father's presence, rejoicing in my achievement from above. It was a profoundly special moment, yet I had no one to share it with, which left a bittersweet ache in my heart.

In addition, I set up my own company and meticulously prepared all the necessary documents to legally practice accounting. My dream of becoming an accountant was slowly taking shape. Over the course of six months, Emma's room became my office, bedroom, and play area—all while I juggled various accounting cases and worked on this book. The room was filled with the sounds of her laughter and the rustling of papers, a chaotic yet comforting symphony that kept me going.

Emma was quite young at the time, so she might not have fully understood the complexities of what was happening. However, children often sense the emotions and atmosphere around them. She likely picked up on the mix of determination, stress, and occasional joy that filled our home. Her laughter and curiosity were a constant reminder of the simple, beautiful moments amidst the chaos.

On one hand, I felt content with my accomplishments and was genuinely delighted by Emma's growth and development. Her innocent joy and curiosity were a constant source of inspiration. On the other hand, a profound sadness lingered. I yearned for all three of us to be happy, celebrating our achievements together. However, communication with Andrew remained fraught with arguments. While I can't say he didn't appreciate my successes or feel pride in my endeavours, it didn't always manifest. He encouraged and supported me in his own way, even though secretly, I longed for more: more attention, more admiration, more encouragement, and more love. The emotional distance between us was a silent, ever-present shadow over my happiness.

As Easter approached, we couldn't afford a vacation. I thought a change of scenery might help us reconnect, but we didn't have the time. My workload was increasing as the company thrived, and I had to manage various accounting cases. Despite my busy schedule, I found time to clean the house and cook traditional dishes from my culture.

On that day, I worked tirelessly and prepared a lot, eagerly waiting for Andrew to return from work so I could serve him. Unfortunately, when Andrew came back, he was drunk, accompanied by his best friend and three other men. They were all intoxicated and insufferable. Despite my efforts to vacuum and tidy up, they walked into the house with their shoes on, leaving marks from the entrance door to the garden gate.

Despite my preparations and the delicious food I had made, Andrew had different intentions for celebrating Easter. In those moments, I was utterly frustrated. I abandoned everything, changed clothes, dressed Emma, and then got into the car to go to church. I knew that my cousin Sibel and her family would be there, and the priest was conducting a special service before Easter day. Although I wasn't particularly interested in the service, I wanted to be as far away from Andrew and his friends as possible—to find some peace.

I felt like screaming and shouting in the church, questioning God why all of this was happening. But I calmed myself down and reminded myself that I was the one responsible for the situation; it wasn't God's fault.

My cousin Sibel is a remarkable person. She's always been a pillar of strength and support for our family. Growing up, she was the one who brought everyone together during family gatherings with her warm and welcoming nature.

Sibel has a natural talent for making people feel at ease. She's incredibly empathetic and always knows the right thing to say to lift someone's spirits. Her faith is also a significant part of her life. She attends church regularly and is actively involved in the community. During special services, like the one before Easter, she often helps organize events and ensures everything runs smoothly.

That Easter service with Sibel was a mix of emotions for me. As I walked into the church, the familiar scent of incense and the soft glow of candlelight created a serene atmosphere. Sibel greeted me with her warm smile, instantly making me feel a bit more at ease.

The church was beautifully decorated with lilies and other spring flowers, symbolizing new beginnings and hope. The choir's harmonious voices filled the air, singing hymns that resonated deeply within me. Despite my initial reluctance, I found myself getting lost in the music and the peaceful ambience.

Sibel stayed by my side throughout the service, her presence a comforting anchor. She held my hand during the prayers, and her gentle squeeze reassured me that I wasn't alone. The priest's sermon focused on forgiveness and renewal, themes that struck a chord with me, given the turmoil I was experiencing at home.

When I returned home from the church, I was bracing myself for whatever awaited me. As I walked through the door, the house was eerily quiet compared to the chaos I had left behind. Andrew and his friends were no longer there, and the remnants of their visit were scattered around—empty bottles, food wrappers, and muddy footprints.

Andrew was slumped on the couch, looking dishevelled and exhausted. He barely acknowledged my presence as I entered. I could see the regret in his eyes, but he didn't say anything. The silence between us was heavy, filled with unspoken words and unresolved tension.

I quietly started cleaning up the mess, trying to hold back my frustration and disappointment. Andrew eventually got up and mumbled an apology, but it felt hollow. He seemed ashamed but also too proud to fully admit his mistake.

Emma, sensing the tension, clung to me, and I focused on comforting her. I realized that night that things needed to change and that I couldn't keep living in this cycle of hope and disappointment. It was a turning point for me, a moment of clarity amidst the turmoil.

The Elegance of Timing

Also, during one of the most challenging periods of my life, something truly captivating happened. It felt as if fate was placing special people in my path, yet I stubbornly continued to follow my own way. My brother Charlie and Katie were looking for someone to rent a room to help cover the rent and bills. One day, a gentleman called Katie expressed interest in the online room rental ad. He mentioned that he worked as a long-distance lorry driver and wouldn't be home much due to his lengthy routes. They arranged a meeting to see the room and discuss all the details.

On the day of the meeting, Charlie was at work, and Katie asked me to be there with her since a stranger was coming to the house. I could sense her nervousness, and it mirrored my own. A few hours before the agreed time, I arrived at Katie's place, my heart pounding with a mix of curiosity and apprehension. As we waited for the gentleman to arrive, the air was thick with anticipation. Every sound seemed amplified, and each passing minute felt like an eternity.

After about ten minutes, the gentleman called Katie to apologize for being late due to traffic. When she put the phone on speaker, I felt an unexpected sense of beauty in his voice. It was soothing, with a rare quality that resonated with calm precision, sending shivers down my spine. His voice had a warmth that seemed to wrap around me, momentarily easing my anxiety. After a brief exchange with Katie, I decided to step outside for some fresh air, hoping to calm my racing heart.

Nervous anticipation gripped me as I awaited his arrival. The minutes seemed to stretch endlessly, each tick of the clock amplifying my unease. Checking the time, I realized it was almost time to pick up Emma and Sophie from school. My mind was a whirlwind of thoughts and emotions, making it hard to focus.

As I stepped out, I found the gentleman standing at the door, looking for the exact address. In my haste, I exited right in front of him, and he mistook my hurried movement for a friendly greeting. Our eyes met, and for a moment, everything else faded away.

"Good afternoon, I apologize for being late," he said, his gaze locking with mine. There was a sincerity in his eyes that caught me off guard, and I felt a strange connection as if we had known each other in another life. His presence was both calming and unsettling, stirring emotions I hadn't expected.

For a fleeting moment, time seemed to stand still. The air was thick with his strong, masculine scent, enveloping me as our eyes met. His gaze was mesmerizing, a captivating blend of blue and green that I couldn't quite decipher. It was as if his eyes held a world of untold stories and secrets. When he apologized, his calm voice and sheepish smile exuded an irresistible charm that made my heart skip a beat. Outwardly, I simply replied, "Yes, indeed, you were late." But inside, I couldn't help but think, "You were about twelve years late."

The gentleman was accompanied by a young man, who I later discovered was his son. They were planning to move into the room together. The father, often away on business, had a commanding presence that suggested a life filled with important engagements and responsibilities. The son, on the other hand, had just arrived in London. He was in his early twenties, with a hopeful yet uncertain look in his eyes, searching for work and a place to stay until he could arrange a more permanent rental. His youthful energy contrasted sharply with his father's seasoned demeanour, hinting at the beginning of his own journey in the bustling city.

Ultimately, I invited them inside and apologized, explaining that I needed to pick up my daughter from school. I mentioned that Katie would show them the room, and they graciously thanked me. As I hurried off to school, my mind was filled with thoughts of those captivating eyes and his distinctive, masculine fragrance that lingered in the air.

When I returned, they had already left, but their decision to move into the available room remained. Katie was also struck by their demeanour, appearance, and conversational style. She described them as polite and well-spoken, with an air of sophistication that was hard to ignore. Curious, I asked Katie for the gentleman's name, but she admitted that although he had introduced himself, she couldn't recall it. She was too distracted by his charming smile and the way he carried himself.

Two days later, the gentleman confirmed the move-in time and arrived with his luggage. Katie invited me to her house so we could both welcome them. I accepted her invitation, eagerly anticipating their arrival. As I walked to her house, I felt a pleasant sense of contentment and curiosity. The anticipation of meeting them again was almost palpable, and I couldn't help but wonder about the stories they might share and the experiences they had lived.

When they finally arrived, the gentleman greeted us warmly, his eyes twinkling with a hint of amusement. He introduced himself again, this time making sure we remembered his name.

I learned their names—Sebastian and his son, Alessandro. They were thrilled to have chosen to rent the room in my brother's house. From the moment they first saw it, they felt a positive energy and an immediate sense of belonging. It didn't feel like they were moving in with strangers; it felt more like joining a family as if we had known each other for years.

From the day they moved in, I felt a delightful warmth whenever I visited Charlie and Katie's home. Sebastian and Alessandro were always polite, well-mannered, and respectful. When Sebastian spoke to me, his gaze would lock onto mine, making me feel uniquely special. His unwavering attention conveyed a genuine fondness as if he had fallen for me at first sight. His smile confirmed what his eyes expressed, seeing beyond the surface and into my soul. Each time our eyes met, it felt as though he could read my entire personality, deciphering all my thoughts and peering deep into my heart.

Whenever I visited, I found myself looking forward to our conversations. Sebastian had a wealth of stories and experiences to share, and he listened with genuine interest when others spoke. His ability to connect on such a deep level was both captivating and comforting. It was as if he had an innate understanding of people, knowing exactly what to say to make them feel seen and appreciated.

However, Sebastian maintained an attentive yet decorous demeanour. He never crossed any boundaries, avoiding suggestive compliments or inappropriate gestures. His elegance was truly captivating. He dressed impeccably, exuding refined sophistication and style. Despite this, I kept an indifferent facade, preserving the boundaries of our friendship. I didn't fully understand why I enjoyed his presence so much, but I didn't want to delve into it—perhaps because Andrew didn't give me as much attention. I relished feeling special, yet I didn't want to reveal any vulnerability. Therefore, I avoided confirming anything to him.

Sebastian was diligent and respectful to everyone, and most importantly, he practised moderation with alcohol. He enjoyed a glass of wine with meals but never overindulged. Our conversations often revolved around cars. Like me, he was passionate about automobiles, particularly BMWs. While I lacked expertise in car components, he patiently taught me about engines and other enhancements we could incorporate to make them even more tuned.

Despite my efforts to remain indifferent, I couldn't help but feel a flutter of excitement whenever Sebastian was around. His presence had a way of making me feel seen and appreciated in a way I hadn't experienced before. There was a warmth in his eyes that made me feel safe as if I could trust him with my deepest thoughts and feelings. Yet, I held back, afraid of what might happen if I let my guard down.

I remember that one sunny afternoon, Charlie, with his usual enthusiasm, suggested that I talk to Andrew so that we could all go fishing together. Both Charlie and I enjoyed fishing, but he didn't have anyone to go fishing with. So, for Charlie's sake, we decided to organize a fishing trip, even though I had only unpleasant experiences with it before.

The week leading up to the trip was a whirlwind of preparation. I knew I had to buy everything we needed: sturdy fishing rods, a variety of baits, and a new tent. I meticulously packed all our gear, making sure not to forget the essentials like a first aid kit and plenty of snacks.

After a week of anticipation, we were finally ready for the fishing trip. Sebastian, always eager for an adventure, learned from Charlie that we were going fishing, and he also wanted to join us. He felt the need for an outdoor adventure and now was his chance. He pleaded with Charlie to take him along, and Charlie happily agreed.

When we arrived at the fishing spot, the air was crisp and filled with the scent of pine and fresh water. I noticed that Sebastian was more prepared for a picnic than for fishing. He had a small fishing rod borrowed from Charlie, but he insisted on catching a little fish. His backpack was filled with sandwiches, a checkered blanket, and a thermos of hot coffee. As I began to set up the tent, the sun started to dip below the horizon, casting a golden glow over the lake. The sound of birds chirping and the gentle lapping of water against the shore created a peaceful ambience. Despite my initial reluctance, I felt a sense of calm and anticipation for the adventure ahead.

Meanwhile, I was left with the unenviable task of setting up the tent and organizing our camping gear. From a distance, Sebastian watched, puzzled as to why neither Andrew nor Charlie offered any help. At one point, I accidentally hurt my finger while anchoring the tent. Seeing this, Sebastian's protective instincts kicked in, and he came over to assist me. However, Andrew seized the moment to make crude jokes about Sebastian, suggesting he was more interested in fishing than helping me. To avoid a confrontation, Sebastian retreated to his fishing spot, enduring Andrew's continued taunts.

That evening, Andrew's attacks on Sebastian escalated, with Andrew trying to intimidate him through both words and threats. I watched as Sebastian handled the provocations with grace, maintaining his composure and responding with politeness. I felt a mix of embarrassment and a strong desire to disappear as Andrew's mocking remarks continued. I also cringed at the amount of alcohol Andrew and Charlie were consuming. Internally, I berated myself for agreeing to this trip, feeling like a servant and witnessing Andrew's excessive drinking. Despite this, Sebastian remained calm, focused on his fishing, and found solace in the tranquillity of nature.

After a few months, Sebastian and his son Alessandro decided to move out of my brother's house. They found a cosy, two-bedroom flat nestled in a quiet neighbourhood, closer to the garage where Sebastian worked and parked his lorry. The new location was more convenient for them, reducing Sebastian's daily commute and allowing him to spend more time with Alessandro.

We remained friends for a while, exchanging greetings and updates on WhatsApp. Our conversations were filled with warmth and mutual respect, but eventually, our messages stopped. Sebastian refrained from writing to avoid any misinterpretation by my husband, Andrew, and I hesitated because I wasn't sure if it was appropriate. Although Sebastian was divorced and single, given my marital status, it felt somewhat inappropriate to continue our correspondence, even as friends.

However, Sebastian remains etched in my memory as a good friend and a perfect man—someone who knew how to appreciate the woman beside him, respect her, and make her feel special. His kindness and attentiveness were like a breath of fresh air. Until I met Sebastian, I didn't know that there were educated, courteous men who wouldn't hesitate to show the world that they love and appreciate the woman by their side. I wasn't aware that there were men proud to love and respect the woman who walks hand in hand with them.

Sebastian's presence in my life, though brief, left a lasting impression. His genuine nature and the way he carried himself with dignity and grace taught me that true gentlemen still exist. Even now, I often find myself reminiscing about our conversations and the way he made me feel valued and respected. He used to tell me, "You're the most beautiful lady," and there was a song he played especially for me: *"Heart is racing here now, never wanna wake up.*

You're a mind reader. A mind reader" from "No Secrets" by DJ Goja and Robert Cristian.

His presence made me feel beautiful and deserving of genuine admiration. Meeting him revealed that I had never truly experienced respect, elegant compliments, or the feeling of being a valued princess until then. We didn't spend much time together, only seeing each other occasionally on weekends. For instance, when we met at Charlie's house and shared meals, he always assisted in setting the table, paying meticulous attention to every detail. He anticipated my needs, often providing utensils before I even asked and neatly folding napkins before I set the plates, knives, and forks on the table.

I felt a pang of sorrow when he left, and our interactions ceased, but I knew it might be for the best. Maybe destiny whispered that he came at the right time and was everything I needed, but he arrived late, very late—about 12 years too late.

The Breaking Point

After some time, Andrew and I found ourselves in yet another argument, this time over our car. I relied on it to take Emma to school and handle our grocery shopping. However, on weekends, when I needed the car for outings with Emma, Andrew wanted it for his fishing trips, leaving me stranded. During the week, when I had the car, his best friend would pick him up, drop him off at work or wherever they went, and then bring him home in the evening.

The car became a major point of contention between us. Andrew insisted it was his car because I hadn't contributed any money when we bought it, while I argued that it was mine since I had paid for half of it. Ultimately, we decided to resolve the issue by selling the car.

This entire situation weighed heavily on my heart, leading me to make the difficult decision to separate from Andrew. The constant arguments had eroded the love and respect we once had for each other. I felt a deep sense of loss and sadness, realizing that our relationship had reached a breaking point. There was no point in staying together and arguing daily. After much contemplation and planning, I decided to live apart for a while—hoping that perhaps, in our time apart, we'd miss each other and learn to appreciate one another again.

The nights were the hardest. I spent countless hours lying awake, my mind racing with memories of happier times and the painful reality of our present. My pillow became a silent witness to my tears, each one a testament to the heartache I felt. The decision to separate was not made lightly, but I knew it was necessary for my own well-being and for Emma's sake. I had reached my limit, and it was time to take a step back and find a way to heal.

I decided to rent a house and move in with Emma. Thanks to a friend at a real estate agency, finding a place was relatively easy. The hard part? Explaining it to Emma. How could I tell our child that Mommy and Daddy no longer understood each other and were going their separate ways? I didn't know where to begin or how she would react. It was traumatic for me, let alone for Emma. Would this change affect her emotionally? Would she cry for her father? And what if I couldn't afford to maintain the house and support both of us? My company was doing reasonably well, but I wasn't prepared for such a significant upheaval. My mind was a whirlwind of thoughts, and I had no clue how to broach the topic with Emma.

I gazed out the window into the velvety night, the stars twinkling like distant promises. The weight of the situation pressed heavily on my chest, making it hard to breathe. I could hear the faint hum of the city outside, a stark contrast to the silence inside the room.

"Mommy, I love you!" Emma's whisper floated from her bed, breaking the stillness.

"Emma, I love you more!" I replied, my voice trembling slightly.

"No, Mommy, I love you more!" she insisted, her voice filled with innocent determination.

"Emma! I love you even more! I love you to the moon and back! I love you beyond the moon and the stars," I said, trying to match her enthusiasm.

As I looked at her, I wondered how much longer I could shield her from the truth. The thought of her little heart breaking was almost too much to bear. I knew I had to be strong for her, but the uncertainty of the future loomed large. Would she understand? Would she forgive me? The questions swirled in my mind, unanswered and relentless.

I settled beside Emma, waiting for her to drift into slumber. The soft glow of the bedside lamp cast gentle shadows on her peaceful face, her rhythmic breathing a soothing lullaby. My mind wandered, pondering why life seemed woven with coincidences. The room was filled with a serene stillness, broken only by the occasional rustle of the curtains swaying in the night breeze. Perhaps solitude was my destiny—to sit alone and seek answers. But how long would I remain in this quiet contemplation? Maybe acceptance was the key: embracing the past with a joyful heart, allowing future days to envelop me, and learning to love the places I'd journey to.

And now, the paradox: How can I confine my soul when it knows no boundaries? How do I instruct my heart to wait patiently when love itself is impatient? Can love remain unmoved, suspended in time, while we unravel the complexities of our existence? Perhaps therein lies the answer—to surrender to love's wild currents, to trust that even amidst chaos, the heart will guide us home.

Real depression, I realized, wasn't merely sadness; it was when the things you once cherished lost their lustre. The vibrant colours of life had faded to dull shades of grey. I had made promises I couldn't keep, and still, the answers eluded me. Yet, I vowed never to lose myself—to miss the days when my smile was genuine. The weight of my own expectations pressed heavily on my shoulders. *"How can I walk with a smile, get on my day, when I deceived myself pretending is all okay?"* (Crying for no reason by Kate B).

I knew Andrew loved me but in his own way. I was convinced he cared for me, yet when I told him I was leaving, he didn't stop me. He didn't plead with me to stay; perhaps he didn't believe I would actually go. When I looked into his eyes, it seemed as if he wanted me to leave. I no longer saw happiness in him. His gaze, cold and distant, convinced me that I was superfluous in his life. His look revealed the harsh truth behind his words—that he stayed with me only because of Emma.

There is no greater joy than cradling in your arms the very person who resides within the deepest chambers of your soul. I yearn to nestle against his chest, feeling the steady rhythm of his heartbeat, where he can hold me with unwavering strength, refusing to release me to the whims of the world. In his embrace, I seek the freedom to gaze upon him, every flutter of my heart echoing happiness and profound love. For when you stand beside a man who whispers, "Together, we shall conquer," nothing remains insurmountable.

I would have loved for Andrew to take my hand, to spin me around, urging me not to leave, assuring me that we would overcome the situation. But it didn't happen that way. I was merely alone, lost in my thoughts, in my pain, in my complexities, my flaws, my ugliness, and all the negativity of the world. The room felt colder, the silence heavier, and the scent of his cologne, once comforting, now only reminded me of what we had lost.

I sat down with Emma and gently explained the situation. Although she wasn't thrilled about our decision, she listened intently and found comfort in knowing she could still see her father whenever she wanted. The house I planned to rent wasn't far, allowing me to take her to visit him anytime. While the proximity of the new house didn't make her happy, the assurance of seeing her father did bring her some solace.

Emma was too young to fully grasp what was happening around her. She couldn't comprehend the turmoil in my heart—the sleepless nights, the endless worries, and the emotional storm I was weathering. She was meant to simply enjoy her childhood, smile, and grow beautifully—not to witness arguments or endure the trauma of her parents' separation. I never wanted her to experience such pain.

I tried to be as strong and resilient as possible, to remain calm and not cry, even though I felt like I had failed as a mother. I searched for the right words to explain the situation to her in terms she could understand. I told her that sometimes, even grown-ups have to make tough decisions to ensure everyone is happy and healthy. I emphasized that both her father and I loved her very much, and that would never change.

Empathy, honesty, and respect are essential qualities, especially when communicating with children. I made sure to listen to her feelings and reassure her that it was okay to feel sad or confused. I promised her that we would navigate this new chapter together and that she would always have both her parents by her side, even if we weren't living under the same roof.

In the next two days, I prepared everything, rented out the house, and, with a heavy heart, decided to continue with the plan and leave. I wanted to start a new life, to be alone for a while, to not feel like an excess in anyone's life, to not force anyone to love me. It would be just me and Emma.

When Andrew was at work, I packed a few essentials, loaded them into the car, and drove away. Arriving at our new home, the turmoil in my heart intensified. It felt as if the tempest at sea had transformed into a tsunami. I felt as if I was running out of air. It felt as though I had robbed a bank and was now being chased by the police. I was desperate, and I couldn't tell anyone what I felt. I couldn't talk to anyone. I didn't want them to think I had gone mad.

No one knew the exact situation between Andrew and me. Everyone thought we were okay and that we would overcome the arguments or rough patches.

In those two days, I meticulously planned every detail. I contacted the landlord, signed the lease, and arranged for the utilities to be set up. I packed Emma's favourite toys, clothes, and some of her books to make the transition easier for her. I also packed my essentials, including important documents and a few personal items that held sentimental value.

The drive to our new home was filled with a mix of emotions. I kept glancing at Emma in the rearview mirror, her innocent face unaware of the magnitude of the changes happening around her. I tried to stay strong for her, but inside, I was a mess. The closer we got to our new home, the more my anxiety grew.

Upon arrival, the reality of my decision hit me like a ton of bricks. The house was empty and unfamiliar, a stark contrast to the home we had left behind. I felt a wave of panic wash over me. The silence was deafening, and the weight of my choices pressed heavily on my chest. I felt isolated and overwhelmed as if I was drowning in a sea of uncertainty.

That evening, when Andrew returned home and realized we weren't there, he called immediately. He had noticed that some things were missing from the house and didn't know what had happened. I calmly told him that I had decided to leave, as I had mentioned so many times before. I asked him to respect my decision and not to make a scene. As we spoke, he calmed down and understood the situation. He seemed affected, yet at the same time, he seemed to know that I would return to him. He was convinced that I wouldn't be able to manage on my own or that Emma would cry for him and that I would return very soon.

After the phone conversation, I realized how much he underestimated me and how little confidence I had in myself, which is why he let me take a few days to calm down and sort out my thoughts. He didn't mention that I should come home, but the way he spoke made it seem like he knew I would return.

I spent the first night unpacking and trying to make the place feel like home. I set up Emma's room first, arranging her toys and books to create a sense of familiarity. I wanted her to feel safe and secure, even if I didn't. As I tucked her into bed, she looked up at me with her big, trusting eyes and asked if everything was going to be okay. I forced a smile and reassured her, even though I wasn't sure myself.

Despite the challenges, I reminded myself why I made this decision. I wanted a fresh start, a chance to rebuild my life and find happiness on my own terms. I knew it wouldn't be easy, but I was determined to make it work for Emma and me. I held onto the hope that, in time, things would get better, and we would find our way.

The next morning, I woke up early and started organizing our new home. To bring joy to Emma and fill her leisure hours, I hatched a surprise plan. She had always longed for a canine companion, so I searched the internet and found Miky, a pure white Bichon Maltese. When I brought Miky home, Emma's joy knew no bounds. Her eyes sparkled with delight, and their connection was instantaneous. Miky's playful energy and affectionate nature brought a new sense of happiness to our lives.

Yet, as I welcomed the puppy into our home, I realized it came with an additional set of responsibilities. Suddenly, I felt like a parent to two—Miky, our tiny bundle of fur, demanded ceaseless attention. Even a brief errand to the store left him distraught and anxious if left alone. His small, fluffy body would tremble, and his big, round eyes would follow me everywhere, pleading for reassurance.

Despite the added challenges, I cherished Miky wholeheartedly. His presence brought a sense of companionship and comfort that I hadn't anticipated. Watching Emma play with Miky, hearing her laughter fill the house, and seeing her cuddle with him at night made all the effort worthwhile. Miky became a source of joy and a reminder that, despite the upheaval in our lives, we could still find moments of pure happiness.

Even with our friend Miky around, after a week in the new house, I had finished cleaning and arranging everything, making it beautiful. The rooms were filled with the scent of fresh flowers, and the sunlight streamed through the spotless windows, casting a warm glow on the newly polished floors. But the quiet began to unsettle me. The silence was so profound that it echoed in my mind, amplifying my anxieties. I had many tasks to complete at work, but my thoughts spiralled out of control, and I couldn't concentrate. "What will people say? What will my mother think? How will my brother Charlie react? People will talk; they'll say I'm immature and irresponsible." These thoughts swirled around my head like a relentless storm. I felt so guilty. So, lost in mi thoughts, I decided to return back to Andrew. It was the worst decision, but the fear of what people would say haunted me. Moreover, my birthday was approaching, and I didn't want to be alone.

I made a few phone calls and arranged to leave the house in the care of my friend Jessica. I knew Jessica from Emma's school. Jessica was a single mother with two children: an older son and a daughter the same age as Emma. Emma was a classmate and friend of Jessica's daughter. Every time we met at school when I picked up Emma, we would talk and share various things. Jessica had a warm, inviting smile and a kind heart, always ready to lend an ear. I knew she needed a place to stay, and although the house was too large for her, she agreed to move in, hoping to find someone to rent a room and help share the cost of the rent. The house, with its spacious rooms and cosy corners, seemed like a perfect refuge for her small family.

Therefore, I returned home the next day. I packed all my things quickly, my hands trembling as I wondered if I was still normal or if I had gone mad. The room felt like it was closing in on me, the walls pressing in with each passing second. I loaded everything into the car, and the trunk and backseat were filled to the brim with hastily packed bags.

Then, I put things back in place as quickly as I could, my heart pounding in my chest, and I waited for Andrew to come home from work as if nothing had happened. As if I had never gone anywhere at all. In my mind, I only had the thought that I had gone mad and that I needed a psychologist. My heart was frozen, a block of ice in my chest. It no longer felt any emotion—not fear, not courage, not joy, not love, not hate. Nothing was felt. I was dead but still living.

Without thinking about my personal life and love anymore, I decided to accept my fate and focus only on Emma, Miky, and work. I no longer hoped or believed that my relationship with Andrew would ever work again. In one way or another, he also tried to be okay, but I couldn't get his words out of my mind when he told me he was with me just for Emma. His words echoed in my mind, a constant reminder of our fractured relationship. I was cold, and no matter what nice things Andrew did, I could no longer see or feel them. That's why I worked a lot, to not think about anything else. My days became a blur of tasks and responsibilities, a way to escape the emptiness inside.

After a brief interval, I realized my long-cherished dream of establishing my own accounting firm. The office became my second home, where I dedicated countless hours. The space was filled with the hum of computers, the rustle of papers, and the soft murmur of client conversations. My days blurred together as I immersed myself in financial statements, tax returns, and client consultations. The satisfaction of solving complex financial puzzles kept me going. As evening approached, I'd reluctantly leave my desk, the glow of the computer screen still lingering in my vision and head home. My mind was still buzzing with numbers and financial matters, making it hard to switch off.

At home, Andrew and I exchanged only a few words, often feeling like we were invisible to each other. The silence between us was heavy, filled with unspoken words and unmet expectations. Sometimes, I missed talking to him and spending time together, but I no longer wanted to be the sole initiator. I waited for him to make a move, to invite me out or plan a vacation. It seemed like I was always waiting for a kind gesture from him, even though nothing he did quite satisfied me. I noticed his flaws more than anything else. It was as if I wanted him but also didn't want him at the same time. Even when he invited me to do things together, it didn't feel fulfilling, and I declined. I had built emotional walls, afraid that getting too close would lead to arguments and hurtful words. The distance between us grew, a chasm that neither of us seemed willing or able to bridge.

Beyond the Silence

After a few months, one evening, Andrew entered Emma's room to let us know he was going fishing alone at the seaside. His face was a mix of excitement and urgency, which struck me as odd. When he returned home from work that evening, he loaded up the car with all his fishing gear, the rods and tackle boxes clattering as he hurriedly prepared. I assumed he was getting ready for an early morning fishing trip, as he usually did. However, it turned out he planned to leave immediately. Something felt off about him leaving in the evening, but I wished him luck and didn't say anything. The unease gnawed at me as I watched him drive away.

As soon as he left, I checked the car's app and noticed he was heading in the opposite direction from where he claimed to be going fishing—toward his friend's house. My suspicion grew, and I continued tracking his movements. After about 30 minutes, I saw the car parked at an unfamiliar address. The location was a quiet residential street, far from any fishing spots. I called Andrew repeatedly, but he didn't answer—probably I called 50 times or more. Each unanswered call heightened my anxiety. I kept monitoring the car through the app, and after 2 hours, he finally headed toward the place he initially said he was going fishing.

At midnight, he called me, insisting he was fishing and hadn't heard his phone. His voice was calm, almost too calm, as he tried to reassure me. Little did he know, I had already figured out his deception. He showed me a grainy image from his video camera, emphasizing that he was indeed fishing. The image was dark and blurry, with barely discernible shapes that could have been anything. But he remained blissfully unaware of the car-tracking app's capabilities. When he noticed my distress, he tried to calm me down, but his friend accidentally spilt the beans, revealing that Andrew wasn't alone as he had claimed before leaving home. The betrayal stung, and the trust between us shattered further.

I was very nervous. My hands were shaking, and my heart was pounding in my chest. I tried to control my nerves, but I couldn't. I imagined that he was having a party on the beach with his friend, accompanied by many other people, especially other women. They would create a romantic bonfire on the beach, the flames dancing in the night, casting flickering shadows. I pictured them listening to music, the sound of laughter and clinking glasses filling the air as they drank and had fun—since they didn't usually go fishing anyway. My mind raced with a thousand ideas, each one more torturous than the last, playing tricks on me.

In those moments of despair, I cradled my laptop and accessed "how to get a divorce." My fingers flew over the keyboard, driven by a mix of anger and heartbreak. I think I completed all the necessary forms in 30 minutes, signed everything, and paid the divorce fee. The process felt surreal like I was watching someone else's life unfold. After receiving confirmation, I messaged Andrew that I had applied for a divorce, and soon we would be officially separated. "I've never borne your family name, and I never will. I've never been your bride, nor will I ever be. Our family was never what I imagined." The words felt like a final, irrevocable step.

He didn't respond to my message; perhaps he didn't believe what I was saying. The silence on the other end was deafening, a void that echoed my own feelings of emptiness and betrayal.

My dreams of being a bride lie shattered. Everything I once hoped for my family feels futile now. The vision of walking down the aisle in a flowing white dress, surrounded by loved ones, has dissolved into a distant memory. I've come to accept that only

Emma truly matters; the rest—the weddings, white dresses, brides, and princes—are mere illusions. I needn't cling to those fantasies any longer. Reality stares me down, and the title of "divorced" defines my path. Our marriage, devoid of wedding traditions and church vows, ended after 13 years under the same roof. Six years after our civil union on December 13, 2013, we divorced.

The truth runs deeper. My heart grapples with questions: "How did we arrive here? Could I have fixed this?" Love transcends mere certificates; it resides in the soul. If asked about Andrew, I'd confess "I stood on love's precipice, ready to surrender my heart." I poured out affection and laid it bare, yearning for our well-being. Yet, it felt insufficient—never quite enough. They say absence reveals the truth: if it doesn't trouble someone, your presence never matters. So, I chose. Tears soaked my pillow as I plotted reclamation. Our story, once vivid, blurred into fiction—a dream left behind. The nights were long and filled with silent sobs, my pillow damp with tears of regret and sorrow. Perhaps I was never a priority, never significant enough. Maybe I wasn't good enough.

The following day, Andrew returned home, and I confronted him. The tension in the air was palpable as we stood in the living room, the weight of our unresolved issues pressing down on us. We needed a solution for sharing the car, especially since I planned to move out with Emma. Our heated argument spanned hours—we hurled insults, raised our voices, and defended our perspectives. The walls seemed to close in as our voices echoed through the house. Eventually, Andrew proposed a compromise: he'd give me a portion of the car's value so I could purchase another one while he retained the current car. Though the car's worth was minimal, I found solace in the division—it was better than receiving nothing at all.

Emotions tangled within me, a puzzle I no longer wished to solve. I busied myself, avoiding introspection. Online car searches yielded nothing that truly resonated. My dream car—the BMW X6—remained out of reach, a luxury beyond my means. Yet, in a spontaneous twist, I resolved to seize the moment. "Life is fleeting," I thought. "Why not find joy?" And so, I embarked on the pursuit of my dream, ready to embrace the road ahead. The thought of driving down the open road in my dream car filled me with a sense of freedom and possibility, a stark contrast to the confinement I felt in my current situation.

The next day, without hesitation, with unwavering confidence in myself, and without pondering the consequences or what might follow, I signed the contract and purchased my dream. The dealership was bustling with activity, the scent of new cars filling the air. I hardly believed I would succeed, but a few hours later, I held the car key in my hand. The key felt cool and solid, a tangible symbol of my achievement. As I looked at the key, uncertainty washed over me—should I be happy or not? I had to face life head-on without any other support. It was a significant responsibility to pay the monthly instalments for such an expensive car, but I encouraged myself, vowing to work day and night to manage everything: Emma, the car finance, rent, and all other expenses. In those moments, as happy as I was, I felt equally sad. The weight of my new responsibilities pressed down on me, mingling with the thrill of my accomplishment.

Despite my thoughts, I eagerly anticipated arriving at Emma's school to greet her after classes with the newest and most beautiful car. I couldn't wait to see Emma's reaction, to share our new "little" car with her, and to take her for a ride in our latest acquisition. I imagined her eyes lighting up with excitement and her joyful laughter filling the car.

I couldn't believe I was driving such a luxurious car, with its sleek design and state-of-the-art features. Not long ago, I couldn't even afford a bus ticket. Now, I drive the most expensive car. Now, I was behind the wheel of my dream car, a symbol of how far I had come. The leather seats were so comfortable, and the engine purred smoothly as I drove. I felt like crying with happiness, overwhelmed by the contrast between my past struggles and my current success. Even though I was worried about the expenses that would come with maintaining such a high-end vehicle, the joy and pride I felt at that moment were indescribable. I put on my favourite song and happily headed towards Emma's school. Music, a timeless language, resonates with the depths of my soul. *"An Ella le gusta la gasolina"* – Daddy Yankee's "Gasolina" blared through the speakers, the upbeat rhythm matching my elevated mood. The drive felt like a celebration, a moment of triumph amidst the challenges.

After a few days, I met Jessica at a cosy cafe. The aroma of freshly brewed coffee filled the air as we sat down at a corner table. I informed her that I would like to move back into the house. The house was ideally located near the park, making it convenient for Emma and me to take Miky for walks. The park's lush greenery and winding paths were perfect for our daily strolls. Additionally, it was close to Emma's school and my accounting office, which would simplify our daily routines.

I asked Jessica how we could resolve the situation and put the plan into action. Jessica, with her usual warm smile and a twinkle in her eye, told me that she had been considering finding a smaller, more affordable house to live in with just her children. She was genuinely happy for me, understanding that I needed to separate from Andrew, spend some time alone, sort out my thoughts and feelings, and then see things differently.

"This house is beautiful, but it's too big and expensive for us," Jessica admitted, her voice tinged with a hint of regret. "Even though we rented a room to a gentleman, the expenses still aren't covered."

Curious, I asked, "And who is this gentleman who has rented a room in this house?"

"His name is Sebastian," she replied, her expression softening as she spoke his name.

At that moment, my heart skipped a beat, and my cheeks flushed with surprise. As Jessica described him, I realized he was the same Sebastian I knew, the one who had rented a room in Charlie's house. Memories of our brief encounters flooded back; each one tinged with unspoken feelings.

"Sebastian is a very nice gentleman," Jessica began, her voice warm and reassuring. "He moved in with his son, but his son left for a few months to Romania. So, he's alone now. He doesn't come home often; he works a lot. He rented the room mainly to have an address where he could safely receive mail. Previously, he lived in a flat, but since his son left for Romania, he decided it wasn't necessary to pay rent for the entire flat."

"I believe I recognize this gentleman, Sebastian," I said, my voice tinged with disbelief. "He rented a room in my brother's house nearly two years ago. It's unbelievable—I never expected to see him again. There was a deep chemistry between us, but we maintained our boundaries and never ventured beyond friendship."

"I can't believe it!" Jessica exclaimed, her eyes lighting up with excitement. "You have a chance to be happy. He is an extraordinary man. I think you're a perfect match."

"I am not ready to start a relationship," I replied, shaking my head. "I think I will ask him to leave. I need some time to be alone.

I don't want anyone in my life, and furthermore, I don't want to give anyone false hope. I no longer believe in love or men; I only believe in myself."

"Are you crazy?" Jessica laughed, her laughter ringing through the cafe like a bell. "The rent for this house is very expensive, and besides, he only comes home once a week. You're mostly alone. You don't need to isolate yourself, and Sebastian is a very polite and hardworking man. Having a helping hand around the house would be beneficial. For instance, if you want to move furniture or rearrange things, you might not be able to lift them, but he can assist you. If something breaks, he can immediately grab a hammer and fix it."

"I'll think about it," I said, sighing deeply. "I really don't know what to do. I no longer want coincidences in my life. What will people say if I live with another man? I don't want to hear gossip and discussions about how I've moved from one man to another."

"Sweetheart, why do you care about what people say?" Jessica asked, her tone gentle but firm. "If you need something, does the world come to help you? Think about yourself, and it's your life. You're still very young; you've just turned 30. Live your life."

I felt a wave of confusion wash over me, reminiscent of the first time I met Sebastian. His voice, calm and soothing, echoed in my mind as if I had been longing for that tranquillity. The memory of his gentle tone brought a sense of nostalgia, making me realize how much I missed it. Unsure of how to proceed, I decided to let things unfold naturally, trusting that the right path would reveal itself in time.

After a brief period of searching, Jessie found a quaint, smaller house nestled in a quiet neighbourhood and decided to move out. The new place had a charming garden and a cosy living room that instantly felt like home to her. She informed Sebastian that I would probably be returning to the house and requested that he take care of it until I made my decision about moving again.

Sebastian was taken aback when he heard Jessica's account of me. He never thought destiny would bring us face to face again. Although he wasn't aware of the entire story or what I was going through, he sensed that I might not be okay. He wanted to reach out, but he lacked the courage to call or text me. He didn't want to intrude or disturb me, fearing that his presence might add to my stress.

Meanwhile, I was extremely busy at the office, buried under piles of paperwork and endless meetings. The most challenging part was finding myself in this situation once more. How could I explain to Emma that we needed to move again? How could I put her through this upheaval once more? The thought of disrupting her life again filled me with dread. Feeling trapped, I desperately wanted to avoid causing any distress to my child. Each day, I wrestled with the decision, hoping to find a way to make things right for both of us.

The day finally arrived, and with a heavy heart, I made the decision to move out. Exhausted by the entire situation, I craved peace, love, and attention—things that had become scarce in my life. At home with Andrew, we barely spoke; he avoided me, engrossed in lengthy video calls with his mother, George, and friends. We coexisted as strangers under the same roof, our life perceptions, dreams, and paths diverging more each day. It was clear that it was time for a fresh start, a new chapter in my life.

I sat Emma down, my heart pounding with anxiety, and emphasized that this move was irreversible. Fearful of her reaction, I was surprised when she responded positively and agreed to relocate once more. Perhaps she, too, was weary of the tension and silence that had become the norm at home. Emma found solace in knowing that wherever we went, our beloved dog Miky would be by her side. I reassured her that whenever she wanted to see her father, I would make sure she could spend time with him.

On the night before our move, I penned a heartfelt letter to Andrew, though I lacked the courage to deliver it. Tears flowed freely as I wrote, each word feeling like a piece of my soul being poured out onto the paper. I wished for a different ending—for us to grow old together—but fate had other plans. Perhaps destiny had whispered long ago that we'd part ways, yet we refused to accept it. As I sealed the letter, I felt a mixture of sadness and relief, knowing that this was the beginning of a new journey for Emma and me. The lyrics of the song ''No-no-no, no-no-no, don't you cry, you can't turn back time'' from 'Will Carry On' by Tommo feat. Melisa resonates deeply in my mind.

Dear Andrew,

I've been thinking about writing to you for a long time, trying to express how I feel. I'm sorry that we're not the same as we used to be and that we can't talk face-to-face to sort things out like adults. I wish things were different—that we could be happy and fix our problems together. But life doesn't always work out that way; people change and sometimes grow apart.

Over the years, I've learned that not everything we want comes true, hard work doesn't always pay off, and not every love lasts forever. Life is full of ups and downs, and each experience shapes us. I'm sorry I wasn't the wife you hoped for—the one you needed. I know I made mistakes.

When we argued, we should have faced our problems together, not against each other. Maybe we were too young to see our mistakes, and now it's hard to fix them. I've faced many storms, mostly of my own making, but I've come out stronger. Every setback taught me something, and I've learned my lessons. I'm not leaving to teach you a lesson; I'm leaving because I've finally understood my own.

I made the choice to trust you, and it was your decision to prove me right. Trust requires time, and I've invested both trust and time. But don't worry—I've learned not to feel wounded when I lose someone who doesn't recognize their luck in having me. Silently, I should have departed the day I realized you wore a happier mask without me. We tried to conceal our emotions, but our eyes betrayed us. Whether we speak or remain silent, the place you hold in my heart remains unchanged. Once, I loved you, and a fragment of my soul will forever be reserved for you. Wherever life takes me, I'll always be close to those I carry within my heart.

Ignorance is like a poison that destroys love, friendship, and everything good. I'm tired of crying alone at night while pretending to be happy during the day because you ignored me without any reason. Our misunderstandings grew, creating a gap between us. I wanted to talk about them, to shout, to let out my frustration. But all I could say was, "I'm okay." I faced my darkest times alone while everyone thought I was fine. So, please don't judge me now. Those silent tears show my deep pain and hidden strength.

Words hurt more than physical wounds; they leave lasting scars that are hard to heal. In my perfect idea of a relationship, even when we were angry or annoyed, we would quickly fix our problems and be happy again. But instead, we stayed silent for days, and we couldn't make up. We should have ignored the fights and disagreements. You should have held me at the end of the day, making me feel safe and loved, showing that we belonged to each other, instilling confidence and the assurance that you were mine, and I was yours.

Once, as a child, I feigned tears; now, I feign smiles. Your silence robbed me of genuine joy. You chose muteness over communication, and in doing so, you extinguished my light. A man who relegates his woman to second place teaches her to exist without him. You repeated this lesson—keeping your distance, instructing me to navigate life without your presence. I heeded your counsel. Loneliness, I discovered, is perilous; it breeds addiction. Once you recognize the weight of solitude, you recoil from interactions with others. Your eyes, once my soulmate's mirrors, now reflect a stranger. And so, I prefer solitude over the company of a stranger by my side. Do not take away my loneliness without offering genuine companionship.

I recall my grandmother's wisdom: when water boils, our reflection vanishes, much like truth eludes us when anger clouds our vision. But your words, spoken in moments of nervousness or intoxication, remain etched in my memory. Love, whether you're clear-headed or not, is about fully cherishing one person. It means making her feel special and valued never putting her down, no matter how hard life gets.

We're not here to be weak or insulted; we're here to be brave and shine. The right person sees the sparkle in our eyes. But even with strength, I felt unappreciated, degraded, and insignificant. Love, appreciation, and support could have helped me through anything, but without them, I felt lost.

As long as someone loves, they can't be defeated. A loving heart forgives easily, even the biggest mistakes. But when love fades, forgiveness is hard to find—even good deeds go unnoticed. I won't ask you to forgive my mistakes; I know what I did wrong and how it hurt you. Every smile cost a tear. Sometimes, I feel like I've taken away the warmth in your heart while trying to find comfort in it.

Maybe the feelings I wanted from you were never there, and I kept asking you to show them, to love me, to prove we were connected. Now, I feel guilty.

Maybe we need to forgive ourselves for loving the wrong person. Remember, God never takes something away without giving us something better. Sometimes, we don't realize how important we are until we're gone. Maybe we need to leave to understand what really matters. Real connections last—they fight, hope, and keep going. But our situation is different. For thirteen years, I stood by you, waiting for a miracle. But if true love isn't there, miracles won't happen. Love itself is the real miracle. We both share the blame—we played with love.

Our hearts drifted apart long ago, even though we stayed together. I hope our feelings don't completely fade because I want to keep the beauty of our shared moments and what we once were. As we move forward, let's cherish the wonderful times we had. Maybe someone better is waiting for each of us.

I'm not an expert on giving advice, but here's something to think about: always show how much someone means to you. Appreciate them without being too critical. Love and hate are very close, and only respect can keep things balanced.

With love, Your ex-ex-wife

P. S. *If you ever miss me, remember that you were the one who decided to let me go.*

Goodbye, Andrew

Thirteen years, a journey long,
Through laughter, tears, where we belong.
We built a life, a family dear,
With Emma's smile, our hearts would cheer.

Through good and bad, we stood our ground,
In love's embrace, we both were bound.
We dreamed of forever, hand in hand,
But fate had plans we hadn't planned.

From lovers close to strangers now,
We part with grace, though we don't know how.
The memories, both sweet and tough,
Remind us that we loved enough.

The nights we laughed, the days we cried,
In each other's arms, we always tried.
To build a world where love could thrive,
But somewhere, somehow, we lost the drive.

The dreams we shared, the plans we made,
In time's cruel hands, they slowly fade.
Yet in our hearts, a spark remains,
Of love once pure, despite the pains.

We'll cherish Emma, our precious light,
In her, our love will still shine bright.
Though paths diverge, our bond stays true,
In every step, she'll see us through.

So, here's to you, and here's to me,
To what we were, and what we'll be.
In this farewell, a silent plea,
For peace, for hope, for clarity.

The seasons changed, as did we,
From spring's first bloom to winter's plea.
We weathered storms, we basked in sun,
But now our shared journey is done.

We learned, we grew, we faced our fears,
Together through the fleeting years.
But somewhere on this winding road,
We lost the way, the love erodes.

Yet in the echoes of our past,
A love that once was built to last.
In Emma's eyes, we'll always see,
The best of you, the best of me.

We'll walk apart, but not alone,
With memories of the love, we've known.
In every laugh, in every tear,
A part of us will still be near.

So, as we say this last goodbye,
With heavy hearts, we won't deny.
The love we had, the life we made,
In Emma's heart, it won't fade.

Here's to the future, bright and new,
To finding strength to start anew.
Though we part, our spirits blend,
in this goodbye, we find the end.

For Emma's sake, we'll find our way,
In separate paths, come what may.
Though we part, our hearts will mend,
In this goodbye, a new start, my friend.

Fragments of Us

I had asked Katie to help me pack my bags quickly so I could leave. Andrew didn't know I was leaving, but after loading my luggage into the car, I sent him a message, finally revealing my decision. I wished him well, urged him to take care of himself, and promised that he could see Emma anytime. Despite feeling agitated and sad, I resisted tears—I simply wanted everything to pass and the pain to fade away.

Upon arriving at the new house, I discovered that Sebastian wasn't home. A small note on the fridge caught my eye:

"I'll be back in about three weeks. I'm going on holiday for a week, then heading straight to work. Please contact me if you need anything. It's nice to know you're here."

The handwriting was hurried yet familiar, bringing a smile to my face. It meant I had time to unpack, tidy up, and heal without anyone seeing me.

I took a deep breath, feeling the weight of the past few months lift slightly. The solitude was a welcome change, giving me the space to process everything. I started by unpacking my belongings, each item finding its place in this new chapter of my life.

Emma was also doing well. During the day, she was at school, and I was at the office. But in the afternoons, when we returned home, we both loved our new house. It offered tranquillity, cleanliness, and freedom. I had customized Emma's room to her liking, painting the walls her favourite colour and filling it with her beloved toys and books. She was thrilled not to share a room with me anymore, especially the bed. She craved her own space, and finally, she had it. She had her room, and I had mine.

The house featured four bedrooms in total: one ensuite with its own bathroom, two double rooms, and one single room. It also boasted a spacious living area with large windows that allowed plenty of natural light to flood in, a large kitchen equipped with modern appliances, and two small bathrooms—one upstairs and one downstairs.

We had a garden, a small but lush green space where Emma and Miky could play. From the garden, we could access the garage, which we used to store items we didn't use frequently. My room was the ensuite, while Emma's room was next to mine. I arranged the single room as a small office, and we rented out the other double bedroom to Sebastian. I was unsure whether to let him stay or ask him to move out.

In the evenings, Emma and I would sit in the living room, enjoying the peace and quiet. We would talk about our day, read stories, or simply sit in comfortable silence. The new house felt like a sanctuary, a place where we could heal and start anew. The silence was comforting, allowing me to process my emotions without interruption.

I sought refuge in solitude, focusing solely on Emma, who was my anchor in this storm. Her laughter and innocent questions were the only things that brought light into my days. She received all my attention, and when she was at school, I immersed myself in work to keep my mind occupied and my heart from breaking.

Andrew was concerned about us, his worry etched into every conversation he had with Emma. Yet, he spoke with Emma every evening, ensuring she was safe and well, his voice a comforting presence in her life. His voice would often crack with emotion, and

I could hear the strain in his words. I had promised him that he could see her every weekend, a small solace in this painful arrangement.

Although this situation was incredibly painful, tearing at my heart every day, it was the best choice for both of us. The weight of my decisions pressed heavily on me like a constant ache that never subsided. But I clung to the hope that, in time, we would all find peace and healing. The quiet moments alone, the sound of Emma's laughter, and the distant comfort of Andrew's voice were the strings that held me together in this fragile state.

After 13 years of living with Andrew, being suddenly alone was incredibly difficult. The separation was a heart-wrenching experience, something I wouldn't have imagined even in my worst nightmares. I wouldn't wish such an ordeal on my worst enemy. I had become so accustomed to him; I knew all his gestures, the way his eyes lit up when he was happy, and even the subtle changes in his tone when he was upset. I was familiar with all his joys and the hurtful insults he sometimes directed at me. I knew everything good and bad about him and had grown used to it all. But everything has its limits in life. It can't be endless days of rain without a single ray of sunshine. That's why I chose to focus on my work and Emma, finding solace in the routine and the love I have for my daughter. The warmth of her smile and the innocence in her eyes became my beacon of hope, guiding me through the stormy days.

I was terrified of what lay ahead, but I clung to the hope that everything would turn out alright. I longed for us to raise Emma together, to be exemplary parents. I envisioned us as a model family, celebrating her milestones and achievements side by side. The guilt over the entire situation weighed heavily on me. Many nights, I found myself unable to sleep, and when I did, I was plagued by the most dreadful nightmares.

I missed Andrew deeply. However, whenever he spoke to Emma on the phone, he only addressed me if he had an urgent and important question, such as inquiries about bills, the rent amount, or where to pay the rent for the house he continued to live in. When I dropped Emma off at his place on weekends, I never stayed longer than ten minutes. We exchanged only a few words, avoiding any arguments, and he regarded me merely as a friend.

He never made any effort to reconcile and seemed uninterested in my presence beyond that of a friend. It was likely that he maintained this friendly demeanour for Emma's happiness. I was content that he respected my decision and refrained from making any gestures that could humiliate or blame me for leaving. Andrew did not contribute financially towards Emma's upbringing. I neither asked for his help nor did he offer it. Since it was my decision to move, he considered it normal for me to bear the costs of rent, bills, food, clothes, shoes, uniforms, and all other expenses. On weekends, when he spent time with Emma, he indulged her every request, especially for sweets, and either cooked or ordered whatever she wanted to eat. I accepted full responsibility for all expenses and was fine with that. He was satisfied seeing Emma well taken care of, nicely dressed, and having everything she needed.

Yes, it's truly heartbreaking. From dreaming big together, from wanting to be a bride and imagining Andrew as the prince in the fairy tale, I envisioned since childhood, to ending up as just friends. I wished for a completely different ending, but if this is how it was meant to be, then so be it. They say that if two people remain friends after a breakup, it means they never truly loved each other. Even this thought haunts me, and I hoped it was just a saying, although we became friends because Emma was between us. Otherwise, I believe that we were just strangers, like we never met.

When Fate Calls

In our new home, Emma and I seemed to be adapting quite well. The spacious rooms and the cosy atmosphere made it easy for us to settle in. Seeing her happy and content in our new surroundings brought me immense satisfaction and peace. It was a reminder that, despite the challenges of moving, we had made the right decision. Her happiness was all that mattered to me, and it made our new house truly feel like home.

After almost one month, Sebastian came home, his face etched with exhaustion from the long haul driving his truck across Europe. I had spent countless hours pondering the situation, yet I still couldn't decide on the best course of action. Should I ask him to leave and find another house to live in, or should I accept him staying with us? He paid rent for the room he occupied for a few days per month, and that money was a lifeline, especially since the rent for the entire house was quite high. Financially, it made sense for him to stay, but deep down, I was plagued by fear. I knew he was a trustworthy man, but the situation had the potential to become complicated.

I was in desperate need of love; my heart felt too sensitive and vulnerable. I craved the comforting presence of a man, someone to share my burdens and joys with, but it was not the right time. The wounds from my past were still fresh, and I didn't want to get involved with anyone. The thought of opening up to someone new was daunting.

Therefore, after much contemplation and calculation, I decided to tell Sebastian to leave when he returned home. However, when he arrived and knocked on the door, my heart skipped a beat. I didn't know how to react. I felt like a little girl, deeply in love, who didn't know how to react after her first kiss. I opened the door and, seeing his tired expression, I smiled. His beautiful green or blue eyes, a mesmerizing blend that seemed to change with the light, gazed deeply into mine, reflecting a mix of exhaustion and relief.

"Good evening, I finally made it home," he said, his voice tinged with exhaustion.

"Good evening," I replied softly, locking the door behind him. The click of the lock echoed in the quiet hallway, a sound that felt both final and comforting.

He circled around me, his movements slow and deliberate, trying to catch my eye. The scent of his perfume enveloped me, mingling with the faint aroma of diesel.

"I thought I would arrive earlier, but I was delayed; I had to wait at the port for my truck to be checked," he explained, his smile weary but genuine, his eyes searching for a connection.

"You are about 12 years late," I replied, my voice carrying a hint of playful sign. I left him with a thousand questions as I headed to the kitchen, the soft glow of the overhead light casting long shadows on the walls.

He followed me into the kitchen, leaving his shoes behind in the hallway.

"At least I was only twelve years late, not my whole life," he said, his smile innocent but his gaze intense, clearly understanding my meaning.

"If you're hungry, there's food in the fridge. You don't need to cook. Help yourself to whatever you like; we have soup and traditional chicken with cream," I offered confidently, changing the subject.

"I'd rather you serve me a portion than rummage through your pots. That way, I won't feel like a stranger. I'll be home for only four days before I leave again. I can cook for myself, but since you mentioned the traditional chicken with cream, please serve me a portion," Sebastian requested.

"You're right, and you shouldn't feel like a stranger; we know each other. Get ready for dinner. I'll prepare everything," I replied, feeling nervous. I worried that he might not like my traditional chicken with cream recipe. As he went to his room to change his clothes, I began preparing his meal, thinking how to maintain a distant demeanour.

He took a quick shower, changed into fresh clothes, and applied his signature perfume that always drove me wild with its captivating scent. After about 20 minutes, he descended the stairs, his stomach growling audibly. With a charming smile, he confessed his hunger. I had thoughtfully set the table for all of us, even though Emma and I had already eaten, believing it was a mark of good manners to dine together.

As I waited, he engaged Emma in conversation, asking her about school and her cousin Sophie, all while gently stroking Miky's fluffy white fur. Miky, our playful and affectionate little dog, seemed to enjoy his attention. Emma, familiar with Sebastian from my brother's house, welcomed him without hesitation. Contrary to my fears that she might reject him or feel uneasy about his presence, she was perfectly at ease.

We all gathered around the table, sharing stories and laughter. The atmosphere was warm and inviting, filled with the aroma of the delicious meal I had prepared. We discussed various aspects of the house, appreciating its proximity to the park, which offered a serene escape and a perfect spot for outings. The evening was a delightful blend of good food, engaging conversation, and a comforting sense of togetherness.

After dinner, Sebastian warmly thanked me for the delicious meal, expressing his appreciation with a genuine smile. He then proceeded to help me clear the table, carefully stacking the plates and utensils. Together, we cleaned the kitchen, wiping down the counters and washing the dishes. Sebastian even took the time to dry and put everything back in its proper place, ensuring the kitchen was spotless and organized.

I longed for the warmth of sharing dinner with someone and feeling like a family. I had hoped for the same when I waited for Andrew to come home from work with the table set, but he never arrived on time. I wished we could sit together, recount our day, share our experiences, laugh, joke, and compliment each other. Sadly, it wasn't meant to be.

After, we both stepped out into the garden, the cool night air wrapping around us as we lit our cigarettes and poured ourselves a glass of wine. The soft glow of the garden lights cast a warm, inviting ambience. His presence was enchanting, yet I kept my mind and heart guarded, unsure of where this evening might lead. I didn't want to break our friendship, and I couldn't bring myself to tell him to leave. Seeing him so tired, I decided to let him stay until I could find the right moment to talk to him.

I was scared of what my family and others might think about me living in another house with another man rather than considering my happiness and the opportunity to save some money. Why not be happy? Because nobody truly cares about what I do. Even when I do the right thing, people judge me. They only see my mistakes, not the good things I've done. It's like they are fixated on the cracks in a beautiful vase, ignoring the intricate designs and craftsmanship that make it unique and valuable.

We began our usual conversation about cars, a topic that always sparked excitement between us. This time, however, the discussion felt different. I now owned the car of my dreams, a sleek, meticulously tuned machine that we had often fantasized about. The car gleamed, every detail perfect, leaving nothing more to add. It was already a masterpiece. By coincidence, Sebastian also owned a BMW X6, though a different model from mine. When I first met him, he had a charming, small, convertible BMW. Therefore, we had a lot to discuss about cars.

As we talked, the atmosphere grew more relaxed and intimate. The gentle rustling of leaves and the distant hum of the city created a serene backdrop. I found myself wishing the night would never end, not wanting to break the spell of our conversation. But as the hour grew late, reality intruded.

"I need to put Emma to bed," I said, reluctantly breaking the moment. "It was a pleasure talking about cars again, especially the BMW brand," I added with a smile, rising from the comfortable garden sofa.

He stood up as well, his movements slow and deliberate. "Next time we have a glass of wine, if we get the chance, we'll discuss another, more important topic," he said confidently, his eyes meeting mine with a promise of future conversations. "I think I'll sleep for about two days; I'm very tired," he added, stepping closer and wrapping his arms around me in a warm embrace. "Good night," he whispered softly, his breath warm against my ear.

"Good night," I replied, my heart pounding in my chest. I stood there for a moment, enveloped in his embrace, unsure of how to react but savouring the closeness. As he pulled away, I felt a mix of emotions, my mind racing with thoughts of what might come next. Should I tell him tomorrow to leave? Maybe I am just confused, and I missed a real hug for so many years. Maybe it was just a friendly hug, and I am crazy for interpreting this wrong. Why am I so scared?" I asked myself, feeling a mix of anxiety and uncertainty.

After I put Emma to sleep and went to my room, lying in bed, feelings of guilt enveloped me, just like Sebastian's scent, which still lingered on my clothes after his embrace. I no longer wanted coincidences in my life, and I no longer wanted to suffer, and I no longer wanted a new beginning. But after three years since Andrew last hugged me, when Sebastian embraced me, my waist felt very small in his hands. His bold touch made me feel vulnerable. I needed love, but I couldn't start a new chapter yet. It wasn't the right time. I should have told him to leave, but instead, I felt shivers when he whispered "good night" while hugging me. I was lost in thoughts and guilt. My brother Charlie didn't even know where I lived, let alone about Sebastian. How could I explain the situation to Charlie? Or to my mother? What would people say? Millions of questions were swirling in my mind.

Eventually, I fell asleep, thinking I would tell Sebastian to leave. But the next day, I hurriedly took Emma to school and then was very busy at the office all day. In the evening, when I returned home with Emma, the soft glow of the setting sun cast long shadows across the living room. Sebastian greeted me warmly at the door, welcoming me home before retreating to his bedroom to meticulously pack his bags for yet another early morning departure. As I walked past his bedroom door, I noticed his neatly folded clothes and perfectly organized travel essentials, a testament to his unwavering dedication to his work.

After I changed my clothes and Emma's school uniform, I walked downstairs into the kitchen, where the aroma of a delicious meal greeted me. Sebastian had gone all out, preparing a mouthwatering beef dish with a rich, savoury sauce that filled the air with its tantalizing scent. Alongside it, he had crafted a fresh, vibrant salad, the colours of the vegetables popping against the white of the plates. I knew he was an excellent cook, but seeing the effort he had put into this meal, from shopping for the ingredients to cooking everything to perfection, left me pleasantly surprised.

We sat down for dinner, the warm light of the dining room creating a cozy atmosphere. As we enjoyed the meal, Sebastian shared the news that his company had called him for an urgent assignment. He explained that he had a demanding route planned, starting from England to Germany, then from Germany to Spain, and finally back to England. He wasn't enthusiastic about going to work, especially since he was exhausted and desperately needed at least four days of rest.

I enjoyed the evening with him again. I didn't tell him to leave; he was leaving to work anyway. We discussed many topics; it was a friendly and decent atmosphere. He never missed a chance to meet my gaze. He had a calm and intense look. His eyes melted me, sending arrows straight to my heart. Sebastian was also very pleased with my and Emma's presence, and we thanked him for the delicious dinner.

After dinner, he invited me for a glass of wine in the garden and a cigarette. The night air was cool, and the stars above seemed to twinkle with a knowing glint. As he had promised the night before, we would discuss more important matters if we had the chance to sit together with a glass of wine. Not wanting to miss the opportunity, while gently pouring wine into the glasses, he asked me, "Will I find you here when I return?"

I looked him straight in the eyes, feeling a mix of curiosity and anticipation, and calmly asked, "Why do you want to find me here?"

He looked at me intensely, his eyes reflecting a depth of emotion that made my heart race. After a few seconds of silence that felt like an eternity, he asked, "Have you ever fallen in love with the most unexpected person at the most unexpected time?"

His question caught me off guard, sending a shiver down my spine. But at that moment, looking into his eyes, feeling the weight of his words and the sincerity behind them, I found myself responding without thinking, "Every time I look into your eyes, I fall more and more in love with you."

The air between us seemed to crackle with electricity, and for a moment, it felt like the world had stopped, leaving just the two of us in that garden, under the stars, sharing a truth that had been unspoken for too long. When I realized what I had said, my cheeks turned a deep shade of red, and a wave of guilt washed over me. I felt a lump in my throat, unsure of what to say next. He looked at me with a mixture of surprise and confusion, his eyes searching mine for any hint of truth. He analysed all my gestures, watching me calmly yet intensely as if trying to decipher a complex puzzle. He probably didn't expect me to respond that way.

To smooth things over, I forced a smile, hoping to lighten the mood. "I was joking. I'm sorry," I said, my voice trembling slightly. "I saw that you wanted to have a serious conversation, but from the way you started, I realized that I'm not yet ready to discuss such a serious topic. I can't promise you'll find me here, but most likely, I will be. I can't promise I'll wait for you. You're my best friend. You know I'm going through a difficult time, and I know you want to be there for me and help, but I can't even be your friend." I said calmly, though my heart was pounding.

His expression softened, but the intensity in his eyes remained. He took a deep breath as if weighing his next words carefully. The silence between us felt heavy, filled with unspoken emotions and unresolved feelings. I could see the concern in his eyes, the desire to understand and support me, but also the hurt that my words had caused. It was a moment of raw vulnerability, where both of us were exposed, unsure of what the future held.

He gazed at me with an intensity that seemed to pierce through my very soul. After a few moments of silence, during which he carefully observed my every gesture, he broke into a warm, reassuring smile. Raising his glass for a toast, he said, "I know you weren't joking. I sense you; I see you, I know you. Don't be afraid to express what you feel. This might be our chance. I believe fate has brought us together, and I trust in destiny and coincidences."

"It feels too late for me to fall in love again," I replied, my voice tinged with melancholy. "But if you wish to enter my heart, do so gently so as not to stir my pain. Within my heart, there exists both a corner of hell and a corner of heaven. I don't want to harm you if you venture into the depths of my heart."

"This is the pathway paradox," he responded, his voice filled with conviction. "It's never too late to fall in love; it happens with the last beat of the heart. I don't merely want to reside within your heart; I aspire to be your heart. I understand this will require time, but even if it brings me pain, I'll continue loving you until the end of the line."

"It is too early for those promises," I said, trying to ground us both in reality. "Let's wake up and face the reality. Let's enjoy this glass of wine and keep our friendship. I don't want to lose you.

Things can get tricky, and even if you try and don't give up, it will still hurt you."

He was watching me intently, his eyes never leaving mine, and he seemed to agree with everything I was saying. After finishing my cigarette and sipping the last of my wine, I slowly got up from the couch. I apologized once again for the joke I had made earlier, trying to assure him that I was just joking and that I wasn't falling in love with his gaze, as I had mentioned without thinking. His expression softened as he listened.

At that moment, he also rose from the couch, his movements deliberate and slow. He reached out and grabbed my hand, his grip firm yet gentle. He pulled me into a tight embrace, his arms wrapping around me with a warmth that made my heart race. He whispered in my ear, his breath warm against my skin, "You are the most beautiful lady I have ever met."

Then, he hugged me even tighter, as if afraid to let go. He cupped my chin in his hand, his touch tender and reassuring. He looked deeply into my eyes, his gaze intense and filled with emotion. Slowly, he leaned in and kissed my lips, a kiss that was both gentle and passionate.

He then whispered "goodnight" softly, his voice barely audible, and asked me to wait for him until he returned from his trip. I didn't know what to say or how to react; I just stood there silently, my mind racing, watching him as he seemed lost in front of me, unsure of what to do next. He thought he had upset me by kissing my lips and didn't know whether to apologize, kiss me again, or run away.

After a few seconds, seeing him agitated and growing sadder with each passing moment, I took his hand, feeling the warmth of his skin against mine. I kissed him gently on the lips, as if returning his kiss, and asked him to drive carefully and come back safely from his trip so we could see what would happen next.

Sebastian looked at me with a gentle smile, his eyes showing a bit of worry. He held my hand tightly as if to say, "Everything will be okay," without speaking. We walked into the house, said goodnight again, hugged each other formally, and then went to our own rooms.

I felt happy about everything that had just happened. A small smile stayed on my lips, and I could still feel his kiss. I didn't want to think about anything else because the future seemed so uncertain, and I couldn't imagine us together. I wasn't looking for any relationship; solitude was what I needed. I didn't want to involve Sebastian in my troubles. It simply wasn't the right time for a new beginning, nor for any romantic entanglements. But even though I felt guilty, a small hope started to grow in my heart.

As I lay in bed, the moonlight softly lighting the room, I kept thinking about the evening. The way Sebastian looked at me, held my hand and made everything feel a bit better. I held onto those memories, letting them fill me with peace and hope.

Even though I didn't know what would happen next, I found comfort in the hope that was growing inside me. It reminded me that even when things seem uncertain, there is always a chance for something good to happen. I drift off to sleep with the lyrics of the song echoing in my mind. *"If you wanna be with me. Baby, there's a price to pay. I'm a genie in a bottle."* – "Genie in a bottle" – by Christina Aqu

Rebirth of the Soul

Behind every strong woman lies a story that compelled her to make difficult choices. As she learns to navigate her emotions, she becomes a force to be reckoned with. In a woman's life, there comes a pivotal moment—a juncture where she sheds old habits, burns away impossible expectations, and shifts her focus from external validation to an internal quest for authenticity.

Sometimes, a woman stops seeking acceptance from others. The world's opinions lose their hold, and the allure of popularity fades. The relentless pursuit of perfection for external validation dissipates. I find myself distancing from those who refuse to acknowledge their own imperfections, those who consistently blame me. It's time to ignite the list of "must-dos" and forge my unique path.

In this fleeting moment, as I face my reflection in the mirror, tears blur the contours of the person staring back at me. How did I stray from my intended course? How did we arrive at this crossroads? Yet, strength must prevail—I must chart a course toward a better existence, a place I can call home. The crossroads beckon, as they do for us all.

A choice awaits, poised to carve a fresh trajectory. I can no longer traverse the well-worn path, feigning contentment. Yes, I've stumbled and made my share of mistakes—after all, who hasn't? But our essence isn't defined by the falls; it's etched in the rise that follows.

The grand tapestry of life unfurls before me, its threads woven with my aspirations. Yet courage eluded me, chaining me to circumstances that bruised my soul. I was myopic, ensnared by unruly emotions. No more. I am more than my frailties. Their indifference doesn't dictate my choices. I possess the strength, intellect, and fervour to tread the arduous path, transcending my former self.

The journey won't yield swiftly, nor will it be painless. Today, tomorrow, or next week—I'll inch forward. Perhaps the anguish I've borne has forged resilience, and the tears I've shed have cleansed my vision. Now, I glimpse my true self and recognize the path that has always lain beneath my feet.

I've undergone a transformation—perhaps growth or sheer weariness. Now, I harbour an aversion to divulging my actions, thoughts, feelings, fears, and vulnerabilities. The compulsion to explain myself to those who misjudge me has waned. Justifying my existence to the discontented, who believe I owe them something, no longer occupies my mind. Convincing others of my intentions and love feels superfluous. Shielding myself from draining debates and needless conflicts—sometimes, I choose silence over advocacy.

I've withdrawn from meddling in others' lives, allowing them autonomy and granting the space of their choice to breathe. Speaking fruitlessly has lost its appeal; I'd rather not be the unwelcome echo of their preferred narratives. No attentive confidant stood by my side, offering counsel. If they thrive without my presence, I'll thrive in their absence. No protector fought my battles, and no mirror reflected my flaws. In moments of confusion, loneliness, and pain, I navigated my path alone, seeking beauty within the chaos.

My name is Hannah, and this is my story. In the end, I discovered the elusive piece of my life's puzzle—it was ME! I had been wandering, lost, seeking external validation to fill my heart and make me whole. But I was mistaken. I hadn't recognized my own worth. I waited for others to shower me with compliments, to offer encouragement, to love me unconditionally. Yet, I failed to grasp my intrinsic value. I neglected self-love.

Staring into the mirror, I scrutinized my imperfections, cataloguing my mistakes. But now, I understand that true fulfilment lies within. I am more than my flaws; I am the sum of my resilience, my growth, and my unwavering spirit.

In the end, we will not remember the words of our enemies but the silence of our friends. I aspire to leave behind something beautiful—a legacy not of stone walls, unspoken emotions, tears, or sorrowful tales. Instead, I yearn to bestow dreams, opportunities, fresh beginnings, laughter, raw emotions, unwavering friendship, trust, love, warm embraces, encouragement, and forgiveness.

The indelible marks left by certain souls remain etched in our hearts—the innocent smiles, the rays of hope. Perhaps I am not perfect, but in a world crowded with fake princesses, I choose to be myself. I embrace the impossible, for there lies less competition, and I welcome every tempest that life hurls my way. An ambitious heart knows no bounds; nothing is truly impossible.

I understand that time doesn't heal everything; it merely teaches us to coexist with pain. Disappointment has tempered my expectations—I no longer anticipate anything from anyone. The consequences and coincidences unfold, and I embrace each moment as it arrives. Tomorrow remains a mystery, but today is a precious gift—the present.

I refuse to justify my life choices or convince others of my worth. While I believe I am a good person, I won't waste time proving it. My company is reserved for those who truly deserve it. People who want to be part of my life will stay without instilling fear of loss or demanding excessive effort to keep them close. When someone truly desires you, no obstacle can separate you; conversely, if they don't, nothing can compel them to stay.

Transparency guides me. I won't hide my emotions, yet I won't burden you with my sadness if you're the cause. A silent ache, an unseen tear—these remain my companions.

Taking risks is a big part of my journey. Sure, I might fall, but without risks, I can't win. Sometimes, I wish I could go back and erase the painful moments, but I can't. So, when things get tough, I don't give up; I start a new chapter. I'll always remember that in the big story of life, we all become stories.

Maybe it's not about happy endings; maybe it's about the story itself. Life, after all, is full of happy accidents. And perhaps, years from now, when I'm but a memory, someone, somewhere, will lift my soul from those pages and acknowledge that once upon a time, there was a little girl—a girl with big dreams. Her eyes sparkled with curiosity, and her heart, beat in rhythm with the universe…

To be continued….

My Guiding Star

In the heart of Italy, you worked so far,
To give us a life, to be our guiding star.
Though fate was cruel and took you away,
Your love and dreams with us always stay.

"My little accountant," you used to say,
A dream you had for me, come what may.
Through numbers and books, I found my way,
Fulfilling your wish, day by day.

Your strength and guidance, my beacon of light,
In every challenge, in every fight.
I wear your name with pride and grace,
In every step, I see your face.

Though you're gone, your spirit remains,
In every joy, in every pain.
Thank you, dear father, for all you've done,
In my heart, you'll always be the one.

You travelled far to earn our keep,
In Italy's embrace, you fell asleep.
A tragic end, a sudden goodbye,
Left us with tears that never dry.

But in your absence, I found my drive,
To honour your wish, to keep your dream alive.
Through sleepless nights and endless days,
I walked the path you paved with praise.

Your voice, a whisper in the breeze,
Guiding me through life's stormy seas.
In every success, in every fall,
I hear your words; I feel your call.

"My little accountant," you called with pride,
In your love, I always confide.
Now I've become what you wished for me,
An accountant, as you dreamed, I'd be.

Your legacy lives on in all I do,
In every number, in every view.
I carry your name, a badge of honour,
In every step, I feel you closer.

Though time has passed, your memory stays,
In the quiet moments, in the busy days.
Thank you, dear father, for all your love,
Watching over us from above.
When you left, we felt so alone,
But your spirit in us had grown.
Me and my brother, side by side,
Determined to honour you with pride.

We faced the world, strong and true,
With every step, we thought of you.
In every challenge, in every test,
We gave our all, we did our best.

We never wanted to let you down,
In your memory, we never frowned.
Through every hardship, through every fight,
We kept your dreams always in sight.

Your absence taught us to be strong,
To find our place where we belong.
In every success, in every tear,
We felt your presence, always near.

Thank you, dear father, for all you've done,
In our hearts, you'll always be the one.
Your legacy lives on in all we do,
Forever grateful, we love you.

"A book read by different thousand people is a thousand different book"

–Andrey Tarkousky.

Life Lessons and Reflections

The most challenging book I've ever read is the one about me. It's not an easy read—there are chapters filled with mistakes I've tried to bury, decisions I wish I could take back, and moments of pain that have reshaped me in ways I didn't always understand. But with each passing year, I've come to realize that accepting my truth is the only way forward. Every scar, every misstep, is a part of the story that makes me who I am. There's no erasing the past, no luxury of rewriting those chapters, but life has offered me something more valuable: the chance to shape the present and create a future that reflects the person I've become.

For so long, I believed that if I just tried harder, if I controlled everything, I could somehow force life to align with my expectations. But life doesn't work that way. It moves at its own pace, teaching me patience, humility, and, more importantly, trust in the unfolding of things. There have been times when I've felt stuck in the same chapter, afraid to turn the page and face what's next. But holding on too tightly keeps the story stagnant. It's when I've had the courage to let go, to trust in the unknown, that my story has truly evolved.

I've learned that life, much like a book, requires us to keep turning the pages, even when we're unsure of what's coming next. And the beauty of it all is that the more I allow myself to embrace each new chapter—with its joys and heartbreaks, its uncertainty and possibility—the more I discover the depth and richness of this journey. Every page I turn reveals another layer of who I am, and that, more than anything, makes this story worth living. Even though the one who caused the pain may forget, the scars remain with the wounded forever. It's easy to let that pain turn into anger, seeking revenge as a way to heal. But true strength isn't in retaliation—it's in transforming that pain into growth and leadership. While revenge may feel satisfying in the moment, it leaves an emptiness behind. Forgiveness, though difficult, brings lasting peace. It's not about erasing the hurt but choosing to rise above it, freeing yourself from the pain's control, and finding the power to lead with compassion and grace.

What's the sweetest revenge? It's simply a smile and a life of happiness. Even though it is not as simple as it sounds, whatever the circumstance arises, you can always find a reason to smile; you just have to look around. A positive mindset will take you to a happy life. Protect your heart and let no one see the depth of your pain. Forgive those who've wronged you, and in that forgiveness, you'll free yourself. Let go of the past, shift your focus toward the future, and embrace the unwritten chapters waiting to unfold. True freedom lies in moving forward with peace and joy.

Don't think you have unlimited time. Time is precious, and life is fleeting. Live your life fully! Treat your soul with care as you interact with others and learn to distance yourself from those who have hurt you in the past. True strength lies in being hurt but still trusting people. Despite disappointments, betrayal, and lies, maintain your belief that there are many other outstanding, loyal, and honest individuals out there. Those who love you will provide strength, while those who envy you will fuel your ambition. Always appreciate the people who stand by you during difficult times.

Judgment of others is a sign of insecurity toward yourself. Refrain from it, as this will indicate toxic behaviour towards others. Everyone is fighting their own battles; you don't know what they are going through. Most of the time, keeping your calm and being silent is louder than words, and for those who are fooling around, there is an idiom dedicated to them. Empty vessels make the most noise.

Remember, the world is filled with frustrated and gossip-prone individuals. Celebrate your achievements and refrain from gossiping about others. Criticism and idle talk often come from those lacking values and morals. Avoid judging others, recognizing that none of us are saints, and no one is perfect.

Pause and reflect before befriending those who begin their day by seeking out negativity, flaws, and ugliness in the world. Individuals who have anchored dissatisfaction and habitually blame others for their failures are not leaders. Even though they are self-proclaimed leaders, people look at them differently. Even when they encounter beauty or good-hearted people, they remain restless until they uncover a flaw to criticize.

A sinner judging another sinner differently. Eventually, you'll grow weary of heeding advice from those who believe they've mastered perfection. Some people may treat you as if you're a failure simply because you haven't married yet, lack of children, reside in a modest home, or you're not driving an expensive car. They might even judge you based on your body size—whether you're too thin or too heavy. You aren't doing anything wrong if no one knows what you're doing.

Here's the truth: some individuals will attempt to diminish your worth, making you feel that your efforts are futile and that you're perpetually off course. In response, learn to shield your pain and safeguard your happiness. Keep it close to your heart, away from the opinions, fears, and prejudices of others. After all, your path is uniquely yours, and your happiness need not be disturbed by external judgments.

Focus on your conscience, not your reputation. Your consciousness defines who you are, while your reputation reflects what others think of you. Remember: their perception of you is their concern, not yours. Prioritize the peace of your mind and soul. If your soul remains untainted and guilt-free, hold your head high and step forward with confidence. The greatest gift you can give yourself is unwavering self-belief.

The world can be harsh, and not everyone is the same. Rejection may come in many forms, but you must hold unwavering confidence in yourself. Your spark of brilliance might cause others to turn away or feel uncomfortable, but don't let that dim your light. Keep shining brightly, no matter what—they may squint, but that's only because your glow is too bright to ignore.

Failure may be a hard pill to swallow, but it holds the power to teach you magnificent lessons. In those moments of struggle, you grow, learn, and discover strength you never knew you had. Each setback is a step toward something greater.

Practice as if you've never won and perform as if you've never lost. Why? Because while no one may notice your sadness or pain, they will always notice your mistakes. Life is a winding, unpredictable journey—a gamble with no guarantees. Giving up is never an option. If you're knocked down, rise up stronger than before. Embrace the challenge, and let every setback fuel your determination to keep moving forward.

Keep learning, work diligently, and fight for your desires— your time will come. What's lost is gone, and no amount of tears will change that. The world can be harsh, and what goes around often comes back around. Let it be and move forward. Inspire yourself to keep going because, as the saying goes, the future is a mystery, the past is history, and the present? It's a gift meant to be cherished. Remember this: a person who wields a pen can alter their fate and even influence the destiny of the entire world.

Fear not to dream, for miracles often emerge from the most minor things. Every time you persist without giving up, you're a winner. Reflect on this: one day, you'll look back and realize that you've fretted excessively over matters that didn't truly matter.

This world is quick to criticize anyone and everyone. While it's okay to listen to others' opinions, don't let them dictate your path. Deep down, you know what's best for you. Trust yourself and stay true to your instincts.

Some people may try to discourage you, but others will inspire you and make you feel unstoppable. As you chase your dreams, the envy of some will only highlight your success. At first, people might question your choices, but soon, they'll be asking how you made it happen. Stand firm in your beliefs, even if it means standing alone. Your courage and perseverance will speak volumes, and eventually, your journey will inspire others.

Remember this about money: it's merely paper, yet many have sacrificed their humanity and dignity for it. Guard your dignity, avoid selfishness, and never sell your soul for wealth. A humble hut where laughter abounds is preferable to a grand castle where tears flow. If you seek richness, count the intangible treasures: love, happiness, time, respect, dignity, and trust. Money can transport you to distant places, but don't let it replace your essence.

No matter your wealth, you cannot purchase true happiness—nor love, time, respect, dignity, or trust.

The happiest people are those who give freely, not those who take. Don't expect others to reciprocate your kindness, as not everyone has a heart like yours. Understand that not everyone will go out of their way for you. Remember, patience has its limits, and kindness has its boundaries. Give with an open heart, but also protect your well-being.

People vary, much like roses: some exude fragrance, while others bear only thorns. Avoid having expectations from anyone; eventually, everyone will disappoint you. Remember this: we inhabit a world where some individuals are willing to trample upon others. Many people neglect justice, sincerity, respect, and moral values. Stay true to your principles, regardless of how others behave.

Don't fight for someone who doesn't want to be fought for. Don't fear losing people who aren't meant to stay. In trying to hold onto them, you might end up losing yourself. When you feel adrift, seek comfort among those who genuinely love you. Never force anyone to make time for you; those who genuinely value your presence will do so willingly.

Remember this: some individuals reveal their true colours only when they no longer require your presence. In life's trials, you'll discern who your true friends are. Avoid causing pain to the person who loves you wholeheartedly. While they may forgive, the scar remains etched in their heart.

Acknowledge the efforts of those who seek you out and strive to stay connected. Few genuinely care, so cherish those who do. Those are the ones who you should stick with.

People who love each other fight together. Those who truly love each other remain unsawed and stand united against the world: against egos, fears, evil, and all adversities. Remember this: only one person can truly teach you what real love is, and you'll yearn to spend your entire life with that person.

When you encounter the right individual, you'll comprehend why other love stories didn't unfold as expected. Life's greatest joy lies in finding someone who knows all your mistakes, flaws, and weaknesses yet still considers you utterly amazing. Wonderful surprises occur when you least anticipate them. Avoid dwelling on the past; don't let it shackle your dreams. Instead, embrace the present and the promise of a future unburdened by past hurts.

Never forget that you don't depend on anyone. Be strong and leave places where you can't find yourself! If you're unhappy in a relationship, just leave! Some people will only realize your true worth after you've departed. A person who genuinely loves you will never let you go.

Don't squander your dreams or beg for love. Avoid waiting endlessly for illusions that may never materialize. If you stay where you don't truly belong, eventually, you'll grow weary of pretending. You deserve more than to be merely someone else's necessity. Remember, beautiful promises can't replace genuine love and happiness. Seek what truly fulfils you, and never settle for less.

Remember, each story is unique, even if love threads them together. Regardless of the ending, never regret following your heart.

Engage your brain to perceive the world as it truly is, not as others describe it. When you heed others' opinions excessively, you risk living in their version of reality. Choose to be human, regardless of how you perceive the world. And don't wait for a special occasion to start doing good—you can begin right now!

In my writing, I hope these words will touch your heart.

Even if we see things differently now, maybe one day, our views will come together.

Life's Gambit: Trust and Betrayal

Two fundamental truths persist in life: we live, and we die. Beyond this, existence becomes a game of chance. Life mirrors a poker game, where everyone yearns to trust their intuition, don a stoic poker face, and take calculated risks. Yet, in this grand gamble, the jackpot remains elusive. Life, like a skilled dealer, shuffles the cards, and until the final hand is played, no certainty exists regarding the ultimate outcome.

In today's world, the notion of love feels unsettling. Beauty is now measured by algorithms of "likes" and "comments," while friendships seem to rest on material wealth—the car you drive, the clothes you wear, or the watch on your wrist. Relationships are often built on self-interest. No money? No friends. You could be there for someone countless times, but the moment you can't help, you're cast aside. Ironically, friends can swiftly turn into enemies, dissecting your character when you're not around. The line between love and hate grows increasingly blurred, making it harder to tell them apart.

Honesty is frequently seen as a vulnerability, while deception is celebrated as a cunning strength. People may greet you with warm smiles, but behind those facades, they lie, harbour grudges, or envy you for having just a bit more than they do. Arrogance and self-praise have become the norm. Take this paradox: some struggle to afford rent and bills, yet still manage to drive expensive cars."

Wisdom is often forged in the fires of suffering, yet some souls remain as dark and impenetrable as coal. Consumed by an unquenchable thirst for wealth, people can transform into beings of selfishness and cruelty.

Within each of us resides an ancient instinct—an echo of primal days when survival meant fangs bared, ready to bite or be bitten. We are all part predator, part prey, navigating a world where trust is scarce and vulnerability a luxury.

Some among us resemble snakes—slithering in shadows, their scales glistening under the dim light, striking from behind with precision, their words dripping with venom that corrodes trust. Others, like bears, pump iron in gyms, their muscles bulging with each rep, sculpting their bodies to impress, yet their hearts remain untouched, encased in a fortress of solitude. Thieves prowl the streets, hungry wolves with eyes that gleam in the night, seeking easy prey, their movements swift and silent. Migratory birds, with wings spread wide, chase elusive dreams in distant lands, their hearts filled with the hope of new beginnings.

Then there are those who sit in sterile offices, their high salaries fattening their wallets like well-fed pigs trapped in a monotonous cycle of work and consumption. Privileged children, wrapped in luxury, live like pampered cats—every whim catered to by wealthy parents, their lives woven from ease and indulgence. Yet, amid this chaotic human existence, a rare breed persists—the loyal and trustworthy dogs. They remain by our side, unwavering, their loyalty shining in their eyes, their love steadfast, a beacon of hope in a world rife with betrayal.

In this intricate tapestry of humanity, we each play our part—a mosaic of light and shadow, virtue and vice. And perhaps, just perhaps, it's within these contradictions that our truest selves emerge, raw and unfiltered, seeking connection and purpose in a world that oscillates between cruelty and grace.

Reflections on Identity, Society, and the Beauty of Romania

*"If you tell the truth,
you don't have to remember anything."*

-Mark Twain

In the eyes of some, I'll forever be a nobody, but no one else can ever be me. I'm like an ant in this vast world—a mere speck. A glass shard amidst a crystal universe. A dust mote caught between fungus flowers. I am no angel; even the earth isn't heaven. I'd rather wear the badge of an open sinner than the mask of a false saint. My personality exudes happiness, yet my soul carries a weighty burden.

I'm the type who understands and forgives, but once I let go, it's for good. I've grown impatient with those who are unclear about what they want—people who make grand promises, deliver little, and always ask for one more chance.

Sometimes, laughter escapes through tears; other times, I cry with a smile on my lips. Pain serves as my teacher, revealing what needs transformation in my life. Only I comprehend the depths I've traversed, and I won't allow anyone to pass judgment. For every dream I've reached, life has demanded its due. I've lost much yet hope remains my steadfast companion.

I come from a place where the government wields control over its citizens, yet many ministers lack even basic education and qualifications. Some grapple with rudimentary reading and writing skills, revealing minimal or non-existent schooling. Their cultural awareness, particularly in language and literature, remains lacking.

Corruption and bribery tarnish our global reputation. Meanwhile, Parliamentary Members often doze off in their offices, contributing little to our country's progress. It's not about who excels at building; it's about who hungers to pilfer and dismantle. In our upbringing, we feared witches more than those who burned them alive.

Our schools, vital educational institutions, should foster learning environments. Unfortunately, insufficient funding plagues our education system, hindering the provision of necessary resources. High rates of early school dropout and underachievement can be traced back to this financial shortfall. Meanwhile, a large audience tunes in to TV shows that peddle idiocy and absurdity. It's disheartening—talentless individuals become overnight stars, while genuine talent often struggles for recognition. Moreover, cultural, artistic, and educational TV programs often appear futile.

Ironically, despite having the highest number of churches per capita, our infrastructure lags behind, and corruption taints our state. Places of worship, meant for prayer and reflection, have at times become centres for business deals. Though we're known as the most devout country in Europe, we struggle with one of the weakest public healthcare systems on the continent. For example, the government allocated a staggering 121 million euros to build the Cathedral of the Salvation of the Gentile, yet our entire country boasts only 1,075 kilometres of motorway and has severely neglected hospital upgrades. Our hospitals are plagued by poor hygiene, outdated equipment, and a critical shortage of specialized staff. Thousands of doctors and nurses have fled to work abroad, leaving our healthcare system on the brink of collapse.

I am currently residing in London, a city brimming with history and culture, but my heart yearns to return to Romania—a country of unparalleled beauty and potential. My unwavering desire is to drive positive change there, transform systems, assist people, and champion a brighter future. I firmly believe that goodness and love ultimately prevail, and together, we can construct a better life for generations to come.

Despite the challenges posed by governmental abuses of power and a flawed system, Romania has birthed numerous heroes and legends. This remarkable country witnessed the birth of the modern jet engine thanks to the ingenuity of Henri Coandă. It is the homeland of the fountain pen, invented by Petrache Poenaru, and the discovery of insulin, a life-saving hormone, by Nicolae Paulescu.

Romania's contributions to the world extend beyond science and technology. It produced the first-ever perfect ten gymnasts in the Olympic Games, with Nadia Comăneci's flawless performance in 1976. The country has also celebrated the achievements of Ilie Năstase, the World's Number One professional tennis player, and Gheorghe Hagi, often hailed as the greatest footballer of all time.

These accomplishments are a testament to the resilience and brilliance of the Romanian people. I am inspired by their legacy and motivated to contribute to a brighter future for Romania. Together, we can overcome obstacles and build a nation that honours its past while embracing a prosperous and inclusive future.

In that cherished place, I discovered the duality of life: kindness and evil, love and hate, beauty and ugliness, poverty and wealth. It was where I learned that love, respect, trust, patience, and goodwill are priceless treasures that money cannot buy. The winding, challenging paths I traversed there led to breathtaking destinations.

I yearn to behold its stunning landscapes, where lush green valley's meet towering, snow-capped peaks, and crystal-clear rivers carve their way through ancient forests. I dream of exploring iconic mountain landmarks, like the majestic Carpathians, and navigating winding mountain highways that offer breathtaking vistas at every turn. I long to feel the soft, warm sand of its pristine white beaches beneath my bare feet, where the gentle waves of the Black Sea kiss the shore.

Even Prince Charles and the British Royal Family share my fascination with its rich cultural and natural heritage. Amidst intriguing history and more than mere legends, ancient medieval castles and historical buildings stand as testaments to its enduring allure. These structures, with their weathered stones and timeless architecture, whisper stories of a bygone era where knights and nobles once roamed.

This place, where Dracula's legend intertwines with reality, exists as both heaven and hell. The eerie, mist-shrouded forests and the imposing Bran Castle evoke a sense of mystery and wonder, while the vibrant, bustling cities showcase the resilience and spirit of its people. It is a land of contrasts, where the past and present coexist in a delicate balance, creating a tapestry of experiences that leave an indelible mark on the soul.

"Imagine there's no heaven. It's easy if you try. No hell below us, above us only sky" (Imagine by John Lennon).

About The Author

Otilia Nicoleta Florea is a passionate storyteller whose love for writing knows no bounds. Born and raised in a small town, Otilia's early life was rich with experiences that ignited her creative spirit. Inspired by the life and experiences of Hanna, Otilia found the courage to bring every detail of Hanna's journey to life in her debut book, The Pathway Paradox. Through her writing, she seeks to empower women, particularly those who feel disrespected or unloved, encouraging them to face life's difficult paths with courage and resilience.

Otilia's commitment to her craft shines through in her attention to detail and her ability to convey deep, complex emotions. She believes in the transformative power of storytelling and hopes her books inspire readers to discover their own strength and voice. Currently, Otilia is working on several new novels, each exploring different aspects of human experience and endurance. She aspires to motivate others through her stories, sharing a message of resilience and hope.

When not writing, Otilia enjoys exploring the outdoors, reading diverse literature, and participating in community activities that support women's empowerment. Her journey as an author is only just beginning, and she is eager to share more stories that resonate with readers across the globe.

www.ingramcontent.com/pod-product-compliance
Lightning Source LLC
Chambersburg PA
CBHW070501120526
44590CB00013B/713